Geography Alive!

Regions and People

Lesson Guide 2

Teachers' Curriculum Institute

Program Directors
Bert Bower
Jim Lobdell

Program Advisors
National Council for
Geographic Education

Curriculum Developers
Julie Cremin
Erin Fry
Amy George
Colleen Guccione
Steve Seely
Kelly Shafsky
Lisa Sutterer

Author
Diane Hart

Contributing Writers
Wendy Frey
Erin Fry
Brent Goff
Holly Melton
Hilarie Staton
Ellen Todras
Julie Weiss

Director of Development: Liz Russell
Editorial Project Manager: Laura Alavosus
Content Editors: John Bergez, John Burner
Production Editors: Mali Apple, Beverly Cory
Editorial Assistant: Anna Embree
Art Director: John F. Kelly
Production Manager: Lynn Sanchez
Senior Graphic Designer: Christy Uyeno
Graphic Designers: Katy Haun, Paul Rebello, Don Taka
Photo Edit Manager: Margee Robinson
Art Editor: Eric Houts
Audio Director: Katy Haun

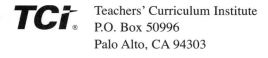

Teachers' Curriculum Institute
P.O. Box 50996
Palo Alto, CA 94303

ISBN13: 978-1-58371-429-4   ISBN10: 1-58371-429-4
 5 6 7 8 9 10 -ML- 12 11 10 09 08

Teacher and Content Consultants

Melissa Aubuchon
Indian Trail Middle School
Plainfield Community Consolidated
School District 202
Plainfield, Illinois

Jim Bredin
Office of the Great Lakes
Lansing, Michigan

Srinivasan Damodharan
New Horizon High School
Bangalore, India

Sarah Giese
Kenmore Middle School
Arlington Public Schools
Arlington, Virginia

Jim Gindling
Willink Middle School
Webster Central School District
Webster, New York

Diana Jordan
Kenmore Middle School
Arlington Public Schools
Arlington, Virginia

Marianne Kenney (NCGE)
Geography Education Consultant
Denver, Colorado

Miles Lawrence
NOAA TPC/National Hurricane
Center
Miami, Florida

Patrick McCrystle
Bellarmine College Preparatory
San Jose, California

Deanna Morrow
Martinez Middle School
Hillsborough County School District
Lutz, Florida

Michael Radcliffe
Greenville High School
Greenville Public Schools
Greenville, Michigan

Betsy Sheffield
National Snow and Ice Data Center
Boulder, Colorado

Stacy Stewart
NOAA TPC/National Hurricane
Center
Miami, Florida

Fred Walk (NCGE)
Normal Community High School
McLean County Unit District No. 5
Normal, Illinois

Department of Geography
Illinois State University
Normal, Illinois

Scholars

Dr. Siaw Akwawua
College of Humanities and
Social Sciences
University of Northern Colorado

Dr. Robert Bednarz (NCGE)
College of Geosciences
Texas A&M University

Dr. James Dunn (NCGE)
College of Humanities and
Social Sciences
University of Northern Colorado

Dr. Bill Fraser
Biology Department
Montana State University

Dr. Patricia Gober (NCGE)
Department of Geography
Arizona State University

Dr. Susan Hardwick (NCGE)
Department of Geography
University of Oregon

Professor Gail Hobbs (NCGE)
Department of Anthropological
and Geographical Sciences
Los Angeles Pierce College

Dr. Phil Klein (NCGE)
College of Humanities and
Social Sciences
University of Northern Colorado

Dr. Gwenda Rice (NCGE)
College of Education
Western Oregon University

Dr. Kit Salter (retired; NCGE)
Department of Geography
University of Missouri

Dr. Earl Scott (retired)
Department of Geography
University of Minnesota

Music Consultant

Melanie Pinkert
Music Faculty
Montgomery College, Maryland

Geography Specialist

Mapping Specialists
Madison, Wisconsin

Internet Consultant

Clinton Couse
Educational Technology Consultant
Seattle, Washington

Researcher

Jessica Efron
Library Faculty
Appalachian State University

Praise for *Geography Alive! Regions and People*

I am excited about the development of this new geography program, *Geography Alive! Regions and People*, which incorporates many of the approaches used in TCI's successful *History Alive!* programs. The innovative, hands-on lessons challenge students to use the tools of geography to view, analyze, and understand the world around them while building on their content area reading skills.

Most world geography texts move from region to region in a predictable sequence, often with superficial coverage. *Geography Alive!* uses a case study approach, allowing students to study geographic issues in greater depth. Each case study, aligned with the National Geography Standards, is framed by an essential question and built around an interactive classroom activity. The activity is tightly integrated with the corresponding chapter in the text and provides students with opportunities to explore and wrestle with geographic concepts and issues. Students examine such topics as spatial inequality in Mexico City, resource consumption in the United States, the impact of the monsoon on South Asia, competing land interests in the Amazon, and the role of women micro-entrepreneurs in Africa.

Embedded in each case study are opportunities for students to develop skills in geographic analysis and geographic inquiry. In addition to providing student editions at both the sixth and ninth grade reading levels, the program includes a mapping lab for each region, a digital teacher resource CD-ROM, and an impressive array of high-quality maps, diagrams, and graphs.

An important component of each case study is the section on Global Connections. Here, students examine the broader global context of issues that arise in the case study. For example, the case study on Japan focuses on how population density affects the way people live. After analyzing how population density impacts transportation, land use, housing, and health in that country, students examine factors contributing to the well-being of people in other countries with a high population density, such as Bangladesh, Singapore, and the Netherlands.

What sets this program apart is that is asks students to use real geographers' skills and strategies to look at critical contemporary geographic issues. This program is a welcome relief from the mind-numbing encyclopedic tour of world regions, still prevalent in many current world geography classes.

Gwenda H. Rice
NCGE President 2004
Chair, Division of Teacher Education
College of Education
Western Oregon University

Contents

UNIT 5 Africa

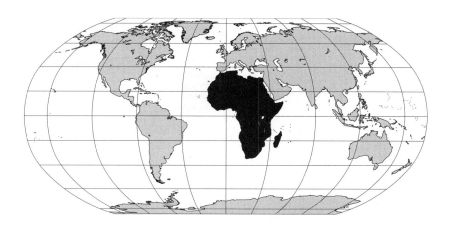

The Nile River: A Journey from Source to Mouth

Overview

In this lesson, students learn about key physical features and human activity that affect river systems as they flow across the surface of Earth. In a **Social Studies Skill Builder,** students examine photographs of important features along the Nile River that show how the river changes in its journey from source to mouth. They use longitude and latitude coordinates to plot the features on a map of the Nile and annotate the map to explain how those features reflect changes in the river.

Objectives

Students will

- define and explain the importance of these key geographic terms: *hydroelectric potential, perennial irrigation, river basin, water cycle.*
- understand key physical features and human activity that affect river systems by identifying how the Nile changes from source to mouth.
- examine how hydroelectric dams impact river systems around the world.

Materials

- *Geography Alive! Regions and People*
- Interactive Student Notebooks
- Transparencies 19A and 19B
- Information Master 19 (1 transparency)
- Placards 19A–19J

Preview

1 Project the satellite image on *Transparency 19A: Preview 19*.
Ask students, *What interesting details do you see? What do you
think this physical feature is?* Explain that this is a satellite
image of the Nile River, and then reveal the map, which is of
the same area.

**2 Have students complete Preview 19 in their Interactive
Student Notebooks.** When they've finished, have them share
their questions. Expect a wide variety of questions. As students
share their ideas, have them each write two additional questions.
Explain that they should keep their four questions in mind
throughout the activity, as they will revisit them later.

**3 Explain the connection between the Preview and the
upcoming activity.** Tell students that it is not surprising that
they have so many questions about the Nile River. At a length
of 4,160 miles, it is generally considered to be the longest river
in the world. In the upcoming activity, students will follow the
path of the Nile as it flows from its sources in the mountains
and highlands of Africa to its mouth on the Mediterranean Sea
and learn about how the river changes along the way.

Essential Question and Geoterms

**1 Introduce Chapter 19 in *Geography Alive! Regions and
People*.** Have students read Section 19.1. Afterward, ask them to
identify at least four details in the mosaic that represent ideas in
the text they just read.

**2 Introduce the Graphic Organizer and the Essential
Question.** Have students examine the map of the Nile. Ask,

- What interesting details do you see?
- Where are the sources of the Nile? At about what parallel of
  latitude is each located?
- Where is the river's mouth? At about what parallel of lati-
  tude is this?
- Through how many countries does the Nile River flow?
- What physical changes do you expect to happen to the Nile
  as it flows from its sources to its mouth?
- What other types of changes might you expect to see as the
  Nile flows from its sources to its mouth?

Transparency 19A   **Preview 19**

Have students read the accompanying text. Make sure they understand the Essential Question, *How do rivers change as they flow across Earth's surface?* You may want to post the Essential Question in the room or write it on the board for the duration of the activity.

3 Have students read Section 19.2. Then have them work individually or in pairs to complete Geoterms 19 in their Interactive Student Notebooks. Ask them to share their answers with another student, or have volunteers share their answers with the class.

Geoterms 19

Social Studies Skill Builder

1 Prepare your classroom for the activity. Create 10 stations along the walls of the room, using two desks for each station. Post one of *Placards 19A–19J: Features Along the Nile River* at each station.

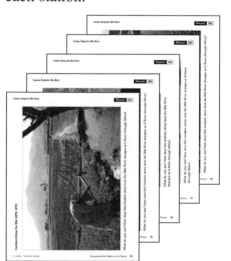

Placards 19A–19E

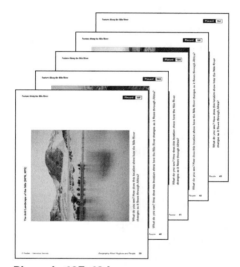

Placards 19F–19J

2 Place students in mixed-ability pairs.

3 Introduce the activity. Have students open their Interactive Student Notebooks to Reading Notes 19. Project a transparency of *Information Master 19: Social Studies Skill Builder Directions,* and review the steps for completing the activity. Keep the steps projected throughout the activity. (**Note:** You may want to copy the third and fourth pages of Reading Notes 19 for each student. Have students tape the copies together and then to the first two pages of the Reading Notes to create one long map of the Nile River on which to take notes. After the activity, students can fold the extra papers into their notebooks.)

Information Master 19

4 Conduct the activity. Assign each pair to a station, and begin the activity. When a pair finishes at a station, have both students raise their hands to indicate that they are ready for you to check their work. Use Guide to Reading Notes 19 to check their answers. If their answers are satisfactory, award them points (optional) and have them move to a new station. Continue until most pairs have visited most of the stations. (**Note:** You may want to model the steps at one station with the entire class before sending pairs of students to individual stations. Also, note that each reading section relates to more than one placard. After students have read a section, they only need to reread the relevant portion when they are directed to that section again.)

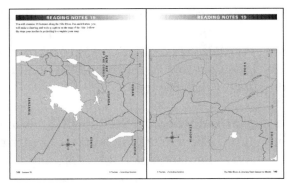

Reading Notes 19

5 Have pairs become "experts" on a station. Once most pairs have visited most of the stations, announce that each pair will become experts on the station they are currently visiting. (**Note:** Some pairs may need to join together to make groups of four.) Tell them to prepare to share information about the location of the feature shown at that station as well as how the Nile changes at that point.

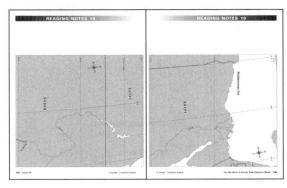

Reading Notes 19

6 Conduct the wrap-up. Have pairs choose one person to represent each station. The representatives should bring the placards to the front of the room. (**Note:** You may want to conduct this wrap-up in a larger space, such as a hallway or playing field. Have students re-create the Nile using an accurate scale to space out the placards. Alternatively, conduct this activity on a set of stairs. Have students stand on the stairs, using elevation to space out the placards.) With the help of the other students, representatives should arrange themselves as if they were the Nile River, beginning with the sources of the river and ending with its mouth. The correct order of the placards is as follows:

- *Placard 19I* (Lake Victoria) and *Placard 19C* (Lake Tana)
- *Placard 19E* (As Sudd)
- *Placard 19J* (Khartoum, Sudan)
- *Placard 19H* ("Great Bend")
- *Placard 19F* (arid landscape)
- *Placard 19B* (Aswan High Dam)
- *Placard 19A* (farmland)
- *Placard 19G* (Cairo, Egypt)
- *Placard 19D* (Nile Delta)

One at a time, have the "Nile River" (students) share information about each feature, its location, and how the Nile changes at that point. (**Note:** Students may decide to place Placard 19C between Placards 19E and 19J because of its latitude. Make sure they explain that Lake Tana is the source of the Blue Nile, which meets the White Nile at Khartoum. Alternatively, they may decide to place Placard 19C somewhat off to the side.)

Processing

1 Have students complete Processing 19. Have students open their Interactive Student Notebooks to Processing 19, and review the directions with them. If they find that they can't answer one of their questions, allow them to substitute another question, either a new one of their own or one that another student has written.

2 Have students share their answers by playing a game. This game will encourage them to review what they learned in the lesson. Follow these steps:

- Divide the class into two teams.
- Have a volunteer from one team read a question and its answer.
- Ask the opposing team if anyone has the same question.
- If the opposing team has the same question, have a volunteer from that team read their answer. Award each team 2 points if the answers are both accurate but share different information. Award each team 1 point if the answers are both accurate but share similar information. Award no points for incorrect answers.
- Continue until all of the questions have been shared or until each student has had a chance to share at least one question.

Processing 19

Global Connections

1 Introduce the Global Connections. Have students read Section 19.7. Tell them that they will now see how some of the issues they encountered in the activity exist in other areas of the world.

2 Project *Transparency 19B: Global Connections.* Help students analyze the map by asking these questions:

- **What interesting details do you see?**

- **What are some of the world's major river systems? Where are they located?**

- **Which river systems have hydroelectric dams? Which do not?**

Transparency 19B

3 **Have students read Section 19.8 and examine the rest of the information in the section.** Then lead a discussion of the following questions. Use the additional information given to enrich the discussion.

- **What are the main benefits of building hydroelectric dams?**

Hydroelectric dams produce clean energy. The Itaipu Dam, for example, on the border of Brazil and Paraguay, supplies 25% of Brazil's energy and 78% of Paraguay's. Hydroelectric power provides 83% of Iceland's energy and almost all of Norway's. Hydroelectric dams don't pollute the air the way power plants that burn fossil fuels do. China is rich in coal reserves, and 75% of China's energy is fueled by the burning of coal. It is not surprising that air pollution is a serious problem in China.

Hydroelectric dams also control flooding and provide water for farms and cities. The Three Gorges Dam project in China is ambitious. An opportunity to increase China's use of a clean energy source, it also is expected to control the hazardous waters of the Yangtze River (Chang Jiang). Stories have been long told about the deadly flooding of this river. In the past 100 years, more than 1 million lives have been lost.

Dams also create lakes that are used for recreation. Lake Mead on the Colorado River was created by the building of the Hoover Dam in 1936. Today, Lake Mead is part of the National Park Service. Visitors can enjoy swimming, fishing, boating, hiking, and other activities there.

- **What are the main costs of building hydroelectric dams?**

Giant dams cost billions of dollars to build. The Itaipu Dam on the border of Brazil and Paraguay cost $18 billion by the time it was completed in 1991.

Hydroelectric dams have environmental costs as well. The lakes that form behind dams flood large areas. Towns, farms, and forests may be submerged by rising water. The Chinese government is relocating 1.2 million people due to the building of the Three Gorges Dam. Some experts believe that even this number falls short by about 700,000 people. People can be relocated, but important archeological and historical sites may not be as lucky. It is estimated that almost 1,300 of these sites will be submerged once the dam is completed.

Wildlife may suffer from the loss of habitat. The Edwards Dam, built in 1837 in Augusta, Maine, on the Kennebec River, provided energy to the mills along its banks. Concern was raised over the ability of fish to swim upstream to spawn. Sure enough, fish almost completely disappeared from the river. The federal government decided that this environmental impact was too much. In 1999, the Edwards Dam was destroyed. It was the first time the U.S. government removed a dam for environmental reasons.

- **Do the benefits of damming rivers outweigh the costs?**

Online Resources

For more information on the Nile River, refer students to Online Resources for *Geography Alive! Regions and People* at www.teachtci.com.

Assessment

Masters for assessment appear on the next three pages followed by answers and scoring rubrics.

Assessment 19

Mastering the Content

Shade in the oval by the letter of the best answer for each question.

1. Which of these is the **best** definition of a river basin?
   - A. the sources of a river and its tributaries
   - B. the delta created by a river at its mouth
   - C. the area drained by a river and its tributaries
   - D. the length of a river from its source to its mouth

2. What is the source of the Blue Nile?
   - A. As Sudd in Sudan
   - B. Lake Nasser in Egypt
   - C. Lake Tana in Ethiopia
   - D. Murchison Falls in Uganda

3. Which of these aspects of life in Egypt depends **most** on the water stored in Lake Nasser?
   - A. annual flooding
   - B. sewage treatment
   - C. population growth
   - D. perennial irrigation

4. Read the text below. What part of the Nile River basin does it describe?

   This area has the richest farmland in all of Africa. Since ancient times, much of Egypt's food has been grown here.

   - A. the As Sudd
   - B. the Nile Delta
   - C. the land around Lake Nasser
   - D. the land where the two Niles meet

5. Which of these created barriers to river travel on the Nile in ancient times?
   - A. cataracts
   - B dams
   - C. floodplains
   - D. wadis

6. What was Egypt's **main** reason for building the Aswan High Dam?
   - A. to encourage water sports on the river
   - B. to flood the river's barriers to shipping
   - C. to stop sewage from flowing into the river
   - D. to develop the river's hydroelectric potential

7. Which of these conclusions is **best** supported by this graph?

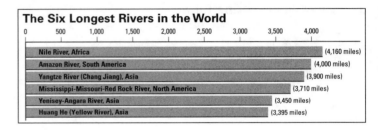

The Six Longest Rivers in the World

Nile River, Africa	(4,160 miles)
Amazon River, South America	(4,000 miles)
Yangtze River (Chang Jiang), Asia	(3,900 miles)
Mississippi-Missouri-Red Rock River, North America	(3,710 miles)
Yenisey-Angara River, Asia	(3,450 miles)
Huang He (Yellow River), Asia	(3,395 miles)

   - A. There are three 4,000-mile-long rivers on Earth.
   - B. The Nile flows through three countries in Africa.
   - C. Three of the world's major rivers flow across Asia.
   - D. The Amazon has three tributaries in South America.

8. All of the following are benefits provided by hydroelectric dams **except**
   - A. habitat loss.
   - B. clean energy.
   - C. flood control.
   - D. irrigation water.

Applying Geography Skills: Reading a Diagram

Use the diagram and your knowledge of geography to complete the tasks below.

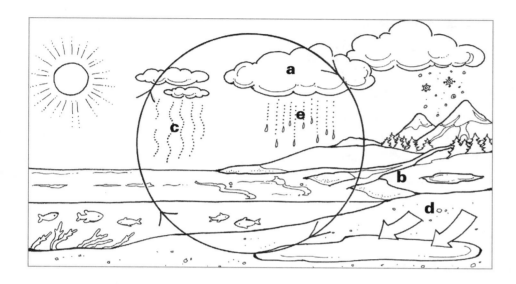

1. Match each letter on the diagram to one of the terms below. Write the letters on the lines.

    _____ condensation

    _____ evaporation

    _____ infiltration

    _____ precipitation

    _____ runoff

2. Give the diagram a title that tells what it shows. Write your title above the diagram.

3. Briefly describe the process shown in the diagram.

Test Terms Glossary
To **describe** means to provide details about something, such as how it works.

To **label** means to attach identification to something.

Exploring the Essential Question

How do rivers change as they flow across Earth's surface?

In Chapter 19, you explored the Nile's journey from its sources to its mouth. Now you will use what you learned. Use the information on the diagram below and your knowledge of geography to complete this task.

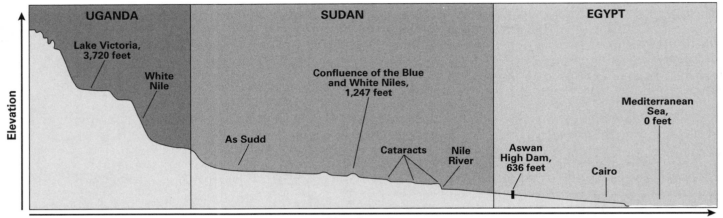

River Length

The Task: Describing the Nile's Journey from Source to Mouth

Step 1: On the elevation profile, label the main source of the White Nile with an **S**. Label the confluence of the White and Blue Niles with a **C**. Label the Nile's mouth with an **M**.

Step 2: Calculate how much the river drops in elevation between **S** and **C**. Do the same for the drop between **C** and **M**. Finally, calculate the total drop in elevation between **S** and **M**.

Step 3: Underline one feature on the river between **S** and **C**. Draw a box around three features between **C** and **M**. Circle the three countries between **S** and **M**.

Step 4: Write a two-paragraph description of the Nile's journey from source to mouth. Describe the White Nile's journey from source to confluence in your first paragraph. In your second paragraph, describe the Nile River's journey from confluence to mouth. Each paragraph should include

A. a topic sentence introducing this part of the river.
B. supporting sentences that include details about the river on this part of its journey. These details may include those you identified in Steps 1–3.
C. a concluding sentence that summarizes the main points of the paragraph.

Writing Tips: Using Sequence Words
Sequence words help readers understand the order in which things occur. As you move from one river feature to another, use words like *first* and *later* to show what comes first, what comes next, and so on. Other sequence terms include *before, next, after,* and *finally.*

Example:
First, the Nile passes through a series of cataracts. *Next,* the river's waters are trapped behind the Aswan High Dam.

Applying Geography Skills: Sample Responses

1. a, c, d, e, b
2. The Water Cycle
3. The water cycle begins when water evaporates from oceans, rivers, and lakes and condenses into clouds. Later the water falls back to Earth as precipitation. Some water flows as runoff into rivers while some soaks into the ground (infiltration). Rivers flow into oceans, where the cycle begins again.

Exploring the Essential Question: Sample Response

Steps 1–3:
Elevation calculations: **S** (source) to **C** (confluence): 2,473 feet; **C** to **M** (mouth): about 1,247 feet; **S** to **M**: about 3,720 feet

Step 4: The paragraphs should include the elements listed in the prompt.

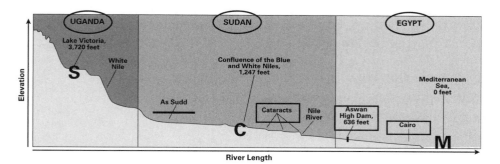

The White Nile is one of the two branches of the Nile River. It begins its journey in Central Africa at the outflow of Lake Victoria. As it travels through Uganda, it drops sharply. Once it reaches Sudan, it slows and spreads out to form a swampy region known as As Sudd. When it reaches the city of Khartoum, the White Nile has dropped more than 2,400 feet in elevation and traveled through a variety of landscapes.

At Khartoum, the White and Blue Niles come together to form the Nile River. Here the Nile enters one of the world's harshest landscapes. Its flow changes several times as it moves through Sudan and Egypt. First, it passes through a series of cataracts. Next, its waters are trapped behind the Aswan High Dam. This dam stores water for generating electricity and irrigating crops. Later, the Nile passes through Cairo. This city takes water out the Nile for drinking and dumps sewage back into it. Just before its journey ends, the river spreads out across the Nile Delta. This area has some of the world's richest farmland. Finally, the Nile empties into the Mediterranean Sea, its long journey over at last.

Mastering the Content Answer Key

1. C	2. C	3. D	4. B
5. A	6. D	7. C	8. A

Applying Geography Skills Scoring Rubric

Score	General Description
2	Student responds to all parts of the task. Response is correct and clear.
1	Student responds to some parts of the task. Response is mostly correct.
0	Response does not match the task or is incorrect.

Exploring the Essential Question Scoring Rubric

Score	General Description
3	Student responds to all parts of the task. Response is correct, clear, and supported by details.
2	Student responds to most or all parts of the task. Response is generally correct but may lack details.
1	Student responds to at least one part of the task. Response may contain errors and lack details.
0	Response does not match the task or is incorrect.

Learn About the Nile River

Follow these steps to learn about the Nile River:

1. Examine the photograph of the Nile River feature at the station. Discuss the question under the photograph with your partner.

2. Turn to the map of the Nile River in your Reading Notes. Use the latitude and longitude coordinates to locate the feature on your map. Mark and label the feature on the map.

3. Find out more about the feature by reading the related section of Chapter 19. Use the feature's latitude coordinate to determine which section to read.

   • If the feature is between 5°S and 4°N, read Section 19.3.
   • If the feature is between 5°N and 19°N, read Section 19.4.
     (**Exception:** For *Placard 19C,* Lake Tana, read Section 19.3.)
   • If the feature is between 20°N and 25°N, read Section 19.5.
   • If the feature is between 26°N and 35°N, read Section 19.6.

4. In an appropriate place on your map, make a drawing of the feature. Write a caption for your drawing. Your caption should describe what the feature is. It should also explain how the Nile River changes at that location.

5. Check your Reading Notes with your teacher. Then move to a different station, and repeat Steps 1–5.

You will examine 10 features along the Nile River. For each feature, you will make a drawing and write a caption on the map of the Nile. Follow the steps your teacher is projecting to complete your map.

Drawings will vary.

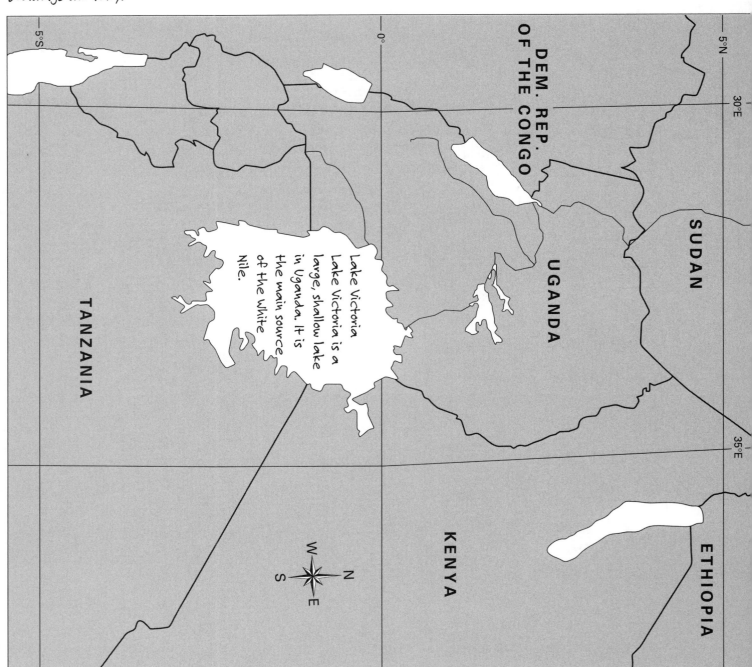

Lake Victoria
Lake Victoria is a large, shallow lake in Uganda. It is the main source of the white Nile.

Drawings will vary.

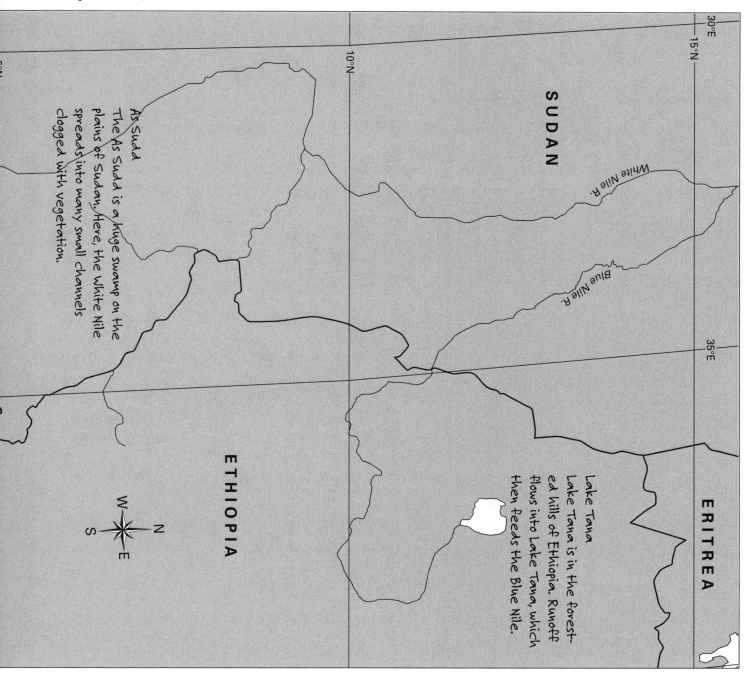

As Suda
The As Suda is a huge swamp on the plains of Sudan. Here, the White Nile spreads into many small channels clogged with vegetation.

SUDAN

White Nile R.

Blue Nile R.

30°E

15°N

10°N

35°E

ERITREA

Lake Tana
Lake Tana is in the forested hills of Ethiopia. Runoff flows into Lake Tana, which then feeds the Blue Nile.

ETHIOPIA

N
W   E
S

Drawings will vary.

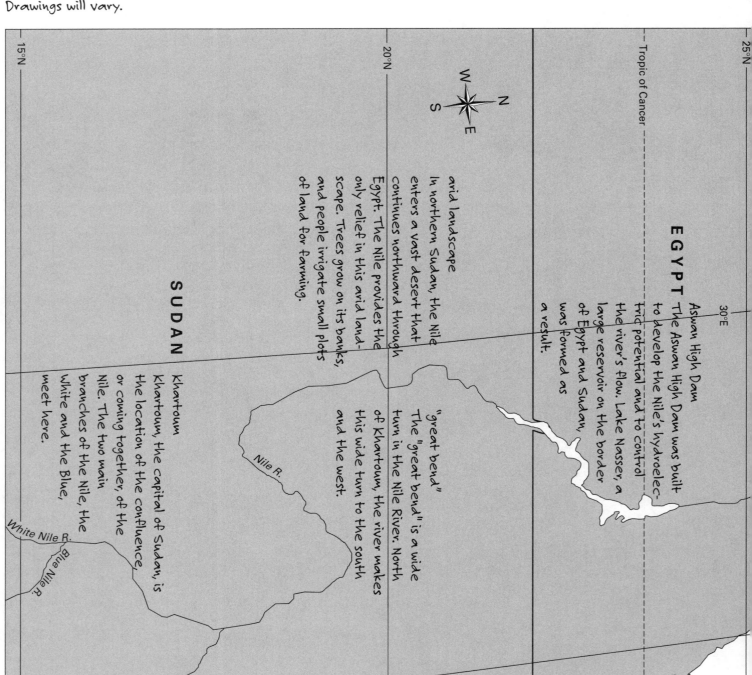

EGYPT

Aswan High Dam The Aswan High Dam was built to develop the Nile's hydroelectric potential and to control the river's flow. Lake Nasser, a large reservoir on the border of Egypt and Sudan, was formed as a result.

"great bend" The "great bend" is a wide turn in the Nile River. North of Khartoum, the river makes this wide turn to the south and the west.

In northern Sudan, the Nile enters a vast desert that continues northward through Egypt. The Nile provides the only relief in this arid landscape. Trees grow on its banks, and people irrigate small plots of land for farming.

avid landscape

SUDAN

Khartoum Khartoum, the capital of Sudan, is the location of the confluence, or coming together, of the Nile. The two main branches of the Nile, the White and the Blue, meet here.

Nile R.

White Nile R.

Blue Nile R.

Tropic of Cancer

25°N

30°E

20°N

15°N

Drawings will vary.

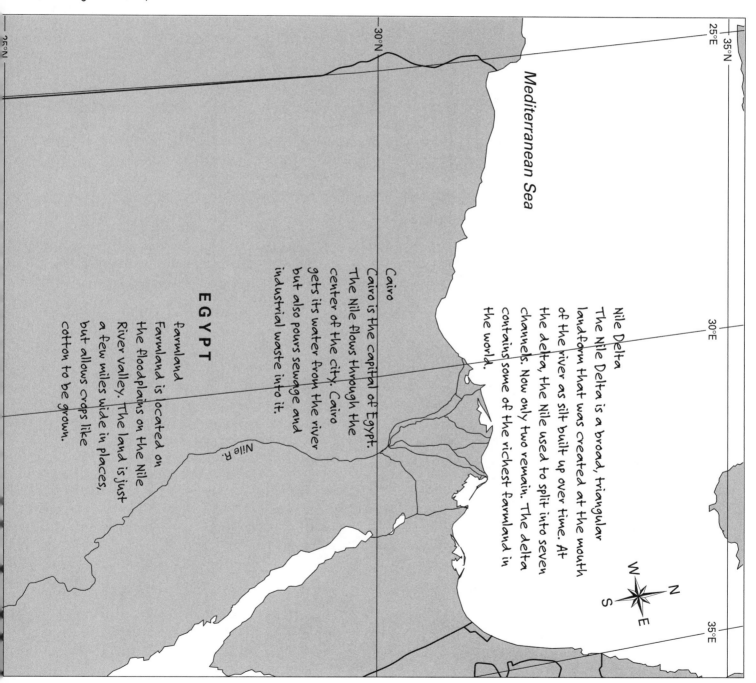

Mediterranean Sea

Nile Delta
The Nile Delta is a broad, triangular
landform that was created at the mouth
of the river as silt built up over time. At
the delta, the Nile used to split into seven
channels. Now only two remain. The delta
contains some of the richest farmland in
the world.

Cairo
Cairo is the capital of Egypt.
The Nile flows through the
center of the city. Cairo
gets its water from the river
but also pours sewage and
industrial waste into it.

EGYPT

Farmland
Farmland is located on
the floodplains on the Nile
River valley. The land is just
a few miles wide in places,
but allows crops like
cotton to be grown.

Nile R.

25°N

30°N

25°E   30°E   35°E

N
W   E
S

Life in the Sahara and the Sahel: Adapting to a Desert Region

Overview

In this lesson, students learn about the ways people have adapted to living in the varied environments of a desert region. In a **Response Group** activity, they investigate three environments of the Saharan region—the desert, the oases, and the Sahel—and make predictions about how people have adapted to life in each. Students then read to determine the accuracy of their predictions. Finally, they examine their own physical environment to identify the ways in which people have adapted to living there.

Objectives

Students will

- define and explain the importance of these key geographic terms: *desertification, drought, marginal land, pastoral nomads*.

- describe the physical characteristics of three environments of the Saharan region: the desert, the oases, and the Sahel.

- identify ways in which people have adapted to life in these three environments.

- analyze the impact of desertification on people living in desert regions around the world.

Materials

- *Geography Alive! Regions and People*
- Interactive Student Notebooks
- Transparencies 20A–20E

Preview

1 **Have students complete Part 1 of Preview 20 in their Interactive Student Notebooks.** Ask several volunteers to share their responses.

2 **Project** *Transparency 20A: A Caravan in the Sahara.* Point out the average temperature and precipitation of the location. Then have students complete Part 2 of Preview 20 and share their ideas.

3 **Explain the connection between the Preview and the upcoming activity**. Tell students that the physical environment is one influence on how people live. People living on a small island in the ocean, for example, might lead very different lives from people living on a continent and near a river because the physical environments are so different. Students may have hypothesized that they would probably not have the same daily routines and activities if they were living in the vast, dry lands of the Sahara. In the upcoming activity, they will learn about the physical characteristics of the Sahara and the Sahel and how people have adapted to the varied environments in this desert region.

Preview 20

Transparency 20A

Essential Question and Geoterms

1 **Introduce Chapter 20 in** *Geography Alive! Regions and People.* Explain that in this chapter, students will learn about how people have adapted to life in the desert region of the Sahara. Have them read Section 20.1. Afterward, ask them to identify at least four details in the photograph of the camel caravan that represent ideas in the text they just read.

2 **Introduce the Graphic Organizer and the Essential Question.** Have students examine the map of the Saharan region. Then ask,

- What interesting details do you see?
- What environments do you see?
- In what ways might the geography of each environment be similar? In what ways might they be different?
- How might people have adapted to living in each of these environments?

Have students read the accompanying text. Make sure they understand the Essential Question, *How do people adapt to living in a desert region?* You may want to post the Essential Question in the room or write it on the board for the duration of the activity.

3 Have students read Section 20.2. Then have them work individually or in pairs to complete Geoterms 20 in their Interactive Student Notebooks. Ask them to share their answers with another student, or have volunteers share their answers with the class.

Geoterms 20

Response Group

1 Arrange students in mixed-ability groups of four. You may want to prepare a transparency that shows them with whom they will work and where they will sit. Arrange the desks so that students in each group can talk among themselves and clearly see the projector screen.

2 Introduce the activity. Explain that students will read about the three environments of the Saharan region—the desert, the oases, and the Sahel—and take on the roles of people living in each one. After discussing the challenges of each physical environment and ways they might adapt to living there, they will read about actual adaptations people have made. Then they will create and perform brief act-it-outs featuring those adaptations. Finally, they will talk about which environment might be the most challenging to live in.

3 Have students learn about the desert environment. Have a volunteer in each group read Section 20.3 aloud. Then ask students to open their Interactive Student Notebooks to Reading Notes 20 and answer the first question for Section 20.3. Use Guide to Reading Notes 20 to review their answers.

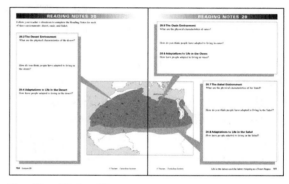

Reading Notes 20

4 Project *Transparency 20B: The Desert.* As a class, review the procedure outlined on the transparency.

5 Have groups brainstorm and record adaptations they might make to life in this environment. Encourage them to examine the image carefully and to use information from their Reading Notes to generate ideas for adaptations they might make to this environment. Allow groups adequate time for discussion. They record their ideas under the second question in the notes for Section 20.3.

Transparency 20B

6 Have students read Section 20.4 and complete the Reading Notes for that section. They will record people's actual adaptations to this environment. Use the Guide to Reading Notes to review their answers.

7 Have groups prepare brief act-it-outs featuring adaptations to the desert environment. Tell each group to choose one adaptation people have made to this environment to bring to life in an act-it-out. Explain that each act-it-out should last 10 to 20 seconds and clearly demonstrate the adaptation. Groups may use simple props and costumes. Allow groups adequate time to create and practice their act-it-outs.

8 Conduct the act-it-outs. Have groups perform their act-it-outs one at a time. To encourage the audience to pay close attention, have each group try to identify the adaptation represented in the act-it-out. Follow these steps:

- After the performance, have each group write the adaptation they think is being demonstrated in big letters on a sheet of scrap paper.
- One at a time, have the audience groups reveal their guess by holding up their paper.
- Ask the group who performed to reveal the adaptation.
- Award points to groups who guessed correctly (optional).

9 Repeat Steps 3 to 8 for the oases and the Sahel. Make these modifications:

- *Oases:* Have students read Sections 20.5 and 20.6. Use *Transparency 20C: The Oases.*
- *Sahel:* Have students read Sections 20.7 and 20.8. Use *Transparency 20D: The Sahel.*

10 Wrap up the activity with a brief discussion. Ask,

- In what ways are the adaptations to each environment—the desert, the oases, and the Sahel—similar? Why do you think those similarities exist?
- In what ways are the adaptations different? Why do you think those differences exist?
- Which of the three environments had the most interesting or unique adaptations?
- Which environment do you think is the most challenging to adapt to? Why?

Transparency 20C   **Transparency 20D**

Global Connections

1 Introduce the Global Connections. Have students read Section 20.9. Tell them that they will now examine the impact of desertification on desert regions around the world.

2 Project *Transparency 20E: Global Connections.* Have students analyze the map by leading a discussion of the following questions. Use the additional information given to enrich the discussion.

Transparency 20E

- **What interesting details do you see?**

- **Where are some of the world's largest desert regions?**
  Nearly 35 percent of the Earth's land area is covered by desert. Desert covers most of northern Africa as well as parts of southern Africa. Desert regions are also found in Southwest and Central Asia. The Gobi is located in East Asia. Much of Australia is covered by desert. Major desert regions are also found in North America and parts of South America.

- **What patterns do you see among the world's deserts?**

3 Have students read Section 20.10 and examine the rest of the information in the section. Then lead a discussion of these questions:

- **Are the world's deserts growing or shrinking?**
  Many marginal areas are being threatened by desertification. According to the United Nations Convention to Combat Desertification, one third of the world's land is at risk. This amounts to 15 million square miles and directly affects 250 million people. All this land could, in time, become desert.

  Not everyone agrees that the world's deserts are expanding. Satellite images are used to study the growth and reduction of the world's deserts. Researchers studied images of the Sahara in the 1980s. In the early part of the decade, the desert expanded. It shrank in 1985 and 1986, but grew again in 1987. After receding in 1988, the Sahara again increased in 1989 and 1990. Overall, the Sahara grew by approximately 245,600 square miles from 1980 to 1990. Some scientists are wary of stating that this evidence indicates a long-term trend because deserts do experience short-term patterns of change.

- **What human activities contribute to desertification?**

- **How might people adapt to living in areas threatened by desertification?**

  People deal with desertification in many ways. One is by being better prepared to deal with drought, which makes desertification more likely. Some countries, like the United States and Australia, have tried cloud seeding. Chemicals are placed in clouds to increase the production of rain. However, experts do not agree on the long-term effectiveness of cloud seeding.

  Another adaptation is to reduce the impact of human activities that contribute to desertification. The Chinese government, for example, is encouraging people to create forest in place of farmland on steep slopes and marginal lands. Doing so will help to prevent the impact of farming on thin, troubled soil.

Processing

Have students complete Processing 20 in their Interactive Student Notebooks.

Online Resources

For more information on the Saharan region, refer students to Online Resources for *Geography Alive! Regions and People* at www.teachtci.com.

Assessment

Masters for assessment appear on the next three pages followed by answers and scoring rubrics.

Processing 20

Mastering the Content

Shade in the oval by the letter of the best answer for each question.

1. Which of these is a **major** difference between the Sahara and the Sahel?

   ◯ A. The Sahara has larger forests.

   ◯ B. The Sahel receives more rainfall.

   ◯ C. The Sahara has more cropland.

   ◯ D. The Sahel records higher temperatures.

2. Marginal land is **best** described as land that is

   ◯ A. watered by an oasis.

   ◯ B. on the edge of a town.

   ◯ C. not well suited for farming.

   ◯ D. best used for raising cash crops.

3. What do ergs, regs, and hammadas have in common?

   ◯ A. They are all desert flora.

   ◯ B. They are all desert fauna.

   ◯ C. They are all desert landforms.

   ◯ D. They are all desert ecosystems.

4. What does this diagram tell about oases?

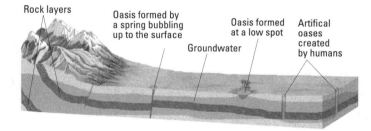

Rock layers

Oasis formed by a spring bubbling up to the surface

Oasis formed at a low spot

Artifical oases created by humans

Groundwater

   ◯ A. Oases are not found in deserts.

   ◯ B. Oases are created in many ways.

   ◯ C. Oases are created only by humans.

   ◯ D. Oases are not fed by natural springs.

5. What is the **main** reason pastoral nomads move from place to place?

   ◯ A. to sell their trade goods

   ◯ B. to care for their date palms

   ◯ C. to clear new land for their crops

   ◯ D. to find fresh pasture for their herds

6. Read the description of date palm groves below. Then choose the statement that **best** explains why these trees are so important to life in the Sahara.

   Those magnificent palm groves are the blood and bone of the desert; life in the Sahara would be unthinkable without them.

   ◯ A. Date palms provide shelter for nomads and their herds.

   ◯ B. Date palms provide food, fuel, and materials for homes.

   ◯ C. Date palms provide drinking water for people and animals.

   ◯ D. Date palms provide a cash crop for farmers on marginal lands.

7. All of the following are major causes of desertification **except**

   ◯ A. overgrazing.

   ◯ B. deforestation.

   ◯ C. long-term drought.

   ◯ D. shifting agriculture.

8. Which of the following are **most** threatened by desertification?

   ◯ A. croplands

   ◯ B. forested areas

   ◯ C. marginal lands

   ◯ D. wilderness areas

Assessment 　20

Applying Geography Skills:
Reading a Physical Features Map

Use this map and your knowledge of geography to complete the
tasks below.

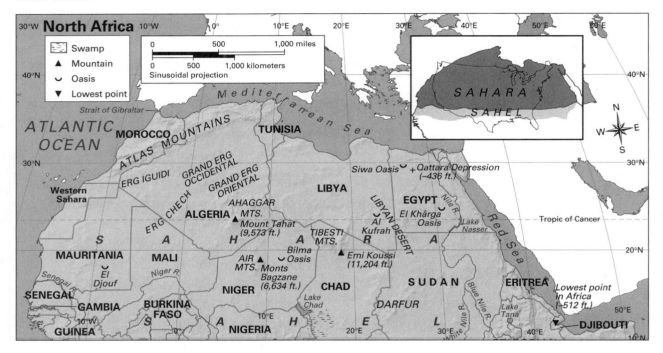

1. Circle Lake Chad and the Atlas Mountains on the map. Use the
   compass rose to determine the direction a camel caravan would
   travel to get from Lake Chad to the Atlas Mountains.

2. Identify one oasis where the caravan might stop on this journey.
   Use the scale to estimate its distance from Lake Chad.

3. Identify two mountain peaks that the caravan could use as landmarks
   on this journey. List each the elevation of each peak. Estimate the
   longitude and latitude of each peak.

4. Draw a route on the map for the caravan from Lake Chad to the
   Atlas Mountains. Include a stop at the oasis. Decide how you
   will deal with ergs, or regions of large sand dunes. Estimate the
   distance of your route in miles.

5. Camels travel about 25 miles a day. Estimate how long this journey
   will take. Include at least one day of rest at an oasis in your estimate.

Test Terms Glossary
To **estimate** means to
make a rough calcu-
lation of something.

Exploring the Essential Question

How do people adapt to living in a desert region?

In Chapter 20, you explored how people have adapted to living in the Sahara and the Sahel. Now you will use what you learned. Use this diagram and your knowledge of geography to complete the task below.

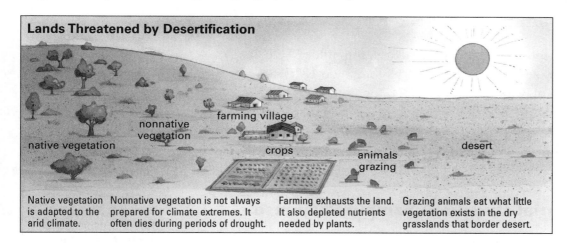

Lands Threatened by Desertification

farming village

nonnative vegetation

native vegetation

crops

animals grazing

desert

Native vegetation is adapted to the arid climate.	Nonnative vegetation is not always prepared for climate extremes. It often dies during periods of drought.	Farming exhausts the land. It also depleted nutrients needed by plants.	Grazing animals eat what little vegetation exists in the dry grasslands that border desert.

The Task: Planning a PSA on Desertification

The diagram shows some of the causes of desertification. Your task is to plan a public service announcement, or PSA, about how people can combat desertification. A PSA is a short ad that appears on radio or television. Its purpose is to give people information about how to deal with a problem. Your PSA will be for television.

Step 1: Think about the people who live in areas like those in the diagram. Identify one group as your target audience. You might choose farmers, herders, homemakers, or schoolchildren. List your target audience below.

Step 2: List two ways your target audience might fight desertification. For example, farmers might plow fields in a new way to reduce erosion. Schoolchildren might make posters to encourage the use of coal for cooking. Underline the way you will talk about in your PSA.

Step 3: On another sheet of paper, outline a plan for your PSA. Your plan should include these things:

A. The setting of your PSA. For example, it might take place in a farm field, a classroom, or someone's home.

B. The characters who will appear in your PSA. At least one of them should represent your target audience.

C. A story line for your PSA. Your story should show your audience what the problem is and what they can do to combat it.

Writing Tips: Identifying Your Audience
The first step in planning a presentation is to identify your audience. This is the group of people who will see what you create. If your audience is young children, you will want to focus on simple ideas. If it is adults, your presentation should include more difficult ideas.

Applying Geography Skills: Sample Responses

Estimates will vary. Accept figures for miles, longitude, and latitude that are close to those below.

1. A caravan would travel northwest to get from Lake Chad to the Atlas Mountains.

2. The caravan might stop at the Bilma Oasis, which is about 400 miles from Lake Chad.

3. Possible peaks:
   Monts Bagzane, 6,634 feet elevation, latitude 18°N, longitude 9°E
   Emi Koussi, 11,204 feet elevation, latitude 19°N, longitude 18°E
   Mount Tahat, 9,573 feet elevation, latitude 23°N, longitude 6°E

4. Total route may be 1,600 to 1,700 miles, depending on whether it goes through or skirts the ergs.

5. The journey could take from 65 to 70 days, depending on the route and length of stop at an oasis.

Exploring the Essential Question: Sample Response

Steps 1 and 2: Accept any reasonable target audience and response to desertification.

Step 3: The plan should include all the elements listed in the prompt.

Example of a PSA for Herders

Setting: A field with some grass and small shrubs, but no tall trees. At the outer edge of the field, sand has begun to cover the grass.

Characters: A herder who is watching his herd of goats, along with his wife and two children

Story line: The herder looks over his dry pasture and announces to his wife and children that it is time to move on to new grazing land. The wife complains that she is tired of moving. She points out that there are still plants for the goats to eat. The children complain that they don't want to leave the friends they have made in the nearby village. The herder explains that if they stay and the goats eat more of the plants, nothing will be left to hold back the desert. He points to the edge of the field where the desert is already taking over. He tells his family that if they don't move on, all of this area will soon be desert. In the last scene, the family is unpacking their belongings in a greener pasture with no sand at its edge. Everyone looks happier, even the goats. The PSA ends with an announcer saying, "If herders are careful to take good care of the land, the land will take care of them and their animals."

Mastering the Content Answer Key

1. B	2. C	3. C	4. B
5. D	6. B	7. D	8. C

Applying Geography Skills Scoring Rubric

Score	General Description
2	Student responds to all parts of the task. Response is correct and clear.
1	Student responds to some parts of the task. Response is mostly correct.
0	Response does not match the task or is incorrect.

Exploring the Essential Question Scoring Rubric

Score	General Description
3	Student responds to all parts of the task. Response is correct, clear, and supported by details.
2	Student responds to most or all parts of the task. Response is generally correct but may lack details.
1	Student responds to at least one part of the task. Response may contain errors and lack details.
0	Response does not match the task or is incorrect.

Follow your teacher's directions to complete the Reading Notes for each of three environments: desert, oasis, and Sahel.

20.3 The Desert Environment

What are the physical characteristics of the desert?

Possible answers: The Sahara has three main landforms: ergs, regs, and hammadas. Only two rivers flow through the Sahara, the Nile and the Niger. Desert temperatures vary greatly between day and night. Rain is unpredictable.

How do you think people have adapted to living in the desert?

Answers will vary.

20.4 Adaptations to Life in the Desert

How have people adapted to living in the desert?

Possible answers: Among those who live in the Sahara are pastoral nomads such as the Tuareg. The Tuareg wear long, loose clothing to protect them from the sun. Tuareg traders use camels for transportation. Drilling machines have reached underground water to create new oases.

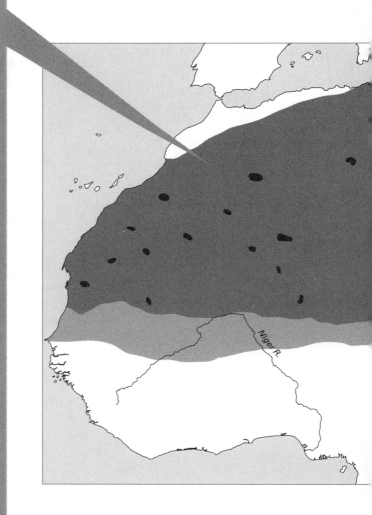

20.5 The Oasis Environment

What are the physical characteristics of oases? Possible answers: Oases are tiny islands of fresh water in the desert. Some oases are natural. Others are made when humans dig or drill into the ground. Date palms are the most important and common oasis plant.

How do you think people have adapted to living in oases?

Answers will vary.

20.6 Adaptations to Life in the Oases

How have people adapted to living in oases?

Possible answers: Farmers grow cash crops like dates and vegetables. Visiting nomads trade their products for water and food. Farmers build windbreaks to protect their fields from the desert. People sometimes must walk to distant wells as an oasis town expands.

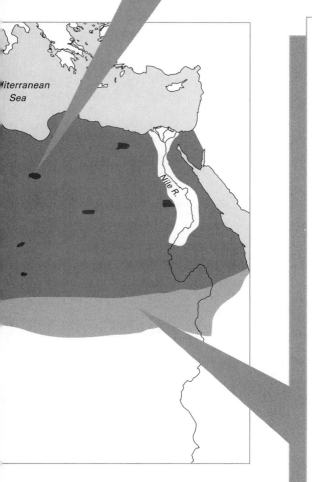

Mediterranean Sea

Nile R.

20.7 The Sahel Environment

What are the physical characteristics of the Sahel?

Possible answers: The land is marginal for farming. The vegetation is a mix of grasslands, acacia trees, baobab trees, and small bushes. Drought is a fact of life. Desertification has begun in some areas.

How do you think people have adapted to living in the Sahel?

Answers will vary.

20.8 Adaptations to Life in the Sahel

How have people adapted to living in the Sahel?

Possible answers: Farmers planted crops, like millet and sorghum, that grow in dry places. Farmers used shifting agriculture. Herders moved their herds from one grazing area to another throughout the year. Farmers today are testing new ways of farming. People are starting to use coal instead of wood for cooking.

Micro-entrepreneurs: Women's Role in the Development of Africa

Overview

In this lesson, students learn how women micro-entrepreneurs are changing the human characteristics of the communities where they live. In a **Writing for Understanding** activity, students read about three women micro-entrepreneurs in Africa. In pairs, they use what they learn to design pamphlets promoting micro-entrepreneurship to other women in developing countries of Africa.

Objectives

Students will

- define and explain the importance of these key geographic terms: *gender-based division of labor, informal economy, micro-enterprise, micro-entrepreneur.*

- explain challenges faced by women in developing countries in Africa.

- describe how African women micro-entrepreneurs have changed the human characteristics of the places where they live and work.

- identify where micro-credit institutions are most active and explain why the majority of their clients are women.

Materials

- *Geography Alive! Regions and People*
- Interactive Student Notebooks
- Transparencies 21A and 21B
- Student Handout 21 (1 copy for every 2 students)
- $8\frac{1}{2}''$ x $11''$ sheets of paper (1 per student)
- colored pencils or markers

Preview

1 Project *Transparency 21A: Preview 21* and have students turn to Preview 21 in their Interactive Student Notebooks. Have students discuss the questions in pairs and record their ideas. Then ask several volunteers to share their ideas about each question. Possible answers are provided below for your reference.

- What interesting details do you notice?
- What kind of information or pictures do you think you might see in this pamphlet?
- Women in developing countries in Africa face many challenges. What might some of them be? *feeding their families, paying for school supplies for their children, paying for medical emergencies, finding and paying for adequate housing*
- What small business—or micro-enterprise—might this woman have created?
- This woman's micro-enterprise affects the lives of her and her family. What might some of those effects be? *having more money, being able to pay for school supplies, being able to buy items like a radio or a television, being able to build or pay for a nicer home*
- This woman's micro-enterprise also affects individuals and families in her community. What might some of those effects be? *This woman may be able to hire others to work for her. People in the community may not have to go so far or pay as much for fresh bread. Others may start up small businesses to complement this one, such as using a bicycle for a bread-delivery business.*

Transparency 21A **Preview 21**

2 Explain the connection between the Preview and the upcoming activity. Explain that in the upcoming activity, students will learn about women micro-entrepreneurs in Africa and how they are changing themselves and their communities.

Essential Question and Geoterms

1 Introduce Chapter 21 in *Geography Alive! Regions and People*. Explain that in this chapter, students will learn how women micro-entrepreneurs are helping to change certain aspects of African culture and society. Have students read Section 21.1. Then ask them to identify at least four details in the photograph of the woman selling bread in an African street market that relate to what they just read.

2 Introduce the Graphic Organizer and the Essential Question. Have students examine the outline map of Africa. Then ask,

- What is the shape of this outline?
- What appears inside this outline of the African continent?
- How might women like this one be changing their lives, and the lives of others, in developing countries in Africa?

Have students read the accompanying text. Make sure they understand the Essential Question, *How are women micro-entrepreneurs in developing countries changing their communities?* You may want to post the Essential Question in the room or write it on the board for the duration of the activity.

3 Have students read Section 21.2. Then have them work individually or in pairs to complete Geoterms 21 *and* the corresponding section of Reading Notes 21 in their Interactive Student Notebooks. Have volunteers share their answers with the class.

Geoterms 21

Writing for Understanding

1 Place students in mixed-ability pairs and introduce the activity. Explain that pairs will be assigned to read one of three case studies of women micro-entrepreneurs in Africa who have helped change their homes, communities, and cities. They will complete Reading Notes for their assigned case studies and use that information to create promotional pamphlets.

2 Assign pairs to read one of the case studies—Section 21.3, 21.4, or 21.5—and complete the corresponding section of Reading Notes. Allow sufficient time for them to read and take notes. Afterward, you may want to have pairs assigned to the same section team up to compare notes. (**Note:** Depending on your class, or for some pairs of students, you may want to have them read and take notes on all three case studies.)

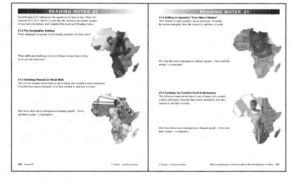

Reading Notes 21

3 Introduce the pamphlets students will create. Give each pair a copy of *Student Handout 21: Creating a Promotional Pamphlet.* Review the instructions with them, and answer any questions. (**Note:** If some or all pairs have taken notes on all three case studies, modify the instructions on Student Handout 21 so that students include information from each case study in their pamphlets. They can use two 8 1/2-by-11-inch sheets of paper or one 11-by-17-inch sheet to create their pamphlets.) Before students begin work, do the following:

- Remind students that the audience for this pamphlet is women in developing countries in Africa, particularly poor women.

Student Handout 21

- Mention that organizations working in developing countries often use a comic-book style for written materials. This format, which uses lots of illustrations and thought and speech bubbles, is often easier to understand for the many adults in developing countries who have little or no formal education.
- Have students identify information in their Reading Notes that they can use directly in their pamphlets.
- As a class or in small groups, have students brainstorm creative touches that would make their pamphlets interesting and engaging.

4 Give pairs one class period to complete their pamphlets. To make sure they include all the required elements, consider having them turn Student Handout 21 into a checklist and check off each required element as they complete it. Alternatively, have pairs bring their work to you when they think they have completed a required element. You can either check off the item or give them further guidance for satisfactorily completing it.

5 Have students complete their Reading Notes using information from pamphlets created by other pairs. Follow these steps:

- Each pair teams up with another pair who was assigned a different case study. They carefully read each other's pamphlets.
- Pairs take turns describing what they learned from the pamphlet about (1) the challenges faced by African women, (2) the micro-enterprises they created, and (3) the ways in which these micro-entrepreneurs changed people's lives and their communities. "Author" pairs then point out any important information in their pamphlets that "reader" pairs may have missed.
- Students fill in the corresponding section of their Reading Notes.
- Each pair teams up with another pair that was assigned the remaining case study and repeats the process.

(**Note:** If the entire class has completed all three sections of Reading Notes, have students go through all the steps above except for completing their Reading Notes.)

6 Conduct a wrap-up discussion. Ask students to discuss the following questions within their final groups of two pairs. Have volunteers share their answers.

- Which of the challenges faced by African women in developing countries are similar to those faced by women in your community? Which are different?

- Which micro-enterprise did you find the most interesting and why?

- Would any of these micro-enterprises work in the United States? Why or why not?

- What are some micro-enterprises or small businesses run by women in your community? How do you think they have changed people's lives and your community?

Global Connections

1 Introduce the Global Connections. Have students read Section 21.6. Then explain that they will now investigate the topic of micro-credit more globally.

2 Project *Transparency 21B: Global Connections.* Help students analyze the map by asking the questions that follow. Use the additional information given to enrich the discussion.

- **What interesting details do you see on this map?**

- **Where and when did micro-credit begin? To what parts of the world has it spread?**

Transparency 21B

The concept of micro-credit began in Bangladesh in the mid-1970s. Muhammad Yunus, a professor of economics from Bangladesh, saw firsthand how very small loans could help poor people and their families survive. His first loan, for $27 and out of his own pocket, was lent to a woman who used it for materials to make simple bamboo furniture. She sold the furniture to support herself and her family.

In 1976, Yunus started the Grameen Bank (Grameen means "rural" or "village" in the Bangla language) to make loans to poor people in Bangladesh. To guarantee that the loans are repaid, the bank uses a system of "solidarity groups." These are small, informal groups that apply together for loans. The members guarantee to repay the loans of any member who does not pay. They also support each other's efforts at economic self-advancement. Grameen Bank's success has inspired similar efforts throughout the developing world and even in industrialized countries. Many micro-credit projects follow Grameen's emphasis on lending specifically to women, since typically more women live in poverty than men. Women are also more likely than men to devote their earnings to serving the needs of their entire family.

- **Notice where micro-credit organizations are most active and least active. What patterns do you notice?**

  Micro-credit institutions are most active in the regions of Monsoon Asia (where Bangladesh is located), Latin America, and Africa. They are least active in Canada and the United States, Europe and Russia, Southwest and Central Asia, and Oceania.

3 **Have students read Section 21.7 and examine the rest of the information in the section.** Then lead a discussion of these questions:

- **In what parts of the world are micro-credit organizations most active? Why might this be so?**

  Micro-credit organizations tend to be concentrated in regions where there are less developed countries, including parts of Asia, Latin America, and Africa. These are areas where, generally, there are more poor people and poor women who can benefit from micro-credit. These also tend to be places where formal banks are unwilling to make the kinds of very small loans that micro-entrepreneurs need to start and grow their businesses.

- **Which gender gets the most micro-credit? Why might this be so?**

- **How do micro-credit institutions help women change their communities?**

  In some African countries, as women's economic power increases, so does their political clout. Two examples in Uganda point this out. First, a new constitution was written in 1995. Women's rights advocates were able to include a provision that states, "Women shall be accorded full and equal dignity of persons with men... laws, cultures, customs or traditions which are against the dignity, welfare or inter-est of women or which undermine their status are prohibited by this constitution." Second, the number of women repre-sentatives in Uganda's parliament has increased from 39 (or 15%) in 1994 to 74 (over 26%) in 2003. As women's political power and representation increases in countries like Uganda, they may force governments to enact more programs to help poor women in their societies.

Processing

There is no Processing assignment for this activity. The promotional pamphlet that students create functions as a Processing assignment.

Online Resources

For more information on women micro-entrepreneurs in Africa, refer students to Online Resources for *Geography Alive! Regions and People* at www.teachtci.com.

Assessment

Masters for assessment appear on the next three pages followed by answers and scoring rubrics.

Mastering the Content

Shade in the oval by the letter of the best answer for each question.

1. What is the **best** definition of a micro-enterprise?
   - A. a successful business run by a woman
   - B. a food business offering home cooking
   - C. a new business started with a small loan
   - D. a small business with few or no employees

2. All of the following have contributed to widespread poverty in Africa **except**
   - A. desertification.
   - B. reforestation.
   - C. disease.
   - D. war.

3. In traditional societies with gender-based division of labor, the kind of work a person does depends mainly on that person's
   - A. age.
   - B. sex.
   - C. income.
   - D. religion.

4. Read the description and then complete the sentence below.

   Kalerwe market is an amazing place to visit. From the center of the market, stalls stretch as far as the eye can see. Kalerwe is known as the "poor man's market." But it attracts all kinds of people who are drawn by its bargain prices.

   Markets like the one described above are part of Africa's
   - A. rural decline.
   - B. vertical trade.
   - C. informal economy.
   - D. shifting agriculture.

5. Which term **best** describes African women who set up street-side restaurants in caravans?
   - A. pastoral nomads
   - B. migrant workers
   - C. indigenous peoples
   - D. micro-entrepreneurs

6. Which of these conclusions about men and women in Africa is **best** supported by the map?

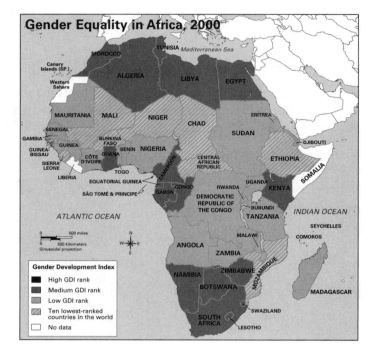

- A. More women graduate from high school than men.
- B. Most men have shorter life expectancies than women.
- C. Women and men are fairly equal in education and income.
- D. Men are better educated and earn more money than women.

7. Which of these is the **most** common problem faced by poor women in developing countries who want to start businesses?
   - A. finding time to start a new business
   - B. finding money to start a new business
   - C. finding customers for a new business
   - D. finding workspace for a new business

8. Which of the following is **not** a benefit provided by women who start small businesses in Africa?
   - A. They create new jobs.
   - B. They raise the price of food.
   - C. They send their children to school.
   - D. They build new homes for their families.

Applying Geography Skills:
Creating Graphs from Data

Use these facts about micro-credit and your knowledge of geography to complete the tasks below.

Fast Facts About Micro-credit

A. About 80% of micro-loans are made to women.

B. About 90% of the income earned by women from micro-loans is used to support their families.

C. About 40% of the income earned by men from micro-loans is used to support their families.

1. Use the data in Fact A to create a circle graph that compares the percent of micro-loans given to men and to women. Give your graph a title. Label each part of the graph.

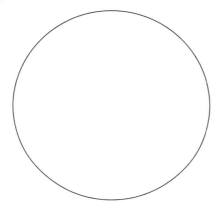

2. Use the data in Facts B and C to create a bar graph that compares how men and women use income earned from micro-loans. Give your graph a title. Label each part of the graph.

Exploring the Essential Question

How are women micro-entrepreneurs in developing countries changing their communities?

In Chapter 21, you explored how women micro-entrepreneurs in African countries are changing their communities. Use what you learned and the information below to complete this task.

A Multifunctional Platform

The multifunctional platform is run by a small engine. Power tools can be attached to the engine to do different tasks. Here are some examples:

- pressing foods for oil or juice
- grinding grains and nuts
- husking grains like rice
- generating electricity
- charging batteries
- pumping water
- welding metal
- sawing wood

The Task: Creating a Micro-Enterprise Using the Multifunctional Platform

People all over the world are using the multifunctional platform to start new businesses. Your task is to create a micro-enterprise using this machine. Your business might be based on one of the tasks listed above. Or you may think of a new way to put the machine to use.

Step 1: Describe the product or service your micro-enterprise will offer.

Step 2: List possible customers for this product or service.

Step 3: Identify three benefits your product or service might provide to your customers.

Design Tips
A flier is a kind of advertisement. Designers of fliers often use illustrations to catch people's attention. They also use large print for the most important information, such as the name of a business. Details appear in smaller print.

Step 4: On another sheet of paper, design a one-page flier that introduces your micro-enterprise to possible customers. Your flier should include these things:

A. the name of your business
B. a description or drawing of your product or service
C. the price of your product or service
D. three benefits your product or service will provide to customers

Applying Geography Skills: Sample Responses

1. The completed circle graph should show that 80% of micro-loans go to women and 20% go to men. The graph should have a title and be accurately labeled.

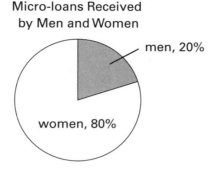

Micro-loans Received by Men and Women

men, 20%

women, 80%

Mastering the Content Answer Key

1. D	2. B	3. B	4. C
5. D	6. D	7. B	8. B

2. The completed bar graph should show that 90% of income from women's micro-loans goes to their families, while only 40% of income from men's micro-loans goes to their families. The graph should have a title and be accurately labeled. It can be either a horizontal or vertical graph.

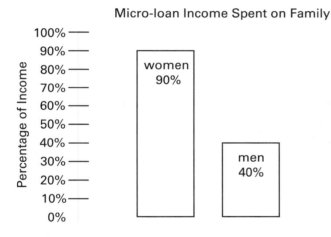

Micro-loan Income Spent on Family

women 90%

men 40%

Percentage of Income

Applying Geography Skills Scoring Rubric

Score	General Description
2	Student responds to all parts of the task. Response is correct and clear.
1	Student responds to some parts of the task. Response is mostly correct.
0	Response does not match the task or is incorrect.

Exploring the Essential Question: Sample Response

Answers will vary. The following example is one possibility.

Step 1: Service: Grinding nuts to make fresh nut butters

Step 2: Possible customers: people with nut trees in their yards, local farmers who grow nuts, people who eat a lot of nuts, school cafeterias, cooks, clubs that want to sell fresh nut butters as fundraisers

Step 3: Benefits: make fresh nut butters without chemicals, use nuts that might spoil, raise money for good causes, save money over store-bought nut butters, make more kinds of nut butters than found in stores

Step 4: Fliers should include the name of the micro-enterprise, a drawing or description of the good or service, a price for the good or service, and three benefits to customers who might buy the good or service.

Exploring the Essential Question Scoring Rubric

Score	General Description
3	Student responds to all parts of the task. Response is correct, clear, and supported by details.
2	Student responds to most or all parts of the task. Response is generally correct but may lack details.
1	Student responds to at least one part of the task. Response may contain errors and lack details.
0	Response does not match the task or is incorrect.

Create a Pamphlet to Promote Micro-enterprises

Picture yourself working for an organization that educates women in developing countries in Africa about micro-entrepreneurs. Your task is to design a pamphlet for these women. It should be engaging and easy to understand. It should also answer the Essential Question: *How are women micro-entrepreneurs in developing countries changing their communities?*

Your organization has a limited budget for this project. So, you must create your pamphlet using just one standard-size sheet of paper. How you fold the paper is up to you.

Your pamphlet must have these things:

- An attractive cover page with a title. The cover page should be eye-catching. It should make the reader want to see what is inside.

- A section about challenges faced by people in developing countries in Africa, especially women who are trying to get out of poverty. (See your Reading Notes for Section 21.2 for ideas.)

- A section that describes one kind of micro-enterprise that African women have developed.

- A section that explains how these women and their micro-enterprise have changed their communities. It should tell how they have affected the women, their families, and the people in and around the community.

- A map that corresponds to some part of the pamphlet.

Also, make sure each section of your pamphlet

- has an appropriate title.

- includes at least one photograph or drawing that helps tell the story of that section.

- has clear, simple text. Remember, your readers might have little or no formal education.

Make your pamphlet as interesting and engaging as possible. For example, you might use a format similar to a comic book. Or you might write it in the voice of an African micro-entrepreneur, telling her personal story.

Read Section 21.2, and answer the questions for that section. Then, for Sections 21.3, 21.4, and 21.5, read only the section your teacher assigns to you and your partner, and complete that section of Reading Notes.

21.2 The Geographic Setting

What challenges do people in developing countries in Africa face? Lack of food is one challenge. Disease, particularly malaria, is another. Natural disasters, like droughts, lead to crop failures and food shortages. And civil wars have left hundreds of thousands dead.

What additional challenges do poor African women face as they try to get out of poverty? Much of the traditional work women do, such as caring for children and growing food on small plots of land, does not earn them money. Another challenge is lack of education. In 2002, nearly half of African women could not read. This limits the jobs they can get.

21.3 Grinding Peanuts in Rural Mali

The African woman shown here is one of many who created a micro-enterprise. Describe their micro-enterprise, how they created it, and how it works. With the help of a UN program, these women bought a machine called a multifunctional platform. The machine can be used to do many things. These women connected it to a grinding tool, which can grind nuts and grains much faster than doing it by hand. Using this machine, these women have created a peanut-grinding business.

How have these micro-entrepreneurs changed people's lives and these women's community? Through their micro-enterprise, these women

- spend far less time grinding peanuts, leaving more time for their families.
- have extra time to grind peanuts and sell the peanut butter in the market.
- earn money by running the machine for their customers.
- have learned new business skills, and many more are taking reading and math classes.
- are sending their daughters to school because they don't need them to help grind.
- have hired men as mechanics to maintain their machine.

In another village, the machine has been connected to a generator to produce electricity. These women have set up a lighting system for their village.

21.4 Selling in Uganda's "Poor Man's Market"

This African woman created a micro-enterprise. Describe her micro-enterprise, how she created it, and how it works. Margaret Saajjabi's first micro-enterprise was selling laundry soap and bottled drinks. By saving her earnings, she was able to purchase land in the Kalerwe market. From that land she has created these micro-enterprises:

- She rents 27 spaces to other micro-entrepreneurs, such as hairdressers, electricians, vegetable sellers, and cooks.
- She sells water in large cans.
- She has a 50-car parking lot and charges people to park there.

How has this micro-entrepreneur changed people's lives and this woman's community? Through her micro-enterprises, Saajjabi

- supports her 6 children and helps raise her 19 nieces and nephews, most of whom are in school.
- hired 6 guards for her parking business.
- sold market space to other micro-entrepreneurs, who in turn are able to provide for their families.

21.5 Cooking Up Comfort Food in Botswana

The African woman shown here is one of many who created a micro-enterprise. Describe their micro-enterprise, how they created it, and how it works. These women have created street-side restaurants that serve traditional Botswana food to city workers. They purchased caravans (small trailers) and converted them into mobile restaurants. They buy plastic patio furniture so their clients can sit while they eat. They park their restaurants where people work and shop.

How have these micro-entrepreneurs changed people's lives and these women's community? Through their micro-enterprises, these women

- earn money to send their children to school.
- are sometimes able to buy land and build a home.
- are sometimes able to hire workers to cook, clean, and transport supplies.
- are sometimes able to create work for other women, such as selling box lunches in other parts of the city.
- provide inexpensive, convenient, and traditional meals to city workers.

Nigeria: A Country of Many Cultures

Overview

In this lesson, students explore the regional differences within the country of Nigeria. In a **Social Studies Skill Builder,** they learn about Nigeria's three regions: northern, eastern, and western. They examine and categorize photographs from the three regions, and read about and record information about each region. They then use the photographs and their research to design a Web page about the regions of Nigeria.

Objectives

Students will

- define and explain the importance of these key geographic terms: *colonialism, cultural region, ethnic diversity, linguistic group.*

- describe the characteristics of the physical environment, ethnic groups, culture, and economic activity unique to each region of Nigeria.

- analyze photographs of Nigeria to determine in which region each was taken.

- analyze potential problems of and possible solutions to the great ethnic diversity that exists within most African countries.

Materials

- *Geography Alive! Regions and People*
- Interactive Student Notebooks
- Transparencies 22A and 22B
- Placards 22A–22D (2 sets)
- Student Handout 22A (1 copy, cut apart)
- Student Handout 22B (1 for every 4 students)
- Information Masters 22A and 22B (1 transparency of each)
- index cards
- scissors
- gluesticks

Preview

1 Project *Transparency 22A: Preview 22.* Help students analyze
the map by asking,

- What physical features do you see?
- What major cities do you see in Nigeria?
- How is the land in the northern part of Nigeria different from
  the land in the southern part?

Transparency 22A

2 Place students in mixed-ability pairs. You may want to prepare a transparency that shows them whom they will work with
and where to sit. Students will remain in these pairs throughout
the activity.

3 Have pairs complete Preview 22. Ask students to open to
Preview 22 in their Interactive Student Notebooks and follow
the directions for dividing Nigeria into three regions. When they
are finished, ask a few to come up to the projector to show how
they divided Nigeria into regions and to explain their reasoning.
(**Note:** Most students will use the Niger and Benue rivers as
physical dividers. Try to have students with other divisions
present their ideas as well.)

Preview 22

**4 Explain the connection between the Preview and the
upcoming activity.** Tell students that Nigeria is a diverse
country. To help understand its complexity, people frequently
describe it as having three regions. In this activity, students will
learn about the three regions of Nigeria. They will read about
each region and examine a series of photographs to determine
in which region each was taken.

Essential Question and Geoterms

1 Introduce Chapter 22 in *Geography Alive! Regions and
People.* Explain that in this chapter, students will learn how
each of Nigeria's three regions is unique. Have students read
Section 22.1. Then ask them to identify details in the photograph of the market in Lagos that relate to what they just read.

**2 Introduce the Graphic Organizer and the Essential
Question.** Have students examine the map of Nigeria. Then ask,

- What are the three regions in Nigeria?
- What kinds of differences might we find among the three
  regions?

Have students read the accompanying text. Make sure they
understand the Essential Question, *How can dividing a diverse
country into regions make it easier to understand?* You may

want to post the Essential Question in the room or write it on the board for the duration of the activity.

3 Have students read Section 22.2. Then have them work individually or in pairs to complete Geoterms 22 in their Interactive Student Notebooks. Afterward, have them share their answers with another student, or have volunteers share their answers with the class.

Social Studies Skill Builder

1 Arrange the classroom and prepare materials.

- Create two "graphics walls" by setting up two identical sets of stations, four on one side of the room and four on the other. Place three desks together to create each station.
- Place one of *Placards 22A–22D: Station Photographs* at each station: Placard 22A at each Station 1, Placard 22B at each Station 2, Placard 22C at each Station 3, and Placard 22D at each Station 4.
- Cut the cards from a copy of *Student Handout 22A: Regions of Nigeria Cards.*

Geoterms 22

Placards 22A–22D

| Station 1 | Station 2 | Station 3 | Station 4 |
| Placard 22A | Placard 22B | Placard 22C | Placard 22D |

| Placard 22A | Placard 22B | Placard 22C | Placard 22D |
| Station 1 | Station 2 | Station 3 | Station 4 |

Student Handout 22A

2 Explain the activity. Tell students that they will be taking on the role of employees at a Web site design company in the United States to create an educational site about Nigeria. The photographer they sent to Nigeria has emailed pictures for use on the site but neglected to identify in which region each was taken. Students will read and take notes about each region of Nigeria and then go to the "graphics wall" in the "layout room" to use what they have learned to identify the photographs from that region. Assign half of the pairs to use the stations on each side of the room.

3 Project a transparency of *Information Master 22A:
Gathering Information to Design a Web Page.* Review the
directions with students. Leave the transparency projected as
students work.

Information Master 22A

4 Give each pair their first region card from Student
Handout 22A, and have them begin. Allow ample time for
completing the activity. Remind pairs to have you check their
completed notes for each region before they begin work on
another. Check the accuracy of their notes, but don't yet reveal
whether the photographs they chose are correct. Instead, allow
them the opportunity to change the images they chose, if they
feel it is appropriate, as they learn about the other regions.

5 After pairs have finished their research, review the entire
set of Reading Notes as a class. Use Guide to Reading Notes
22 for examples of notes students might have taken and as a
guide to how the photographs should be categorized.

6 Conduct a game to debrief the activity. Project a transparency of *Information Master 22B: Game Directions,* and
explain that students will now participate in a game called *Two
Truths and a Lie* to assess their understanding of Nigeria's three
regions. Give three index cards to each pair, and review the
directions for the game. Have pairs fill out their three cards and
then join with another pair to play the game. (**Note:** You may
want to circulate as students work to spot-check their statements
for accuracy.)

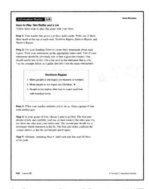

Information Master 22B

Global Connections

1 Introduce the Global Connections. Have students read
Section 22.6. Then explain that they will now learn more
about some of the problems facing the very diverse countries
of Africa.

2 Project *Transparency 22B: Global Connections.* Help students analyze the map by discussing and sharing their answers
to the following questions. Use the additional information given
to enrich the discussion.

- **What interesting details do you see on the map?**

- **What do the red lines represent? The black lines? The
  explosion symbols?**
  *The red lines represent the boundaries of various ethnic
  groups on the African continent. The black lines represent
  the political boundaries of the countries of Africa. Some*

Transparency 22B

countries have many ethnic groups, and some have fewer. Some ethnic groups are located in multiple countries. The explosion symbols represent major armed ethnic conflicts that occurred between 1995 and 2001.

- **Which countries appear to have the most ethnic groups within their borders? The least?**

The countries in Central Africa have the most ethnic groups. Nigeria, Sudan, Democratic Republic of the Congo, Chad, Cameroon, Ethiopia, Tanzania, and Zambia have a wide variety of ethnic groups. The countries in northern Africa, such as Algeria, Libya, and Egypt, have fewer ethnic groups. The same is true of very small nations, like Gambia, Lesotho, and Swaziland, whose populations are almost entirely composed of one ethnic group.

- **Why do you think there are so many ethnic groups within each country?**

In Africa, it is rare for ethnic group boundaries and political boundaries to match. This is a result of European countries dividing up Africa into colonies in the 18th and 19th centuries. When European countries rushed to "claim" portions of Africa, they paid little attention to the ethnicities of the people living in the region. Colonialism did not end completely in Africa until the mid-20th century, and today's political boundaries are a result of those colonial boundaries.

3 Have students read Section 22.7 and examine the rest of the information in the section. Then lead a discussion of these questions:

- **Why do most African countries have so many cultural regions?**

- **What problems do countries with many cultural regions face?**

- **What are some ways governments might reduce cultural conflicts?**

Processing

Before students begin the Processing assignment, cut one set of three photographs from *Student Handout 22B: Web Page Photographs* for each student. Review the directions for Processing 22, and answer any questions students have. Students may cut apart the three photographs and tape or glue them into their notebooks or onto separate sheets of paper to create storyboards of their Web page designs.

Student Handout 22B   **Processing 22**

Online Resources

For more information on Nigeria, refer students to Online Resources for *Geography Alive! Regions and People* at www.teachtci.com.

Assessment

Masters for assessment appear on the next three pages followed by answers and scoring rubrics. Students will need colored pencils or markers for the constructed-response portion of this assessment.

Mastering the Content

Shade in the oval by the letter of the best answer for each question.

1. What does the graph below illustrate?

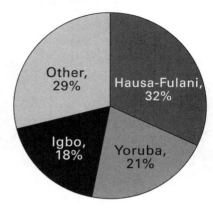

⭘ A. Nigeria's ethnic diversity
⭘ B. Nigeria's spatial inequality
⭘ C. Nigeria's migration streams
⭘ D. Nigeria's economic activities

2. A cultural region is **best** defined as a region whose people share the same
⭘ A. standard of living.
⭘ B. life expectancy.
⭘ C. climate zone.
⭘ D. way of life.

3. Choose the statement that is true of the Hausa and Fulani peoples of Northern Nigeria.
⭘ A. Both groups are herders.
⭘ B. Both groups live in cities.
⭘ C. Both groups are Muslims.
⭘ D. Both groups speak Hausa.

4. Although many Yoruba dialects are spoken in Nigeria, the Yoruba belong to one
⭘ A. consumer group.
⭘ B. linguistic group.
⭘ C nomadic group.
⭘ D. occupation group.

5. Which ethnic group was rewarded by the British for their willingness to learn English and attend British schools?
⭘ A. Fulani
⭘ B. Hausa
⭘ C. Igbo
⭘ D. Yoruba

6. Which of these is an important legacy of British rule in Nigeria?
⭘ A. the movement of the national capital from Lagos to Abuja
⭘ B. conflict between the Igbo and other ethnic groups
⭘ C. state legal systems based on Islamic law
⭘ D. the rapid shrinking of Lake Chad

7. Which of these is the **most** important economic activity in the Niger River Delta?
⭘ A. cattle herding
⭘ B. commercial fishing
⭘ C. oil production
⭘ D. subsistence farming

8. Which of these was **most** responsible for the borders shown on the map below?

Africa, 1914

⭘ A. colonialism
⭘ B. nationalism
⭘ C. immigration
⭘ D. desertification

Applying Geography Skills:
Comparing Data on a Map and Graph

Use this map, graph, and your knowledge of geography to complete the tasks below.

1. Circle the capital of Nigeria on the map. What do you observe about its location?

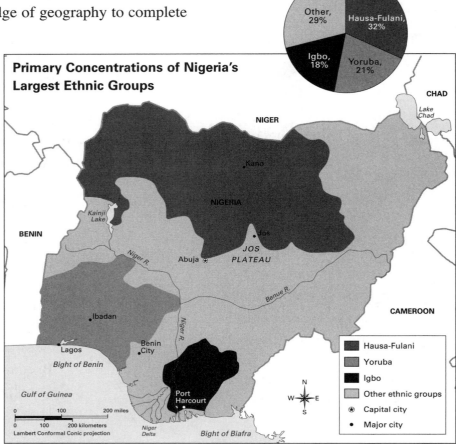

2. Look at the size of the Hausa-Fulani ethnic group on the graph and the region in which this group mostly lives on the map. What do you observe about the size of this group compared to the size of its cultural region?

3. Look at the size of the Igbo ethnic group on the graph and the region in which this group mostly lives on the map. What do you observe about the size of this group compared to the size of its cultural region?

Test Terms Glossary
To **observe** means to notice something after looking at it carefully.

Exploring the Essential Question

How can dividing a diverse country into regions make it easier to understand?

In Chapter 22, you explored how geographers use cultural regions to help them study a complex country like Nigeria. Now you will use what you learned.

The Task: Mapping the Regions of Your School

Regions come in all sizes. They can be as large as a continent or as small as a neighborhood. Your task is to divide your school campus into regions and then map those regions.

Step 1: Make a mental map of the buildings and grounds that make up your school campus. List all of the different rooms, buildings, and outside areas you can think of. Include classrooms, playing fields, and special-purpose buildings such as the library.

Step 2: Think about ways to group the places in your list above. Look for characteristics that different places have in common. For example, you might group together places that are used in similar ways, such as for sports. Or you might group places according to the grade levels of the students who use them. Identify at least three groups of places. These are your school regions. Give each region a name, and assign each region a color.

Step 3: On another sheet of paper, draw a regional map of your school. Your map should include the following:
A. a title
B. a key that lists your regions and their colors on your map
C. the buildings and/or outdoor areas in each region

> **Test Terms Glossary**
> A **mental** map is a map you form in your head.

Applying Geography Skills: Sample Responses

1. Abuja, the capital of Nigeria, is located in the center of the country.

2. The Hausa-Fulani make up about a third of the population of Nigeria. This is roughly equal to the size of their cultural region.

3. The Igbo make up the about a fifth of the population of Nigeria. However, the Igbo cultural region covers much less than a fifth of the country.

Exploring the Essential Question: Sample Response

Step 1: Answers will vary, but students might include the playground, gym, lunchroom, offices, classrooms, library, and computer lab.

Step 2: Answers will vary, but students might group classrooms and the computer lab together, the playground and gym together, and offices and the teacher's room together. Each list should have a functional title, such as Play Region, Eating Region, Teacher Region, and Study Region.

Step 3: The map should include the elements listed in the prompt.

Mastering the Content Answer Key

1. A	2. D	3. C	4. B
5. C	6. B	7. C	8. A

Applying Geography Skills Scoring Rubric

Score	General Description
2	Student responds to all parts of the task. Response is correct and clear.
1	Student responds to some parts of the task. Response is mostly correct.
0	Response does not match the task or is incorrect.

Exploring the Essential Question Scoring Rubric

Score	General Description
3	Student responds to all parts of the task. Response is correct, clear, and supported by details.
2	Student responds to most or all parts of the task. Response is generally correct but may lack details.
1	Student responds to at least one part of the task. Response may contain errors and lack details.
0	Response does not match the task or is incorrect.

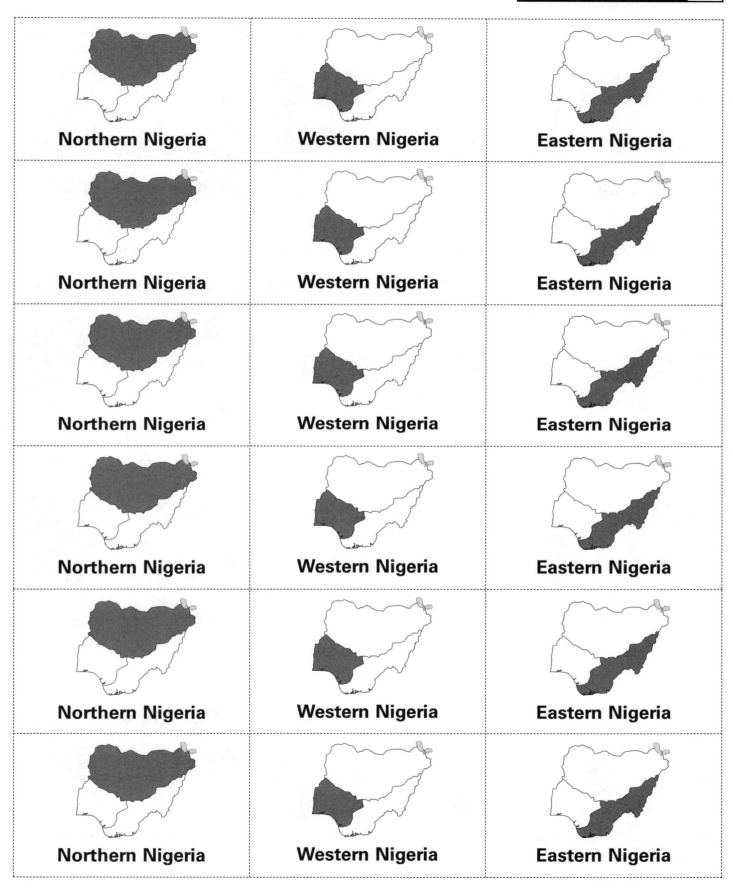

Northern Nigeria	**Western Nigeria**	**Eastern Nigeria**
Northern Nigeria	**Western Nigeria**	**Eastern Nigeria**
Northern Nigeria	**Western Nigeria**	**Eastern Nigeria**
Northern Nigeria	**Western Nigeria**	**Eastern Nigeria**
Northern Nigeria	**Western Nigeria**	**Eastern Nigeria**
Northern Nigeria	**Western Nigeria**	**Eastern Nigeria**

Aerial View of Lagos

Savanna Near the Jos Plateau

Mangrove Swamp in the Rainforest

Aerial View of Lagos

Savanna Near the Jos Plateau

Mangrove Swamp in the Rainforest

Aerial View of Lagos

Savanna Near the Jos Plateau

Mangrove Swamp in the Rainforest

Aerial View of Lagos

Savanna Near the Jos Plateau

Mangrove Swamp in the Rainforest

Gather Information for Your Web Page on Nigeria

Follow these steps to learn about Nigeria's three regions. You will use the information you gather to design a Web page on Nigeria.

Step 1: Get a Regions of Nigeria Card from your teacher. Read the section of Chapter 22 that matches the region on the card (northern, western, or eastern).

Step 2: Turn to Reading Notes 22 in your Interactive Student Notebook. Complete the row of the table for your region.

Step 3: Bring your Reading Notes to your teacher to make sure you have correctly recorded all of the information for the region. If you have, go on to Step 4. If not, go back to Step 2.

Step 4: Go to the graphics wall with your partner. At each of the four stations, determine which photograph was taken in the region you are studying. Write the letter of that photograph in the box for the appropriate topic in that region.

Step 5: Get a new Regions of Nigeria Card, and repeat Steps 2–4. As you work on new regions, you might need to review the photographs you chose for previous regions. You might change your mind about the region in which a particular photograph belongs.

Step 6: When you've completed the Reading Notes for all three regions, have your teacher check that you chose the correct photos.

How to Play *Two Truths and a Lie*

Follow these steps to play this game with your class:

Step 1: Your teacher has given you three index cards. Write one of these three heads at the top of each card: *Northern Region, Eastern Region,* and *Western Region.*

Step 2: Use your Reading Notes to create three statements about each region. Write your statements on the appropriate index card. Two of your statements should be obviously true of that region (two truths). One should not be true (a lie). Put a star next to the statement that is a lie. Use the example below as a guide (but don't use the same statements).

Northern Region

1. Many people in my region are farmers or herders.

2. Most people in my region are Christian. ★

3. People in my region often live in round mud huts with thatched roofs.

Step 3: When your teacher instructs you to do so, form a group of four with another pair.

Step 4: In your group of four, choose a pair to go first. The first pair should slowly and carefully read one of their cards to the other pair. Do not show the other pair your index card. The second pair should try to determine which statement is the lie. The first pair either confirms the correct answer or has the second pair guess again.

Step 5: Alternate, repeating Step 4, until each pair has read all three of its cards.

Work with your partner to gather information about Nigeria. You will use the notes you take to design a Web page about Nigeria's three regions. Follow the instructions your teacher has projected.

For each region, read the corresponding section of your book: Section 22.3, 22.4, or 22.5. Fill in the matching row of the table below. List several ideas about each of the four topics. Then have your teacher check your work.

Northern region

Western region   Eastern region

	Physical Environment	Ethnic Groups
Northern Nigeria (Section 22.3)	• During the six-month dry season, from October to March, little rain falls and lakes and rivers dry up. • Lake Chad, one of Nigeria's most important water sources, is much smaller than it once was. • High, flat plains are used for farming. The Jos Plateau rises above them and is cooler and wetter. The harmattan blows from the north, bringing dust from the Sahara. Photograph [B]	• The two largest ethnic groups are the Hausa and Fulani. The Hausa came to the region 1,000 years ago. The Fulani arrived in the 1200s. • The Hausa tend to live in cities, the Fulani in the country. • A third of Nigerians speak Hausa. • The groups are both Muslim, but Christians live here too. Sometimes there is conflict over shari'a, or traditional Islamic laws. Photograph [J]
Western Nigeria (Section 22.4)	• This region sits on the Gulf of Guinea. The Niger River forms its northern and eastern borders. • The coast used to be tropical rainforest, but trees have been cleared for farming. • Most of this region is a savanna with tall grasses and scattered trees. • Many people live in cities. Lagos and Ibadan are the largest. Photograph [A]	• The largest ethnic group is the Yoruba. • The ancient Yoruba developed many kingdoms ruled by kings. • Historically there were many dialects of Yoruba, but today they are becoming more alike. • Many Yoruba are Christian, though some follow Islam or traditional beliefs. Photograph [K]
Eastern Nigeria (Section 22.5)	• This region sits on the Gulf of Guinea. The Benue River forms the northern edge; the Niger forms the western edge. • The region has more rainfall than the rest of Nigeria. • Rainforests used to cover the land. Today, swamps line the coasts. • The Niger Delta is rich in oil. Photograph [C]	• The Igbo are the largest ethnic group here. • The ancient Igbo lived in villages ruled by councils of elders. • The Igbo had special privileges during British colonialism. After independence, the Igbo fought to create their own country, but lost. • Most Igbo are Christian. • There are over 300 dialects of Igbo, but only 1% of Nigerians speak Igbo. Photograph [L]

Now go to the graphics wall with your partner. At each of the four stations, determine which photograph was taken in the region you are studying. Write the letter of that photograph in the box for the matching topic in that region.

	Culture	Economy
Northern Nigeria (Section 22.3)	• In the city, people have houses with flat roofs. In the country, they have round houses of mud with roofs of reeds or palm leaves. • Men and women wear loose clothes, usually robes that cover the body. Muslim women wear the hijab, a headscarf; other women wear a cloth headdress. • Tension drums are popular instruments that make sounds like the spoken language. Photograph I	• Many people are farmers and herders. • Hausa farmers grow crops like corn and millet to feed their families and sell at markets. • Fulani herders sell milk and butter. • The Hausa have traditionally made cloth and leather goods. Today, some Hausa are traders and merchants. Photograph D
Western Nigeria (Section 22.4)	• Many people live in cities—the well-off in one-story houses or apartments, the poor in shacks on the city outskirts. • Homes in the country are made of mud bricks with steep tin or iron roofs. • Yoruba are known for their colorful cloth and beadwork. • Yoruba art includes wood and ivory masks, bronze or clay statues, and drums. Photograph G	• Many Yoruba live in cities and work in factories and offices. Some commute back to the country to work on farms. • Yoruba women also work in street markets selling food, cloth, baskets, and other tourist goods. Photograph F
Eastern Nigeria (Section 22.5)	• In the cities, homes are built from mud bricks, with metal roofs, and often on stilts in swampy areas. • Men and women wear colorful cloth wrapped around their bodies. • The Igbo make masks of wood or leather and decorate them with teeth, hair, fur, and other materials. • Masked dancing is popular. Photograph H	• Oil is the Igbo's main economic activity. • Foreign oil companies run Nigeria's oil industry. • The Igbo have used education to improve their lives, and today some are doctors, lawyers, and teachers. • Oil spills have done a lot of environmental damage. Photograph E

Resources and Power in Post-apartheid South Africa

Overview

In a **Visual Discovery** activity, students examine photographs of the new South Africa and read about post-apartheid changes regarding politics, employment, education, and living conditions. They discuss how well each image represents the new South Africa and then work in small groups to bring two of the images to life in act-it-outs. Finally, they evaluate how much progress South Africa has made toward achieving equality for people of all races since the end of apartheid.

Objectives

Students will

- define and explain the importance of these key geographic terms: *apartheid, distribution, multiracial, segregation.*

- describe how apartheid has affected South Africans of various ethnicities.

- analyze the redistribution of power and resources in post-apartheid South Africa.

- evaluate South Africa's progress toward equality for all South Africans since the end of apartheid.

- examine the effects of the worldwide HIV/AIDS epidemic.

Materials

- *Geography Alive! Regions and People*
- Interactive Student Notebooks
- Transparencies 23A–23E
- Student Handouts 23A and 23B (1 of each for every 4 students)
- $8\frac{1}{2}"$ x $11"$ sheets of paper (1 for every 2 students)
- markers
- masking tape

Preview

1 Prepare students for the Preview. Have students open *Geography Alive! Regions and People* to Chapter 23 and inspect the photograph of a "whites only" sign in South Africa in the 1980s. Then ask,

- What do you think the purpose of this sign is?
- How do you think whites felt about this sign? How do you think blacks felt?
- When do you think this photograph was taken? What details in the image might be clues about when it was taken?

2 Have students complete Preview 23. Have students turn to Preview 23 in their Interactive Student Notebooks and follow the directions to create a list of ways their lives would change if their government instituted apartheid-like laws. Ask several volunteers to share their ideas.

3 Explain the connection between Preview and the upcoming activity. Tell students that, in the upcoming activity, they will learn about the resources that attracted Europeans to South Africa and about the system that was implemented there to separate whites and nonwhites in all spheres of life. They will then learn how this system finally came to an end and, most importantly, what progress has been made toward equality in South Africa in the years since.

Preview 23

Essential Question and Geoterms

1 Introduce Chapter 23 in *Geography Alive! Regions and People*. Explain that in this chapter, students will learn about the South African government's policy of separating racial groups and the redistribution of power and resources since the end of that policy. Have students read Section 23.1.

2 Introduce the Graphic Organizer and the Essential Question. Have students examine the circle graph. Then ask,

- What does the circle graph show?
- How many primary ethnic groups are in South Africa?
- What does the graph tell us about the four main ethnic groups in South Africa?

Explain that each of these four broad groupings is actually made up of many ethnicities; for example, the native Zulu, Xhosa, and Swazi are three of the many ethnic groups that have been labeled as black South Africans and were denied equality by the South African government until 1994. Ensure that students understand that in South Africa, "coloreds" are people of mixed-race. Have students read the accompanying text. Make

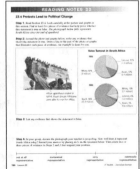

sure they understand the Essential Question, *How might ethnic group differences affect who controls resources and power in a society?* You may want to post the Essential Question in the room or write it on the board for the duration of the activity.

3 Have students read Section 23.2. This will give them a general background on the natural resources that attracted European settlers to South Africa, how the country of South Africa was formed, and when the policy of apartheid was implemented. Then have them work individually or in pairs to complete Geoterms 23 in their Interactive Student Notebooks. Have volunteers share their answers with the class.

Geoterms 23

Visual Discovery

1 Arrange students in mixed-ability pairs. You may want to prepare a transparency that shows them with whom they will work and how to arrange their desks.

2 Explain the activity. Tell students that in this activity they will examine a transparency image that shows significant progress in South Africa in the area of politics, employment, education, or living conditions. Then they will read a section in their book and analyze other images and graphs to determine how well the transparency image represents South Africa today.

3 Have students read Section 23.3. This will give them background information on the policy of apartheid and its effects on South African society. To check their understanding, ask,

- How were nonwhites in South Africa treated under apartheid?
- Why were homelands and townships created?
- Who benefited from apartheid?
- How do you think that whites, despite being a small minority of the population, were able to keep apartheid laws in place?

4 Project *Transparency 23A: Political Power in South Africa Today.* (**Note:** The photograph shows Nelson Mandela campaigning for the office of president during the first free elections, held in 1994.) Help students analyze the image by asking,

- What interesting details do you see?
- What do you think is happening here? Support your answer with at least one detail from the image.
- How *might* this photograph show how things are different in South Africa today compared with the apartheid era?

5 Have pairs complete the Reading Notes for Section 23.4. Have pairs turn to Reading Notes 23 in their Interactive Student Notebooks and complete the notes for Section 23.4.

Transparency 23A   **Reading Notes 23**

6 Have groups prepare to bring the image to life in an act-it-out. Combine pairs into groups of four, and give each group *Student Handout 23A: Directions for Act-It-Out 1.* Assign each group a character, and have them complete the steps on the handout from that character's perspective. Encourage them to use information from their Reading Notes to generate ideas for how to bring their character to life. Give groups several minutes to prepare and practice as you circulate among them. (**Note:** Depending on the class size, you might assign more than one group to each character and then choose one actor from among the groups to perform in the act-it-out. Or you might assign one group to each character and have the remaining groups become reporters. Tell "reporter groups" to brainstorm one or two questions for each character. Remind them that good reporters ask open-ended questions that the person can answer. If an actor can simply answer yes or no, the question is not a good one.)

7 Conduct the act-it-out. Call up one actor to represent each character. Have the actors stand in front of the appropriate characters on the screen, taking on their postures and facial expressions. For characters not in the image, actors might step off to the side as if they are part of the broader scene. As the on-scene reporter, interview the characters, asking questions like those they discussed in their groups. Once you have interviewed all the actors, allow student reporters to ask a few more questions. Have students return to their pairs when the act-it-out is finished.

8 Have students analyze *Transparency 23B: Job Opportunities in South Africa Today* **by following Steps 4 and 5 above.** (**Note:** The photograph shows Emmanuel Lediga, the owner of South Africa's first black-owned stock brokerage, making his first trade at the new offices of Legae Securities in 1996.) After pairs analyze the photograph and complete the Reading Notes for Section 23.5, debrief the image by asking, *How well does this photograph represent job opportunities in South Africa today?*

9 Have students analyze and then perform an act-it-out for *Transparency 23C: Education in South Africa Today* **by following Steps 4–7 above.** (**Note:** The photograph shows students of all races being taught by a black teacher at Sacred Heart College, an integrated private school in Johannesburg). After pairs analyze the photograph and complete the Reading Notes for Section 23.6, have them reconvene in their groups of four from the previous act-it-out. Distribute *Student Handout 23B: Directions for Act-It-Out 2* to each group. Following the steps on the handout, have students prepare for and perform the second act-it-out.

Student Handout 23A

Transparency 23B

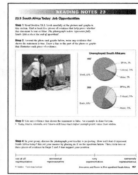

Reading Notes 23

Transparency 23C

Reading Notes 23

Student Handout 23B

10 Have students analyze *Transparency 23D: Living Conditions in South Africa Today* by following Steps 4 and 5. (**Note:** The photograph shows the daughter of two of South Africa's successful new black elite playing with a friend in her toy car in the driveway of their home in 2004. The family lives in Cedar Lake, an upper-class gated community in Johannesburg.) After pairs analyze the photograph and complete the Reading Notes for Section 23.7, debrief the image by asking, *How well does this photograph represent living conditions in South Africa today?*

Transparency 23D   **Reading Notes 23**

11 Prepare the class to create a human spectrum. Place a 10- to 15-foot strip of masking tape across the floor at the front of the room. On the board above either end, write "Benefited the Most from the End of Apartheid" and "Benefited the Least from the End of Apartheid." Explain the purpose of a spectrum, and tell students they will now rank the various ethnic groups in South Africa according to how much or how little they benefited from the end of apartheid. Assign each pair to represent one of the four ethnic groups: whites, blacks, coloreds, or Asians. Give each pair a sheet of paper and a marker and have them quickly write the name of their ethnic group on the paper in large letters.

12 Have students create a human spectrum. Give pairs one to two minutes to discuss where on the spectrum they would place their ethnic group. Then have one person from each pair stand on the spectrum, holding their name cards in front of their chests, where they think their ethnic group belongs. Encourage discussion among the "audience" about where the ethnic groups should be placed, challenging students to identify groups they believe are misplaced. (**Note:** The purpose of this activity is not to determine the "correct" locations but to have students support their opinions with appropriate evidence.)

Global Connections

1 Introduce the Global Connections. Have students read Section 23.8. Then explain that they will now learn more about how one of South Africa's most challenging problems is affecting all of Africa and the world.

2 Project *Transparency 23E: Global Connections.* Help students analyze the map by asking the questions that follow. Use the additional information given to enrich the discussion.

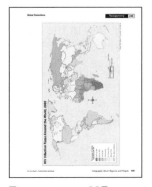

- **What interesting details do you see?**

- **What do the various colors on the map represent?**
  They represent the percentage of adults infected with HIV/AIDS.   **Transparency 23E**

- **Which parts of the world have been most affected?**

  According to the World Health Organization, sub-Saharan Africa has been most affected. On average, 7.5% of adults in this region are infected. The far southern portion of Africa has been the greatest affected, with between 15% and 39% of adults infected.

- **Which parts of the world have been least affected?**

  Oceania, North Africa, and Southwest Asia have had very low infection rates, with an average of only 0.2% of adults infected. Latin America, the United States, Canada, Southeastern Asia, Europe, and Central Asia are also among the least affected.

3 **Have students read Section 23.9 and examine the rest of the information in the section.** Then lead a discussion of these questions:

- **Why has Africa been more affected than other regions?**

- **What factors have contributed to the global spread of this disease?**

- **How might HIV/AIDS hurt the countries that are most severely affected?**

Processing

Have students complete Processing 23 in their Interactive Student Notebooks. Review the directions, and answer any questions they have.

Online Resources

For more information on post-apartheid South Africa, refer students to Online Resources for *Geography Alive! Regions and People* at www.teachtci.com.

Assessment

Masters for assessment appear on the next three pages followed by answers and scoring rubrics.

Processing 23

Mastering the Content

Shade in the oval by the letter of the best answer for each question.

1. Which was the central purpose of South Africa's apartheid policy?
   ○ A. conflict resolution
   ○ B. division of labor
   ○ C. racial segregation
   ○ D. sustainable development

2. Which statement below is **best** supported by the graph?

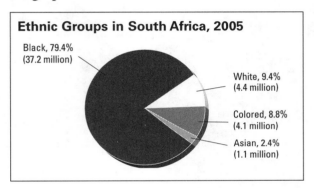

Ethnic Groups in South Africa, 2005

Black, 79.4%
(37.2 million)

White, 9.4%
(4.4 million)

Colored, 8.8%
(4.1 million)

Asian, 2.4%
(1.1 million)

   ○ A. South Africa is a developed country.
   ○ B. South Africa is a multiracial country.
   ○ C. South Africa is a democratic country.
   ○ D. South Africa is a mostly urban country.

3. During apartheid, which ethnic group was moved to the dark areas shown on the map below?
   ○ A. blacks
   ○ B. whites
   ○ C. Asians
   ○ D. coloreds

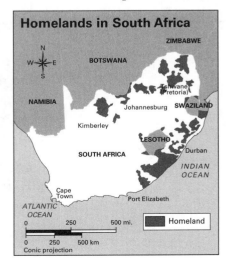

Homelands in South Africa

ZIMBABWE

BOTSWANA

Tshwane (Pretoria)

NAMIBIA

Johannesburg   SWAZILAND

Kimberley

LESOTHO

Durban

SOUTH AFRICA

INDIAN OCEAN

Cape Town

ATLANTIC OCEAN

Port Elizabeth

0   250   500 mi.   ■ Homeland

0   250   500 km
Conic projection

4. How did the apartheid policy affect Asians and coloreds in South Africa?
   ○ A. It forced them to leave the country.
   ○ B. It gave them fewer rights than blacks.
   ○ C It treated them as the equals of whites.
   ○ D. It restricted their rights and opportunities.

5. How did the end of apartheid affect the distribution of political power in South Africa?
   ○ A. Whites continued to control the government.
   ○ B. Coloreds and Asians refused to vote in elections.
   ○ C. Whites left the country rather than give up power to blacks.
   ○ D. Blacks gained control of the government through free elections.

6. How has the Employment Equity Act affected job opportunities in South Africa since 1998?
   ○ A. It has opened jobs to all ethnic groups.
   ○ B. It has increased pay for all government jobs.
   ○ C. It has decreased the number of jobs available.
   ○ D. It has put limits on who can apply for most jobs.

7. Which of these educational goals has South Africa emphasized since the end of apartheid?
   ○ A. sending every student to college
   ○ B. preparing all students for good jobs
   ○ C. setting up special schools for gifted students
   ○ D. teaching most students in their native language

8. Millions of people are infected with HIV each year. Most of these victims are which of the following?
   ○ A. elderly people
   ○ B. young children
   ○ C. working-age adults
   ○ D. health care workers

Applying Geography Skills:
Analyzing an Economic Activity Map

Use the map and your knowledge of geography to complete the tasks below.

1. List three natural resources that are important to South Africa's economy.

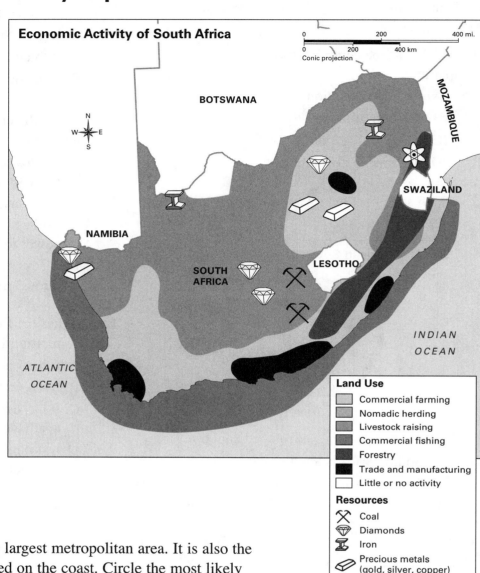

Economic Activity of South Africa

2. List three economic activities that can be found near South Africa's coastline.

Land Use
- Commercial farming
- Nomadic herding
- Livestock raising
- Commercial fishing
- Forestry
- Trade and manufacturing
- Little or no activity

Resources
- Coal
- Diamonds
- Iron
- Precious metals (gold, silver, copper)
- Uranium

3. Johannesburg is South Africa's largest metropolitan area. It is also the only large city that is not located on the coast. Circle the most likely location of Johannesburg on the map. Explain why this major city is located where it is.

Test Terms Glossary
To **list** means to write down a series of related terms, one after the other.

To **explain** means to make the relationship between two things clear.

© Teachers' Curriculum Institute

Exploring the Essential Question

How might ethnic group differences affect who controls resources and power in a society?

In Chapter 23, you explored the distribution of power and resources in South Africa during and after apartheid. Now you will use what you learned. Use the information in the graphs below and your knowledge of geography to complete this task.

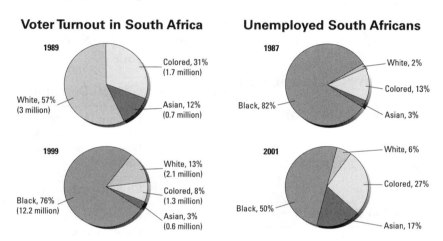

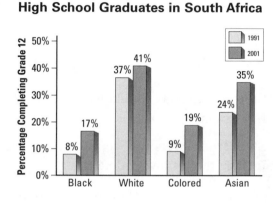

The Task: Comparing Life During and After Apartheid

These graphs show information about South Africa's four major ethnic groups during and after apartheid. Your task is to write a newspaper article about how life has changed for one of these groups since apartheid ended in 1991.

Step 1: On each graph above, circle the name of the group that you will write about.

Step 2: Use the table below to organize information about your group.

Topic	During Apartheid	After Apartheid
Voting Rights		
Job Opportunities		
Educational Opportunities		

Step 3: Write a short article that contrasts life during and after apartheid for your group. Your article should have a headline telling what it is about. It should cover the three topics listed in the table above and include any other information you can add.

Applying Geography Skills: Sample Responses

1. Possible resources include coal, diamonds, iron, precious metals, and uranium.
2. Possible economic activities located near the coast include commercial farming, trade and manufacturing, commercial fishing, forestry, nomadic herding, and mining diamonds and precious metals.
3. Students should have circled the inland area of trade and manufacturing in the northeast part of South Africa as the location of Johannesburg. Johannesburg is located there because of the wealth of precious metals and diamonds. It is also the center of a commercial farming area.

Exploring the Essential Question: Sample Response

Step 1: Students should have circled the name of one group on all five graphs.

Step 2: Answers will depend on the group chosen. Data for blacks might include the following details.

Topic	During Apartheid	After Apartheid
Voting Rights	Could not vote	12.2 million voted in 1999 election
Job Opportunities	made up 82% of the unemployed in 1987	made up 50% of the unemployed in 2001
Educational Opportunities	8% completed high school in 1991	17% completed high school in 2001

Step 3: The article should include all the elements listed in the prompt.

Apartheid's End Changes Life for Blacks in South Africa

Life for South African blacks has changed in many ways since apartheid ended in 1991. During apartheid, blacks could not vote. By 1999, 76% of the voters were black. As a result, black leaders have gained control of South Africa's government.

Economic conditions have improved too. During apartheid, blacks were kept out of many jobs. They made up 82% of the unemployed. Now all jobs are open to them. By 2001, they were only 50% of the unemployed. But slow economic growth still kept many out of work.

Educational opportunities improved as well. During apartheid, schools were segregated. Only 8% of blacks finished high school. By 2001, schools were open to all students. The graduation rate for blacks had doubled. More blacks were attending college. Still, they had a long way to go to catch up with other groups in education as in other areas of life.

Mastering the Content Answer Key

1. C	2. B	3. A	4. D
5. D	6. A	7. B	8. C

Applying Geography Skills Scoring Rubric

Score	General Description
2	Student responds to all parts of the task. Response is correct and clear.
1	Student responds to some parts of the task. Response is mostly correct.
0	Response does not match the task or is incorrect.

Exploring the Essential Question Scoring Rubric

Score	General Description
3	Student responds to all parts of the task. Response is correct, clear, and supported by details.
2	Student responds to most or all parts of the task. Response is generally correct but may lack details.
1	Student responds to at least one part of the task. Response may contain errors and lack details.
0	Response does not match the task or is incorrect.

Prepare for Act-It-Out 1: Politics in South Africa

You will work in your group to bring to life an image that illustrates a political change in post-apartheid South Africa. Your teacher will assign a character to your group. When it's time, one member of your group will be asked to play that character. Your teacher will interview the actors. Reporters will ask the actors questions about the characters' views.

Step 1: Circle the character your group has been assigned.

- Black South African

- White South African

- Colored South African

- Asian South African

- Nelson Mandela

- Reporter

Step 2: Discuss how your character would respond to the questions below. Make sure everyone in your group can answer the questions from your character's perspective. Everyone should be prepared to be the actor.

- What was your life like during apartheid? What are some of the political changes you have seen or experienced since the end of apartheid?

- What do you think of the political changes since the end of apartheid?

- How well does this image represent South Africa today?

Reporters, come up with one question for each character listed above.

Step 3: Discuss how to make your character come alive. Use visual and written information from your Reading Notes to brainstorm ways to make the character realistic.

Prepare for Act-It-Out 2: Schoolchildren in South Africa

You will work in your group to bring to life an image that illustrates an educational change in post-apartheid South Africa. Your teacher will assign a character to your group. When it's time, one member of your group will be asked to play that character. Your teacher will interview the actors. Reporters will ask the actors questions about the characters' views.

Step 1: Circle the character your group has been assigned.

- Black South African student

- White South African student

- Colored South African student

- Asian South African student

- Teacher

- Reporter

Step 2: Discuss how your character would respond to the questions below. Make sure everyone in your group can answer the questions from your character's perspective. Everyone should be prepared to be the actor.

- How has your educational experience changed since apartheid ended?

- Do you think your future will be different because of these changes? Why or why not?

- How well does this image represent South Africa today?

Reporters, come up with one question for each character listed above.

Step 3: Discuss how to make your character come alive. Use visual and written information from your Reading Notes to brainstorm ways to make the character realistic.

23.4 Protests Lead to Political Change

Step 1: Read Section 23.4. Look carefully at the picture and graphs in this section. Find at least five pieces of evidence that help prove whether this statement is true or false: *The photograph below fully represents South Africa since the end of apartheid.*

Step 2: Around the photo and graphs below, write any evidence that shows the statement is true. Draw a line to the part of the photo or graphs that illustrates each piece of evidence. An example is done for you.

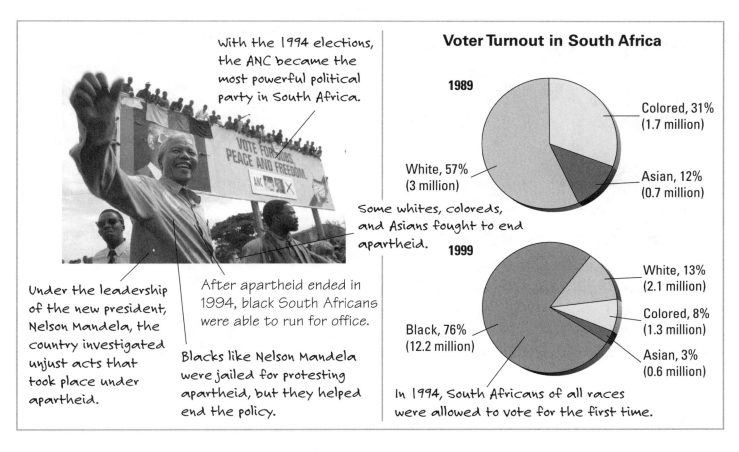

With the 1994 elections, the ANC became the most powerful political party in South Africa.

Some whites, coloreds, and Asians fought to end apartheid.

Under the leadership of the new president, Nelson Mandela, the country investigated unjust acts that took place under apartheid.

After apartheid ended in 1994, black South Africans were able to run for office.

Blacks like Nelson Mandela were jailed for protesting apartheid, but they helped end the policy.

Voter Turnout in South Africa

1989
- Colored, 31% (1.7 million)
- Asian, 12% (0.7 million)
- White, 57% (3 million)

1999
- White, 13% (2.1 million)
- Colored, 8% (1.3 million)
- Asian, 3% (0.6 million)
- Black, 76% (12.2 million)

In 1994, South Africans of all races were allowed to vote for the first time.

Step 3: List any evidence that shows the statement is false.

There is no evidence in Section 23.4 that shows this statement is false.

Step 4: In your group, discuss the photograph your teacher is projecting. How well does it represent South Africa today? Record your answer by placing an X on the spectrum below. Then circle two or three pieces of evidence in Steps 2 and 3 that support your position. Answers will vary.

not at all representative	somewhat representative	very representative	extremely representative

23.5 South Africa Today: Job Opportunities

Step 1: Read Section 23.5. Look carefully at the picture and graphs in this section. Find at least five pieces of evidence that help prove whether this statement is true or false: *The photograph below represents fully South Africa since the end of apartheid.*

Step 2: Around the photo and graphs below, write any evidence that shows the statement is true. Draw a line to the part of the photo or graphs that illustrates each piece of evidence.

In 2001, only 50% of unemployed people in South Africa were black, compared to 82% during apartheid.

In 1998, the government passed the Employment Equity Act, opening job opportunities to all. It requires businesses to hire blacks, coloreds, Asians, women, and the disabled.

The government encourages blacks to start businesses and wants 25% of them to be run by blacks by 2010.

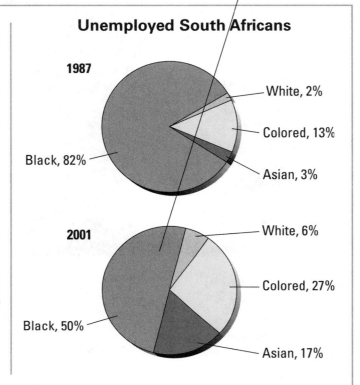

Unemployed South Africans

1987
- White, 2%
- Colored, 13%
- Asian, 3%
- Black, 82%

2001
- White, 6%
- Colored, 27%
- Asian, 17%
- Black, 50%

Step 3: List any evidence that shows the statement is false. An example is done for you.
- Today, blacks, coloreds, and Asians still have much higher unemployment rates than whites.
- In 2005, half of South Africa's population lived in poverty.
- South Africa's economy is growing slowly, and there are not enough new jobs.

Step 4: In your group, discuss the photograph your teacher is projecting. How well does it represent South Africa today? Record your answer by placing an X on the spectrum below. Then circle two or three pieces of evidence in Steps 2 and 3 that support your position. Answers will vary.

| not at all representative | somewhat representative | very representative | extremely representative |

23.6 South Africa Today: Education

Step 1: Read Section 23.6. Look carefully at the picture and graphs in this section. Find at least five pieces of evidence that help prove whether this statement is true or false: *The photograph below represents fully South Africa since the end of apartheid.*

Step 2: Around the photo and graph below, write any evidence that shows the statement is true. Draw a line to the part of the photo or graph that illustrates each piece of evidence. An example is done for you.

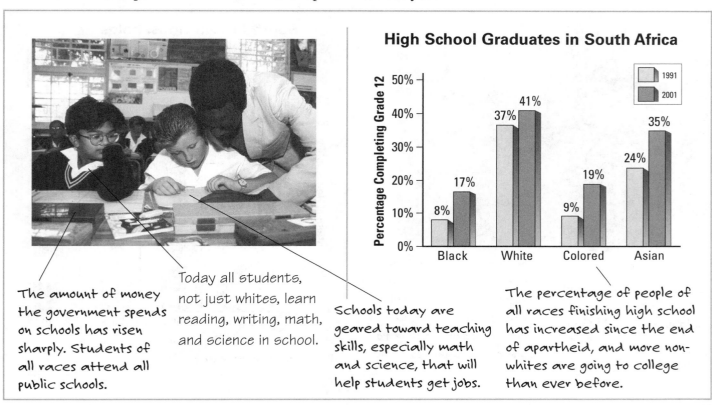

High School Graduates in South Africa

The amount of money the government spends on schools has risen sharply. Students of all races attend all public schools.

Today all students, not just whites, learn reading, writing, math, and science in school.

Schools today are geared toward teaching skills, especially math and science, that will help students get jobs.

The percentage of people of all races finishing high school has increased since the end of apartheid, and more non-whites are going to college than ever before.

Step 3: List any evidence that shows the statement is false.

- Because of apartheid, over 10 million nonwhites never went to high school, and over 4 million had no schooling at all. This has led to high levels of poverty among nonwhites.

- In the past few years, because of slow economic growth, college enrollment has gone down.

Step 4: In your group, discuss the photograph your teacher is projecting. How well does it represent South Africa today? Record your answer by placing an X on the spectrum below. Then circle two or three pieces of evidence in Steps 2 and 3 that support your position. *Answers will vary.*

| not at all representative | somewhat representative | very representative | extremely representative |

23.7 South Africa Today: Living Conditions

Step 1: Read Section 23.7. Look carefully at the picture and graphs in this section. Find at least five pieces of evidence that help prove whether this statement is true or false: *The photograph below represents fully South Africa since the end of apartheid.*

Step 2: Around the photo and graphs below, write any evidence that shows the statement is true. Draw a line to the part of the photo or graphs that illustrates each piece of evidence. An example is done for you.

Although few in number, some nonwhites live in formerly white-only, nice neighborhoods in South Africa's cities.

In the 10 years after apartheid, the government provided 1.6 million homes to the poor. South Africa is still working to improve housing conditions.

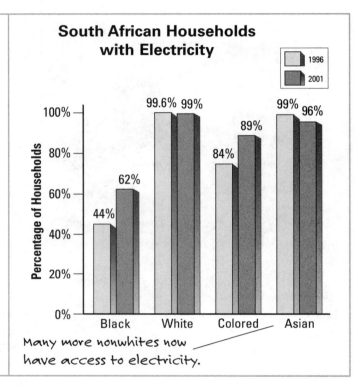

South African Households with Electricity

1996
2001

Percentage of Households

	1996	2001
Black	44%	62%
White	99.6%	99%
Colored	84%	89%
Asian	99%	96%

Many more nonwhites now have access to electricity.

Step 3: List any evidence that shows the statement is false.

• After apartheid, people could live anywhere. But many nonwhites still could not afford to move to the nice cities. They still often live in areas with a lot of crime.

• There are still not enough doctors in rural areas.

• HIV/AIDS continues to be a huge challenge to South Africa's future.

Step 4: In your group, discuss the photograph your teacher is projecting. How well does it represent South Africa today? Record your answer by placing an X on the spectrum below. Then circle two or three pieces of evidence in Steps 2 and 3 that support your position. *Answers will vary.*

not at all representative	somewhat representative	very representative	extremely representative

UNIT 6 Southwest and Central Asia

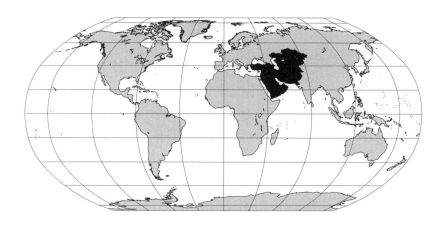

Lesson 24
Oil in Southwest Asia:
How "Black Gold" Has Shaped a Region

Lesson 25
Istanbul: A Primate City Throughout History

Lesson 26
The Aral Sea:
Central Asia's Shrinking Water Source

Oil in Southwest Asia: How "Black Gold" Has Shaped a Region

Overview

In this lesson, students learn how oil has influenced Southwest Asia. In a **Response Group** activity, they analyze geographic data to answer a series of critical thinking questions about how oil has affected 10 countries in the region. Classroom discussion is driven by a map of the region that is projected onto a wall. Students read to discover the answers to those questions and then examine other trends in world energy resources.

Objectives

Students will

- define and explain the importance of these key geographic terms: *crude oil, nonrenewable resource, oil reserves, renewable resource.*
- understand how oil is formed.
- understand how oil is distributed in Southwest Asia.
- investigate the effects of large oil reserves on Southwest Asian countries.
- explore alternative energy resources.

Materials

- *Geography Alive! Regions and People*
- Interactive Student Notebooks
- Transparencies 24A and 24B
- Student Handouts 24A–24C (1 of each for every 3 students)
- Information Master 24 (1 transparency)
- large sticky notes

Preview

1 Project *Transparency 24A: Southwest Asia's "Black Gold."*
Have students analyze the photograph by asking,

• What do you see? Describe the physical environment of this place.

• Where do you think this photograph was taken? Why?

• What do you think the structures shown here are used for?

• What valuable resource do they extract?

Tell students that this photograph is of an oil-drilling rig in the sand dunes of Saudi Arabia. Explain that Southwest Asia contains almost two thirds of the world's known oil supplies and that having such a valuable natural resource affects the region in many ways.

2 Have students complete Preview 24 in their Interactive Student Notebooks. When they are finished, have them share their ideas with another student. Then ask a few volunteers to share theirs with the class. Explain that in the upcoming activity, students will analyze how oil has affected Southwest Asia.

Essential Question and Geoterms

1 Introduce Chapter 24 in *Geography Alive! Regions and People*. Explain that in this chapter, students will learn how a valuable natural resource, oil, impacts the countries of Southwest Asia. Have students read Section 24.1. Then ask them to identify at least two details in the two photographs of Dubai that might reflect the impact of oil on this United Arab Emirates state and city.

2 Introduce the Graphic Organizer and the Essential Question. Have students examine the illustration. Ask,

• What do you see?

• What countries are shown here? Which region of the world are they from?

Have students read the accompanying text. Make sure they understand the Essential Question, *How might having a valuable natural resource affect a region?* You may want to post the Essential Question in the room or write it on the board for the duration of the activity.

3 Have students read Section 24.2. Then have them complete Geoterms 24 in their Interactive Student Notebooks, individually or in pairs. Have them share their answers with another student, or have volunteers share their answers with the class.

Transparency 24A

Preview 24

Geoterms 24

Response Group

1 Place students in mixed-ability groups of three. You may want to prepare a transparency that shows them with whom they will work and where they will sit. Have them arrange their desks so that group members can talk among themselves and clearly see the projector screen.

2 Introduce the activity. Explain that students will answer a series of questions about oil and Southwest Asia. Groups will begin researching the answer to each question by analyzing data and will need to be able to justify their conclusions to the class based on those data. They will then discover the actual answers to the question, and learn more about the topic, by reading a section of *Geography Alive! Regions and People.*

3 Have groups explore the first topic: the geology and geography of oil. Give each group a copy of *Student Handout 24A: Questions About the Geology and Geography of Oil,* and quickly review the directions with the class. Then have students work in their groups to discuss all the questions on the handout, including Critical Thinking Question A. (**Note:** It is essential that students not open *Geography Alive! Regions and People* while they work, as answers to the critical thinking questions are found there.)

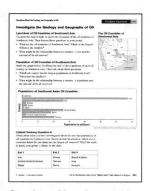

Student Handout 24A

4 Have groups prepare for a class discussion of Critical Thinking Question A.

• Project a transparency of *Information Master 24: Oil Countries of Southwest Asia* as large as possible on a wall of the classroom.

• Give three large sticky notes to each group. Assign each group a number, and have them write their group number, as large as possible, on each note.

• Choose someone from each group to place their three sticky notes on the projected map to identify the set of countries they think are the top oil producers.

Information Master 24

5 Conduct a student-centered discussion of Critical Thinking Question A. Follow these steps:

• Appoint a Presenter in each group.

• Select one Presenter to stand and explain which set of countries his or her group selected and why.

• Ask all other Presenters to raise their hands. Have the first Presenter call on one of them by name.

- Have the new Presenter and all subsequent Presenters begin their presentations as follows: *(Name of previous speaker), our group agrees/disagrees with your group because....*
- Encourage lively debate by having students call on Presenters whose answers differ from theirs.

6 **Have students discover the answer to Critical Thinking Question A.** Explain that students will now find out how oil is formed and which countries in the region actually have the most oil reserves. Have them read Section 24.3 and complete the corresponding Reading Notes. When they have finished, use Guide to Reading Notes 24 to review the main points with them.

7 **Repeat the procedure for the topic of oil wealth and people's well-being.** Distribute *Student Handout 24B: Questions About Oil Wealth and People's Well-Being* to each group and repeat Steps 3–6 above. Make these modifications:

- *Step 3:* Have groups discuss the questions on Student Handout 24B, including Critical Thinking Question B.
- *Step 4:* Assign new students to move their groups' sticky notes to the set of countries they think rank highest in the Human Development Index.
- *Step 5:* Rotate the role of Presenter to a new student in each group.
- *Step 6:* Have students read Section 24.4 and complete the corresponding Reading Notes.

8 **Repeat the procedure for the topic of the price and flow of oil.** Distribute *Student Handout 24C: Questions About the Price and Flow of Oil* to each group and repeat Steps 3–6. Make these modifications:

- *Step 3:* Tell students that this handout looks at the effects of oil not only on countries in Southwest Asia but around the world. Point out that this time groups must prepare answers to two questions, Critical Thinking Questions C and D.
- *Step 4:* Assign new students to move their groups' sticky notes to the set of countries they think are not OPEC members.
- *Step 5, Critical Thinking Question C:* Rotate the role of Presenter to a new student. At the end of the class discussion, reveal that the non-OPEC countries are Oman, Syria, and Yemen. Tell them that Bahrain is also not an OPEC member. See if anyone has a hypothesis about why these are the four non-OPEC oil-producing countries in Southwest Asia.
- *Step 5, Critical Thinking Question D:* Have groups reposition their sticky notes to show which Southwest Asian countries they think contributed the most resources to the 1991 Persian Gulf War. Then conduct the last class discussion.

Reading Notes 24

Student Handout 24B

Reading Notes 24

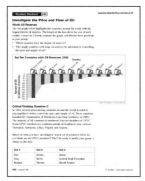

Student Handout 24C   **Reading Notes 24**

- *Step 6:* Have students read Section 24.5 and complete the corresponding Reading Notes.

Processing

Have students turn to Processing 24 in their Interactive Student Notebooks, and review the directions with them. When they've finished, have them share their annotations with another student, or have volunteers share theirs with the class.

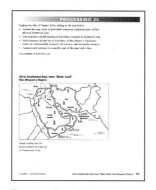

Processing 24

Global Connections

1 Introduce the Global Connections. Have students read Section 24.6, which moves from the topic of a nonrenewable energy source, oil, to a renewable one, solar energy.

2 Project *Transparency 24B: Global Connections.* Have students analyze the map by discussing and sharing their answers to the questions below. Use the additional information given to enrich the discussion.

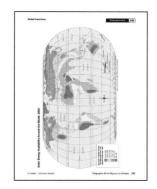

Transparency 24B

- **What can we learn from this map?**

- **What do the various colors represent?**

  The colors represent the average annual solar energy available per square meter. In other words, the colors show which areas of the world receive the most energy from the sun. These numbers help determine how much power solar energy can generate in various locations around the world.

- **Which areas of the world have the most potential for solar power? How could this valuable natural resource affect the futures of these countries?**

  The countries nearest the Tropics of Cancer and Capricorn have the most potential for using solar energy. Countries such as Peru, Namibia, Oman, and Australia may gain power and wealth if they can provide energy to others.

- **Which areas of the world have the least potential for solar energy? How might their futures be affected by the lack of this natural resource?**

  The northern portions of North America, Europe, and Asia have the least potential for solar energy. Countries such as Russia may need to rely on other countries for their energy needs if solar energy becomes the main resource.

3 Have students read Section 24.7 and analyze the additional information in the section. You may want to read the section as a class so you can facilitate discussion of these questions:

- **What energy sources is the world using to meet most of its energy needs? What do they have in common?**

- **Why isn't the world getting more of its energy from renewable resources?**

- **How might having renewable energy resources affect a region in the future?**

Online Resources

For more information on oil and Southwest Asia, refer students to Online Resources for *Geography Alive! Regions and People* at www.teachtci.com.

Assessment

Masters for assessment appear on the next three pages followed by answers and scoring rubrics.

Mastering the Content

Shade in the oval by the letter of the best answer for each question.

1. Why is oil considered a nonrenewable resource?
   - ○ A. It is found deep in the ground.
   - ○ B. It is used to produce electricity.
   - ○ C. It creates pollution when burned.
   - ○ D. It takes millions of years to form.

2. Which of these forces slowly turns the remains of plants and animals into oil?
   - ○ A. solar energy and wind power
   - ○ B. the mixing of water and gases
   - ○ C. underground pressure and heat
   - ○ D. the movement of tectonic plates

3. Which statement **best** describes how oil is distributed among the countries of Southwest Asia?
   - ○ A. One country has all the proven oil reserves.
   - ○ B. Some countries have far more oil than others.
   - ○ C. Every country draws oil from one large deposit.
   - ○ D. Oil is evenly distributed to all countries in the region.

4. What do the countries in this list have in common?

Country
United States
Saudi Arabia
Kuwait
United Arab Emirates
Japan
Germany
United Kingdom
South Korea

   - ○ A. They all belong to OPEC.
   - ○ B. They all export or import oil.
   - ○ C. They all rank low in the HDI.
   - ○ D. They all have large oil reserves.

5. Which of the following is a renewable energy resource?
   - ○ A. coal
   - ○ C. natural gas
   - ○ B. uranium
   - ○ D. wind

6. A Southwest Asian country that spends much of its oil earnings on education and health care is **most likely** to have which of the following?
   - ○ A. a high HDI ranking
   - ○ B. a low life expectancy
   - ○ C. a large rural population
   - ○ D. a small per capita GDP

7. Which of these is a **major** goal of the Organization of the Petroleum Exporting Countries (OPEC)?
   - ○ A. to find new oil deposits
   - ○ B. to keep oil prices steady
   - ○ C. to decrease oil pollution
   - ○ D. to increase oil consumption

8. Which conclusion about world energy production from 1970 to 2003 does the graph below **best** support?

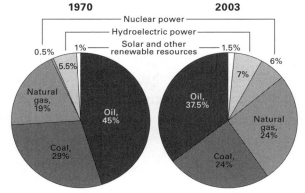

World Energy Production

   - ○ A. The cost of generating electricity rose year by year.
   - ○ B. The nuclear power industry declined during this period.
   - ○ C. The need for energy in developing countries rose sharply.
   - ○ D. The use of renewable energy resources grew very slowly.

Applying Geography Skills: Analyzing Data Tables

Use the tables and your knowledge of geography to complete the tasks below.

The Top Ten Oil Reserves in Southwest Asia, 2004

Rank	Country	Proven Oil Reserves (in millions of barrels)
1	Saudi Arabia	261,700
2	Iran	130,800
3	Iraq	112,500
4	United Arab Emirates	97,800
5	Kuwait	96,500
6	Qatar	16,000
7	Oman	5,500
8	Yemen	4,000
9	Syria	2,500
10	Bahrain	126

Per Capita GDP of Southwest Asian Oil Countries, 2001

Rank	Country	Per Capita GDP (in U.S. dollars)
1	United Arab Emirates	$25,200
2	Qatar	$23,200
3	Kuwait	$21,300
4	Bahrain	$19,200
5	Oman	$13,100
6	Saudi Arabia	$12,000
7	Iran	$7,700
8	Iraq	$3,500
9	Syria	$3,400
10	Yemen	$800

HDI* Ranks in Southwest Asia, 2002

Rank	Country
1	Bahrain
2	Kuwait
3	Qatar
4	United Arab Emirates
5	Oman
6	Saudi Arabia
7	Iran
8	Syria
9	Yemen

* Human Development Index

1. Identify the country that ranks first in proven oil reserves. Compare that rank with its ranking on the per capita GDP table. Discuss why you think the two rankings are not the same.

2. Identify the country that ranks last in proven oil reserves. Compare that rank with its ranking on the HDI table. Discuss what the HDI ranking shows and why you think the two rankings are not the same.

Test Terms Glossary
To **discuss** means to consider different sides of a question or problem and come to a conclusion.

Exploring the Essential Question

How might having a valuable natural resource affect a region?

In Chapter 24, you explored the importance of oil in Southwest Asia. Now you will use what you learned. Use the diagram below and your knowledge of geography to complete this task.

The Task: Writing "The Story of Oil" for a Young Reader

The diagram below shows how crude oil is formed, pumped out of the ground, and used. Your task is to write a book that explains this process to young readers. You will illustrate your book with the six drawings below.

Step 1: Fold a blank sheet of paper in half lengthwise. Fold it again in thirds. The boxes formed by the folds will be the six pages of your book.

Step 2: Cut out the six drawings below. Paste or tape one drawing in each box, keeping them in the correct order. Leave room around each drawing to write an explanation of it.

Step 3: Explain each step in the story of oil in simple words that a young reader can understand.

Writing Tips: Creating Text for Young Readers
Young readers do best with simple text. Keep sentences short. Use easy-to-read words when you can. For example, use *make* instead of *produce*. Define terms readers may not understand, such as *crude oil* and *natural gas*.

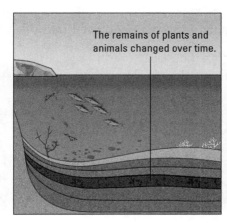

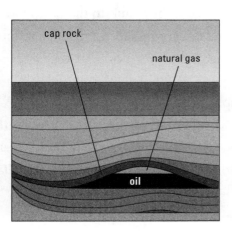

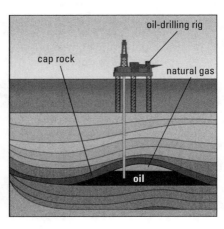

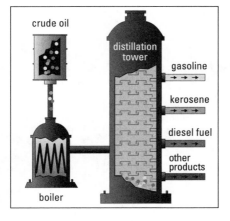

Applying Geography Skills: Sample Responses

1. Saudi Arabia has the most oil reserves, but its per capita GDP is sixth in the region. There are many possible reasons for this. Saudi Arabia may not be producing as much oil per person as other countries in the region. This would lower its GDP per capita. Or it may have a large population compared to its oil reserves and production. Even if its total GDP were high, Saudi Arabia's per capita amount would be lower when divided among so many people.

2. Bahrain has the lowest oil reserves, but it ranks first in the region in HDI. Its high HDI ranking shows that Bahrain's people have the highest level of health care and education in Southwest Asia. One reason for this may be Bahrain's small population. Even though its reserves are small, money from oil sales does not have to be divided among a very large number of people. Another reason is that Bahrain chooses to spend its oil wealth to improve the lives of its people.

Exploring the Essential Question: Sample Response

Possible explanations of the six drawings:

- Long ago, tiny plants lived in the sea. Animals lived there too. When they died, they sank to the bottom of the sea.
- Sand covered the dead plants and animals. Slowly they turned into oil.
- Rock covered the oil and kept it trapped deep in the ground.
- People drill holes through the rock to reach the oil. Then they pump it up to the surface of Earth.
- The oil goes to a refinery. This is a factory that turns oil into things people need. One of those things is gasoline for cars.
- Some oil is sent to other factories. It is used to make things like plastic. Do you have a plastic toy?

Mastering the Content Answer Key

1. D	2. C	3. B	4. B
5. D	6. A	7. B	8. D

Applying Geography Skills Scoring Rubric

Score	General Description
2	Student responds to all parts of the task. Response is correct and clear.
1	Student responds to some parts of the task. Response is mostly correct.
0	Response does not match the task or is incorrect.

Exploring the Essential Question Scoring Rubric

Score	General Description
3	Student responds to all parts of the task. Response is correct, clear, and supported by details.
2	Student responds to most or all parts of the task. Response is generally correct but may lack details.
1	Student responds to at least one part of the task. Response may contain errors and lack details.
0	Response does not match the task or is incorrect.

Investigate the Geology and Geography of Oil

Land Area of Oil Countries of Southwest Asia

Examine the map at right. It shows the locations of the oil countries of Southwest Asia. Then discuss these questions in your group:

- What are the oil countries of Southwest Asia? Which is the largest? Which is the smallest?

- What might be the relationship between a country's size and the amount of its oil reserves?

Population of Oil Countries of Southwest Asia

Study the graph below. It reflects the size of the population of each oil country in Southwest Asia. Then talk about these questions:

- Which oil country has the largest population in Southwest Asia? Which has the smallest?

- What might be the relationship between a country's population and the amount of its oil reserves?

The Oil Countries of Southwest Asia

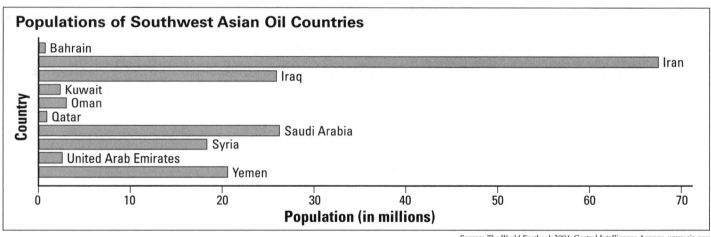

Source: *The World Factbook 2004*, Central Intelligence Agency, www.cia.gov.

Critical Thinking Question A

Think about what you have investigated about the size and population of oil countries in Southwest Asia. Based on that information, which set of countries below do you think has the largest oil reserves? Why? Be ready to justify your group's choice to the class.

Set 1	Set 2	Set 3
Iran	Oman	Saudi Arabia
United Arab Emirates	Yemen	Iraq
Qatar	Syria	Kuwait

Investigate Oil Wealth and People's Well-Being

Gross Domestic Product

Gross domestic product (GDP) is the value of all the goods and services produced in a country in a year. The table lists the GDP of each oil country of Southwest Asia, from highest to lowest. Analyze the table, and discuss these questions in your group:

- Which oil countries have the highest GDP? Which have the lowest?
- What might be the relationship between a country's GDP and the well-being of its people?

GDP of Southwest Asian Oil Countries, 2001

Rank	Country	GDP (in U.S. dollars)
1	Iran	$516,700,000,000
2	Saudi Arabia	$310,200,000,000
3	United Arab Emirates	$63,670,000,000
4	Syria	$60,440,000,000
5	Iraq	$54,400,000,000
6	Kuwait	$48,000,000,000
7	Oman	$38,090,000,000
8	Qatar	$19,490,000,000
9	Yemen	$16,250,000,000
10	Bahrain	$13,010,000,000

Source: *The World Factbook 2004*, Central Intelligence Agency, www.cia.gov.

Per Capita GDP

Per capita GDP is a country's total GDP divided by its population. The next table lists the per capita GDP of each oil country of Southwest Asia, from highest to lowest. Analyze the table, and discuss these questions in your group:

- Which oil countries have the highest per capita GDP? Which have the lowest?
- Are the rankings on this table the same as on the GDP table above? Why or why not?

• Which type of information—GDP or per capita GDP—do you think might give better information about the well-being of a country's people? Why?

Per Capita GDP of Southwest Asian Oil Countries, 2001

Rank	Country	Per Capita GDP (in U.S. dollars)
1	United Arab Emirates	$25,200
2	Qatar	$23,200
3	Kuwait	$21,300
4	Bahrain	$19,200
5	Oman	$13,100
6	Saudi Arabia	$12,000
7	Iran	$7,700
8	Iraq	$3,500
9	Syria	$3,400
10	Yemen	$800

Source: *The World Factbook 2004*, Central Intelligence Agency, www.cia.gov.

Critical Thinking Question B

One way to measure people's well-being is through the Human Development Index, or HDI. This index is used by the United Nations. It combines a variety of information, including per capita GDP, life expectancy, literacy, and level of education.

Think about what you've investigated about the GDP and per capita GDP of the oil countries in Southwest Asia. Based on that information, which set of countries below do you think would rank the highest in the Human Development Index? Why? Be ready to justify your group's choice to the class.

Set 1	Set 2	Set 3
Syria	Oman	Bahrain
Iran	Saudi Arabia	Qatar
Iraq	United Arab Emirates	Kuwait

Investigate the Price and Flow of Oil

World Oil Reserves

The bar graph below highlights the countries around the world with the largest known oil reserves. The length of the bars show the size of each country's reserves. Closely examine the graph, and discuss these questions in your group:

• Which countries have the largest oil reserves?

• Why might countries with large oil reserves be interested in controlling the price and supply of oil?

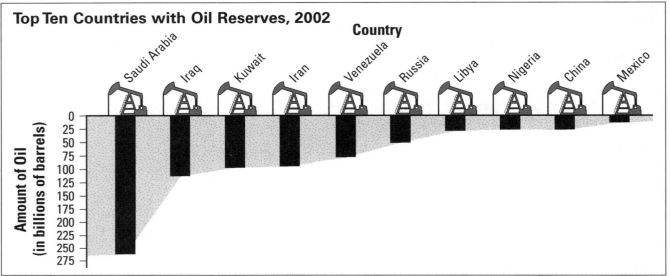

Source: *NationMaster*, www.nationmaster.com.

Critical Thinking Question C

In 1960, several oil-producing countries around the world decided to join together to better control the price and supply of oil. These countries founded the Organization of Petroleum Exporting Countries, or OPEC. The majority of oil countries in Southwest Asia are members of OPEC. Some OPEC members are countries outside of Southwest Asia, such as Venezuela, Indonesia, Libya, Nigeria, and Algeria.

Based on what you have investigated, which set of countries below do you think are *not* OPEC members? Why? Be ready to justify your group's choice to the class.

Set 1	Set 2	Set 3
Iran	Oman	Qatar
Iraq	Syria	United Arab Emirates
Kuwait	Yemen	Saudi Arabia

© Teachers' Curriculum Institute

World Oil Consumption

The graph below highlights the countries in the world that consume the most oil. The height of the bars reflects the amount of oil each country uses each day. Analyze the graph, and discuss these questions in your group:

- Which countries consume the most oil? What is similar about them?

- Why might countries that consume lots of oil be interested in controlling the price and supply of oil?

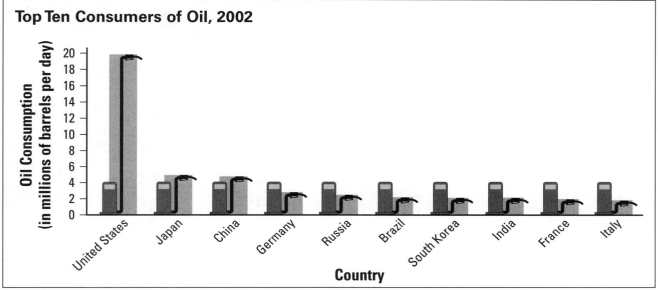

Top Ten Consumers of Oil, 2002

Source: *NationMaster,* www.nationmaster.com.

Critical Thinking Question D

In 1990, Iraq invaded the neighboring country of Kuwait. This invasion threatened the flow of oil from this part of Southwest Asia. In response, the United States and many other countries worked together to drive Iraq out of Kuwait. This became the 1991 Persian Gulf War.

Some countries contributed soldiers, equipment, and money to the war. Top contributors included the United States, Germany, and Japan. Many oil countries in Southwest Asia were also big contributors.

Based on what you have learned, which set of countries below do you think contributed the most toward the costs of the Persian Gulf War? Why? Be ready to justify your group's choice to the class.

Set 1	Set 2	Set 3
Iran	Saudi Arabia	Yemen
Oman	Kuwait	Bahrain
Qatar	United Arab Emirates	Syria

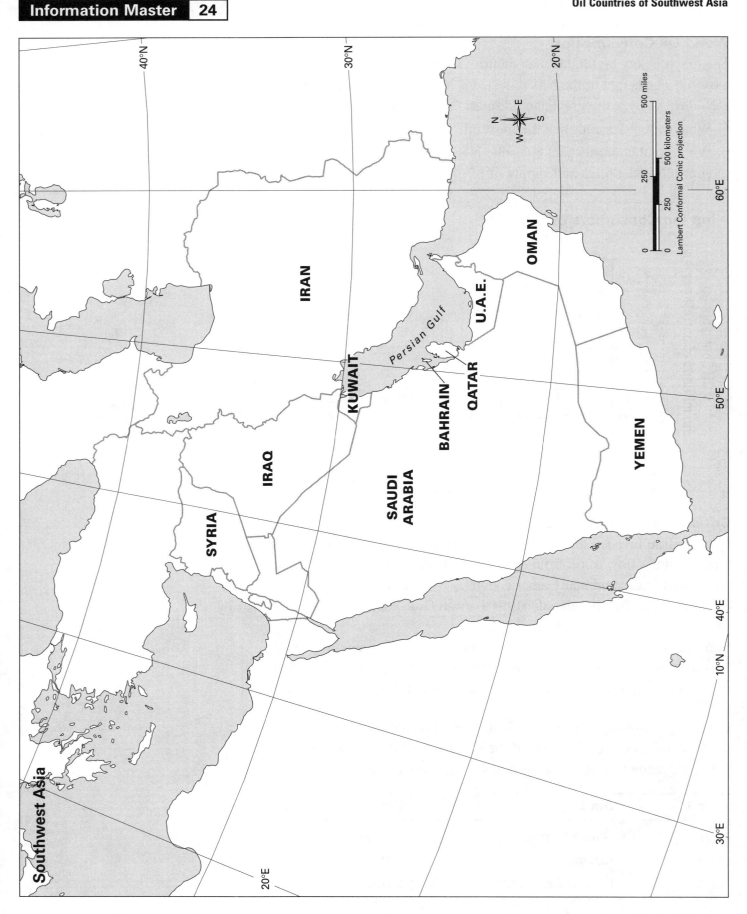

Southwest Asia

40°N

30°N

20°N

60°E

50°E

40°E

30°E

20°E

10°N

IRAN

OMAN

U.A.E.

Persian Gulf

KUWAIT

BAHRAIN

QATAR

SAUDI
ARABIA

IRAQ

SYRIA

YEMEN

N
W · E
S

500 miles

500 kilometers

250

250

0

0

Lambert Conformal Conic projection

24.3 The Geology and Geography of Oil

Read Section 24.3. Then, on the map, rank each of Southwest Asia's oil countries according to the size of its proven oil reserves. Label them from 1 (largest reserve) to 10 (smallest reserve). Shade the three countries with the largest oil reserves.

Southwest Asia: Who Has the Oil?

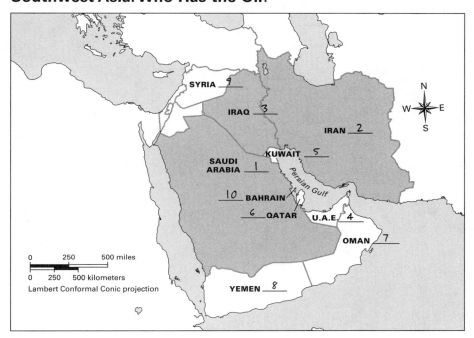

Answer these questions:

- How does oil form? Explain the process in at least three steps.

  The process begins with tiny plants and animals that died in the oceans millions of years ago. Over time, most of them turned to rock. The weight of the water, heat from Earth's core, and chemical changes turned some of the remains into oil and natural gas.

- Why is so much oil buried under Southwest Asia?

  Oil can be found under Southwest Asia because millions of years ago the area was under water. When the Iranian and Arabian tectonic plates hit, they created spaces where oil was formed and trapped.

- Are oil reserves distributed equally among the countries of Southwest Asia? Explain.

  Oil is not distributed equally among these countries. The region's largest country, Saudi Arabia, contains about one quarter of the world's known oil reserves. But smaller countries like Kuwait also possess much oil. Other countries, like Syria and Yemen, have much less oil than others in the region.

24.4 Oil Wealth and People's Well-Being

Read Section 24.4. Then, on the map, rank each of Southwest Asia's oil countries according to its Human Development Index (HDI) rank. Label them from 1 (highest rank) to 10 (lowest rank). Shade the three countries with the highest HDI ranks.

Southwest Asia: Measuring Well-Being with HDI

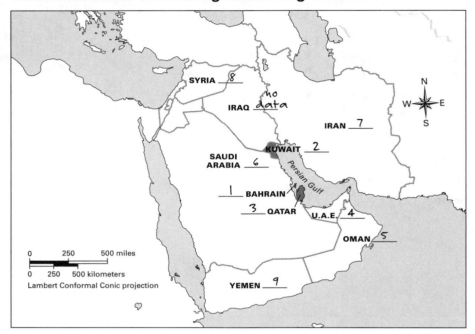

Answer these questions:

- How has oil made the people of Southwest Asia better off?

  Oil money has improved the lives of people in Southwest Asia. Over the past 30 years, life expectancy has increased and the number of infants who die in their first year has decreased.

- Why isn't per capita GDP always an accurate reflection of people's wealth?

  Per capita GDP assumes that a country's wealth is divided equally among its citizens, but that isn't really true.

- What are some examples of why some oil countries haven't been able to end poverty?

  Oil money has not been able to end poverty in Yemen or Iraq. The combination of low oil revenues and a large population has left Yemen poor. And Saddam Hussein used oil money to buy weapons and pay for wars instead of improving life for ordinary Iraqis.

24.5 The Price and Flow of Oil

Read Section 24.5. Then, on the map, place an X on the lines for the countries that are OPEC members. Circle the names of the Southwest Asian countries who were top contributors to the costs of the Persian Gulf War.

Southwest Asia: OPEC Members and Persian Gulf War Contributors

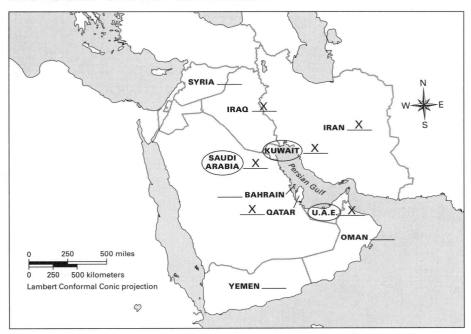

Answer these questions:

- What have been the goals of Southwest Asian OPEC members?

  One goal is to have a steady supply of oil flowing out and money flowing into their countries. Another goal is to keep oil prices steady—not too high or too low.

- What two realities have limited OPEC's power?

  OPEC can't control all of the world's oil sales; it exports less than half of the world's crude oil. And OPEC countries don't always act as a group.

- What were the two types of coalition members in the Persian Gulf War? Why were they coalition members?

  Two types of coalition members were oil-importing countries who did not want their oil supplies threatened and oil-exporting countries who did not want to lose control of their oil reserves.

Istanbul: A Primate City Throughout History

Overview

In this lesson, students examine the city of Istanbul to learn about the unique traits of primate cities. In an **Experiential Exercise,** students develop an appreciation for the importance of location, as defined by site and situation, by playing a game in which they discover the best trading location among several designated areas in the room. They then read about Istanbul and compare and contrast their experience in the game with various aspects of this primate city, which has thrived for centuries.

Objectives

Students will

- define and explain the importance of these key geographic terms: *capital city, primate city, site, situation.*

- experience the importance of site and situation by playing a trading game that begins with students in scattered locations and ends with them congregated in a single location best suited for trading.

- investigate the role of geography in the development of primate cities.

- examine the traits of primate cities.

- analyze the location and importance of primate cities worldwide.

Materials

- *Geography Alive! Regions and People*
- Interactive Student Notebooks
- Transparencies 25A and 25B
- Information Master 25 (1 transparency)
- masking tape
- blue, orange, yellow, red, and green transparency markers
- 30 sheets of colored paper: 7 blue, 2 orange, 5 yellow, 6 red, and 10 green

Preview

There is no Preview for this lesson. The Experimental Exercise functions as a preview to the geography.

Experiential Exercise

1 Before class, prepare materials and arrange the room. The classroom configuration and associated trading game are designed to simulate Istanbul's site and situation and reveal the key features that make it and other cities primate cities. The trading game begins with students distributed at several locations. As it progresses, more and more students will concentrate in one location to complete their trades. Follow these steps to create a series of cities, towns, and rural villages in which students will play the trading game:

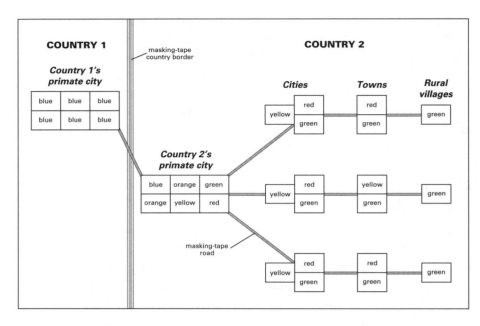

- Arrange desks as shown in the diagram. Do not tell students what these locations represent. (**Note:** If you prefer, have students arrange the room when they view Information Master 25 in the next step.)

- Create a border between the two fictitious countries by taping a double line across the floor, separating the six desks on the far left from the rest.

- Use masking tape to create roads as shown in the diagram.

- Place a sheet of colored paper on each desk. In all, there are 30 sheets of paper in five colors: 7 blue, 2 orange, 5 yellow, 6 red, and 10 green. Their distribution represents the relative availability of goods in various parts of the two countries.

- Use transparency markers to color-code the diagram on the transparency of *Information Master 25: Game Directions.*

(**Note:** The diagram assumes a class size of 30 students. If your class is larger or smaller, reduce or enlarge the number of desks in the two primate cities. If you have fewer than 25 or more than 35 students, remove or add one city–town–rural village "spoke" from Country 2.)

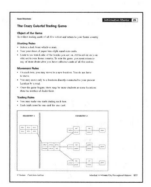

Information Master 25

2 Introduce the game and distribute materials. Have students stand along the edges of the room so that they can see the projection screen. Explain that they will now play a trading game. Project Information Master 25, and review the game objectives and rules with them. Emphasize these game basics:

- The object of the game is to collect the greatest variety of colored cards. There are five colors in all.

- A "location" is a single desk or a group of desks separated from other locations by a masking-tape road.

- Students will always have eight cards, but by trading they can collect a variety of colors. Demonstrate how to fold and tear a sheet of paper to create eight cards.

- Students may make one move and one trade per turn. Each trade must be one card for one card.

- The two sides of the tape represent two different countries. To be able to win, students must be back in their starting country when the game ends. This means they must be on the same side of the tape as they were at the beginning.

- Heighten students' interest by explaining that if they want to win the game, they need to think carefully about which desks are best to start from. Only one student may start at each desk.

3 Conduct the game. Follow these steps:

- Release students in groups of five to select their starting desks. Expect some to go quickly to key strategic desks and others to choose desks at random. Have students tear the sheet of paper at their chosen desk into eight cards.

- Signal when each turn begins by announcing "Turn 1," "Turn 2," and so on. Time each turn to be about 30 seconds. Begin the game by announcing "Turn 1." Play the game for six to eight turns.

- Expect that as the game proceeds, Country 2's primate city will become more and more crowded. As you announce "Last turn," remind students that to be eligible to win, they must end the game in their starting country.

4 Debrief the game. Have students return to their starting desks and sit down. Project the map on Information Master 25 again, and discuss these questions:

- How many students were able to collect all five colors and end the game in their home country?

- *Winners:* What factors helped you to win? What feelings did you experience during the game?

- *Nonwinners:* Who ended with the fewest colors? Why was it difficult for you to win? What feelings did you experience during the game?

- Where was the best place to trade? Why?

- Suppose you were allowed to make a rule change during the game but needed to get the agreement of most of the players to make that change. In what location would it be easiest to make such a decision? Why? Why would other locations—say the three single desks that were farthest from the best place to trade—be poor places to make such decisions?

- Suppose the different colors represented different aspects of culture—such as music, religion, food, clothing, and entertainment—and that the greater the variety of colors at a location, the more rich and varied the culture there. Which location has the richest and most varied culture? Why?

- (Point out Country 1 and Country 2 on the diagram.) Which location do you think best represents each of these descriptions: the most important city in Country 2? The rural villages in Country 2? Towns in Country 2? Other cities in Country 2? An important city not in Country 2?

Tell students that in Chapter 25, they will learn about the concept of a primate city. Primate cities are powerful places and are often capital cities where key decisions are made. They are places where trade and other economic activities flourish. And they are cultural capitals with a wide variety of cultural features. Ask, *Which location do you think is Country 2's primate city?*

Essential Question and Geoterms

1 Introduce Chapter 25 in *Geography Alive! Regions and People*. Explain that in this chapter, students will learn about primate cities through the study of one example, Istanbul, Turkey. Have students read Section 25.1. Afterward, ask them to identify at least three ways in which the text and the photograph of Istanbul reflect aspects of the busiest location of the trading game.

2 Introduce the Graphic Organizer and the Essential Question. Have students examine the map of Turkey. Then ask,

- What do you see?
- What do the different size dots represent?
- Which dot represents Turkey's primate city? What about this city's location might have helped it to become a primate city?

Have students read the accompanying text. Make sure they understand the Essential Question, *Where are primate cities located, and why are they important?* You may want to post the Essential Question in the room or write it on the board for the duration of the activity.

3 Have students read Section 25.2. Then have them complete Geoterms 25 in their Interactive Student Notebooks, individually or in pairs. Have them share their answers with another student, or have volunteers share their answers with the class.

4 Make connections between the reading and the experience.

- Project the map on Information Master 25 again. Ask, *Based on your experiences in the game, which location in Country 2 represents a primate city? Why?*

- Project the physical map at the top of *Transparency 25A: Istanbul's Favorable Site and Situation* while keeping the second map covered. Point out Istanbul, and remind students that *site* refers to a location's place, including its physical setting. Have volunteers come up to the map and point out features of Istanbul's site. Then ask, *How did Istanbul's site help it develop into Turkey's primate city?* Students may point out that Istanbul is located on a peninsula, has a protected harbor, and is near two bodies of water.

- Now project the second map, which shows trade routes during the Byzantine Empire. Remind students that Istanbul was formerly called Constantinople and that *situation* refers to a location's position in relationship to its wider surroundings. Have volunteers come up to the map and point out features of Istanbul's situation. Ask, *How did Istanbul's situation help it develop into Turkey's primate city?* Students may point out that Istanbul's situation allows trade to reach it by water and overland from Africa, Asia, Europe, and other locations in Southwest Asia. Then ask, *How does this map of trade routes remind you of the trade patterns developed during the game?*

- Project Information Master 25 once more. Ask, *Which was more important when you chose a starting location for the trading game: site or situation? Explain.* Students may say that situation was more important because, to win, one needed to start in or near the primate city of Country 2.

Reading for Understanding

Have students read Sections 25.3 to 25.5 in *Geography Alive! Regions and People* and complete Reading Notes 25 in their Interactive Student Notebooks. As they finish each section of notes, use Guide to Reading Notes 25 to review the answers with them. You might then challenge them to describe any other connections between the reading and the game that they can think of.

Geoterms 25

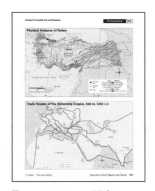

Transparency 25A

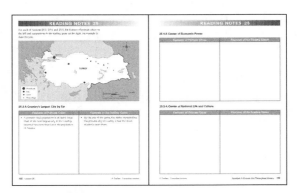

Reading Notes 25

Global Connections

1 Introduce the Global Connections. Have students read Section 25.6. Then ask, *In what ways are Istanbul, Paris, and Bangkok similar?*

2 Project *Transparency 25B: Global Connections.* Help students analyze the map by asking,

Transparency 25B

- **What can we learn from this map?**

- **What patterns do you see in the locations of primate cities?**

3 Have students read Section 25.7 and examine the rest of the information in the section. You may want to read this section as a class so you can facilitate a discussion of these questions:

- **What role do site and situation play in the development of primate cities?**

- **What relationship do you see between primate cities and capital cities?**

- **What might explain why some countries do not have a primate city?**

Processing

Have students complete Processing 25 in their Interactive Student Notebooks. Afterward, have students share their state maps with another student, or have volunteers share their maps with the class. (**Note:** The approximate population of each state's largest cities can be found at www.mapquest.com/atlas/.)

Processing 25

Online Resources

For more information on Istanbul and primate cities, refer students to Online Resources for *Geography Alive! Regions and People* at www.teachtci.com.

Assessment

Masters for assessment appear on the next three pages followed by answers and scoring rubrics.

Mastering the Content

Shade in the oval by the letter of the best answer for each question.

1. What defines the largest city in a country as a primate city?
   ○ A. It is the country's official capital city.
   ○ B. It is the city with the greatest ethnic diversity.
   ○ C. It has more tourist attractions than any other city.
   ○ D. It has twice as many people as the next largest city.

2. What aspect of the **site** of Constantinople helped the city withstand many attacks?
   ○ A. It was a center of business and culture.
   ○ B. It was the capital of three empires.
   ○ C. It was surrounded on three sides by water.
   ○ D. It was founded more than 2,500 years ago.

3. What aspect of the **situation** of Constantinople is shown on the map below?

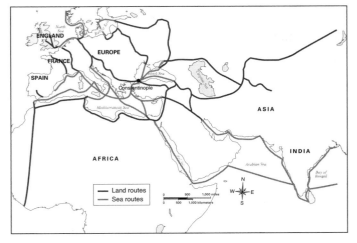

   ○ A. It was built on a flat peninsula.
   ○ B. It was not conquered until 1453.
   ○ C. It was the capital of three empires.
   ○ D. It was located on important trade routes.

4. Where does the capital city of Ankara stand in Turkey's urban hierarchy?
   ○ A. at the top
   ○ B. near the top
   ○ C. at the bottom
   ○ D. near the bottom

5. Which of these is **most likely** to draw someone from a rural area to a primate city to live?
   ○ A. historic sites
   ○ B. sporting events
   ○ C. job opportunities
   ○ D. shopping bazaars

6. Which of these is a **major** difference between Istanbul and Ankara?
   ○ A. Ankara has more people.
   ○ B. Istanbul attracts more tourists.
   ○ C. Istanbul is a much younger city.
   ○ D. Ankara attracts more seagoing trade.

7. The Hagia Sophia, Topkapi Palace, and Blue Mosque all reflect Turkey's
   ○ A. site and situation.
   ○ B. history and culture.
   ○ C. trade and agriculture.
   ○ D. government and military.

8. Which of these generalizations is true of **most** primate cities?
   ○ A. They are located on bodies of water.
   ○ B. They are many thousands of years old.
   ○ C. They are poor compared to other cities.
   ○ D. They are limited to developed countries.

Applying Geography Skills: Analyzing Site and Situation with a Physical Features Map

Use this map and your knowledge of geography to complete the tasks below.

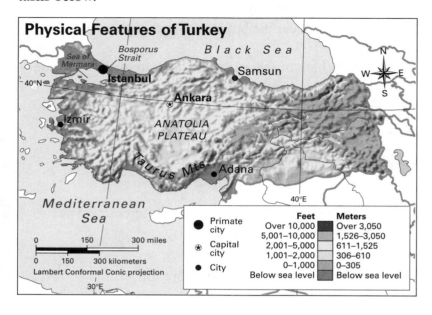

1. Draw a box around Turkey's capital city. Describe the site, or physical setting, of this city.

2. Circle four other Turkish cities. Examine the sites of these cities. Identify two things these sites all have in common.

3. Examine the situation, or position, of the capital in relation to the other four cities. Explain how its situation makes this city a good choice to be the center of Turkey's government.

Test Terms Glossary
To **examine** means to study or analyze a subject in detail.

© Teachers' Curriculum Institute

Exploring the Essential Question

Where are primate cities located, and why are they important?

In Chapter 25, you explored how site and situation affected the growth of Istanbul, Turkey. Now you will use what you learned. Use this diagram and your knowledge of geography to complete the task below.

The Task: Illustrating the Site and Situation of Your Community

This diagram illustrates the urban hierarchy. You task is to place your own community in that hierarchy. Then you will create a poster that illustrates key facts about your community's site and situation.

Step 1: Circle the part of the diagram that best illustrates where your community ranks on the urban hierarchy.

Step 2: List three facts below about the site, or physical setting, of your community that make it a good place to live. These facts might include information about its land-forms, bodies of water, vegetation, climate, or natural resources.

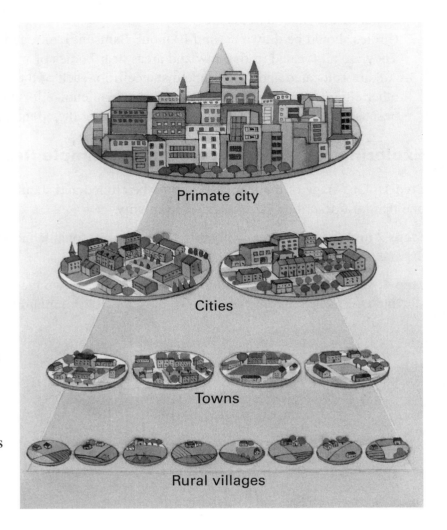

Primate city

Cities

Towns

Rural villages

Step 3: List three facts below about the situation, or position of your community relative to other things, that make it a good place to live. These facts might include information about nearby farms, factories, businesses, highways, airports, scenic attractions, historic sites, colleges, or parks.

Design Tips
Choose facts for your poster that are easy to show in simple pictures or a few words. Arrange them in an interesting way. Also be sure your title stands out.

Step 4: On another sheet of paper, create a poster about your community. Title your poster "The Site and Situation of (your community's name)." Use pictures and words to show at least two facts about your community's site and two facts about its situation.

Applying Geography Skills: Sample Responses

1. A box should be drawn around Ankara. Its site is a hilly region in the center of the Anatolia Plateau.

2. Circles should be drawn around Istanbul, Samsun, Izmir, and Adana. They are all located in flat, lowland areas near bodies of water.

3. Ankara is located about the same distance from each of the four other cities. Its central location makes it a good choice for the capital because it is fairly easy to reach from any part of the country.

Exploring the Essential Question: Sample Response

Step 1: One stage of the hierarchy should be circled and should be the one that best describes the student's community.

Steps 2 and 3: Responses will vary. Accept any reasonable facts about the site and situation of the student's community.

Step 4: The poster should include a title and illustrate two facts about the site and two facts about the situation of the student's community.

Mastering the Content Answer Key

1. D	2. C	3. D	4. B
5. C	6. B	7. B	8. A

Applying Geography Skills Scoring Rubric

Score	General Description
2	Student responds to all parts of the task. Response is correct and clear.
1	Student responds to some parts of the task. Response is mostly correct.
0	Response does not match the task or is incorrect.

Exploring the Essential Question Scoring Rubric

Score	General Description
3	Student responds to all parts of the task. Response is correct, clear, and supported by details.
2	Student responds to most or all parts of the task. Response is generally correct but may lack details.
1	Student responds to at least one part of the task. Response may contain errors and lack details.
0	Response does not match the task or is incorrect.

The Crazy Colorful Trading Game

Object of the Game
To collect trading cards of all five colors and return to your home country

Starting Rules
- Select a desk from which to start.
- Tear your sheet of paper into eight equal-size cards.
- Look to see which side of the border you are on. All locations on your side are in your home country. To win the game, you must return to any of those desks after you have collected cards of all five colors.

Movement Rules
- On each turn, you may move to a new location. You do not have to move.
- You may move only to a location directly connected to your present location by a road.
- Once the game begins, there may be more students at some locations than the number of desks there.

Trading Rules
- You may make one trade during each turn.
- Each trade must be one card for one card.

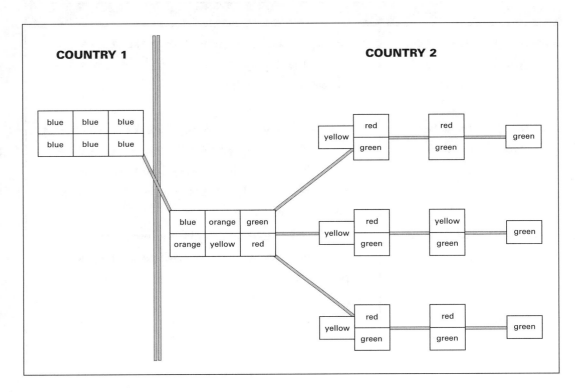

For each of Sections 25.3, 25.4, and 25.5, list features of primate cities on the left and comparisons to the trading game on the right. An example is done for you.

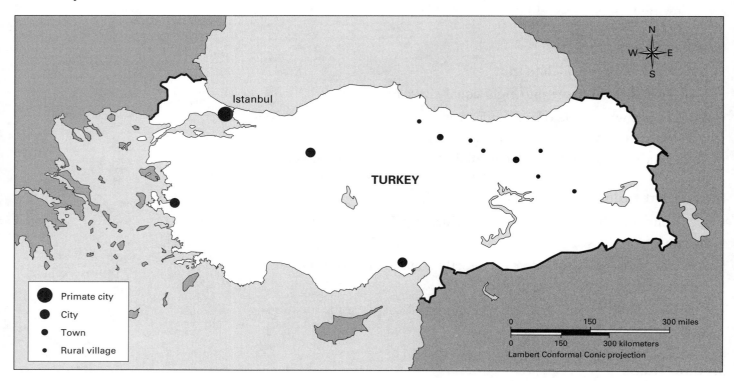

25.3 A Country's Largest City by Far

Features of Primate Cities	Features of the Trading Game
• A primate city's population is at least twice that of the next largest city in the country. Istanbul has more than twice the population of Ankara.	• By the end of the game, the desks representing the primate city in Country 2 had the most students near them.
• People from rural areas migrate to primate cities. They are looking for jobs, education, and excitement.	• Students who started near desks representing rural villages migrated to desks representing the primate city in Country 2 so that they could more easily collect the trading cards they needed.
• A primate city can become overcrowded and develop problems.	• The desks representing the primate city in Country 2 became overcrowded as the game progressed.

25.4 A Center of Economic Power

Features of Primate Cities	Features of the Trading Game
• Primate cities are economic centers for business and trade.	• The desks representing the primate city in Country 2 were where most of the trading took place.
• As a center for plane, ship, and train travel, Istanbul connects Turkey with the rest of the world.	• The roads used for transportation in the game all led through one location: the desks representing the primate city in Country 2. This location was also connected to a large city in Country 1.
• Many primate cites are also capital cities.	• We discussed that it would be easiest to change the rules of the game from the desks representing the primate city in Country 2.

25.5 A Center of National Life and Culture

Features of Primate Cities	Features of the Trading Game
• Primate cities are cultural capitals. In Istanbul, one can find goods and landmarks that highlight Turkey's culture.	• As a class, we discussed that the colors of trading cards could represent different aspects of culture. The place in the game with the most colors was at the desks representing the primate city in Country 2.

The Aral Sea: Central Asia's Shrinking Water Source

Overview

In this lesson, students examine how the shrinking of the Aral Sea in Central Asia has affected the nearby physical environment and the humans who live there. In a **Problem Solving Groupwork** activity, students prepare and present "documentaries" on how a particular group of people has been affected by the changes to the Aral Sea. Using information gathered from charts, graphs, maps, and readings, they then analyze how changes to the physical environment affect human interactions.

Objectives

Students will

- define and explain the importance of these key geographic terms: *environmental degradation, groundwater, salinization, water stress*.
- discover why the Aral Sea has shrunk significantly in the last 40 years.
- examine how the shrinking of the Aral Sea has affected people in Kazakhstan and Uzbekistan.
- investigate irrigation in other parts of the world and its effects on people in those areas.

Materials

- *Geography Alive! Regions and People*
- Interactive Student Notebooks
- Transparencies 26A and 26B
- Student Handout 26A (1 copy for every 4 students, plus 1 transparency)
- Student Handout 26B (a different version for every 4 students)
- butcher paper or poster board
- markers

Preview

1 Project the first image on *Transparency 26A: Landsat Images of the Aral Sea in 1964 and 2005.* Have students turn to Preview 26 in their Interactive Student Notebooks and, in pairs, complete Step 1. Then briefly discuss the four questions in Step 1. In response to the last question *(Would you expect this area to look any different if the image were taken today?)*, students might mention, among other things, more evidence of infrastructure, more houses, more industry, and more pollution.

2 Project the second image on Transparency 26A, and have students compare it to the first. Have pairs complete Step 2 of the Preview and then share their answers to the three questions in Step 2.

3 Explain the connection between the Preview and the upcoming activity. Explain that the Aral Sea has decreased in size by almost 60 percent over the last 40 years. Students will explore the many reasons for this decline in this lesson, but more importantly, they will examine the impact that this loss of water has had on the surrounding environment and the people who live there. Students will discover why the Aral Sea has shrunk and how people in Kazakhstan and Uzbekistan are trying to cope with the problems that have resulted.

Transparency 26A   **Preview 26**

Essential Question and Geoterms

1 Introduce Chapter 26 in *Geography Alive! Regions and People.* Explain that in this chapter, students will learn about the shrinking of the Aral Sea and the impact it has had on nearby residents. Have them read Section 26.1. Then have them examine the photograph of the stranded boat, and ask,

- What details do you notice about this image?
- What do you think happened to cause this boat to be left where it is?
- What kinds of people are most likely to be affected by this situation? In what ways?

2 Introduce the Graphic Organizer and the Essential Question. Have students examine the illustration of the shrinking Aral Sea. Then ask,

- What do you see?
- What is the setting of this illustration?
- The illustrations in the arrows represent groups of people who might be affected by changes to the Aral Sea. What group of people does each represent?

Have students read the accompanying text. Make sure they understand the Essential Question, *How are humans affected by changes they make to their physical environment?* You may want to post the Essential Question in the room or write it on the board for the duration of the activity.

3 Have students read Section 26.2. Then have them work individually or in pairs to complete Geoterms 26 in their Interactive Student Notebooks. Ask them to share their answers with another student, or have volunteers share their answers with the class.

Problem Solving Groupwork

1 Arrange students in mixed-ability groups of four. You might prepare a transparency that shows them with whom they will work and where they will sit. (**Note:** For a smaller class, you may want to use groups of three and adjust the roles within the groups.)

2 Introduce the activity. Tell students that they will work in their teams to create a short piece for a documentary that could be used to educate people about the causes and consequences of the shrinking of the Aral Sea. (You might explain that a *documentary* is a film made to educate people about a particular topic.) Each team will be assigned to represent a group of people who lived or live near the Aral Sea and have been affected by the loss of water and the resulting damage to the environment. They are to find an engaging way to present the story of their assigned group.

3 Review the steps for creating the documentary. Give each team a copy of *Student Handout 26A: Preparing a Documentary,* and project a transparency of each page of the handout as you review the directions and as teams complete each step of the activity. Assign each team to one of the following groups of people by giving them the appropriate version of *Student Handout 26B: Background Information on a Group in the Aral Sea Region:*

- Farmers in the Aral Sea Region Before 1970
- Farmers in the Aral Sea Region Today
- Fishing Industry in the Aral Sea Region Before 1960
- Fishing Industry in the Aral Sea Region Today
- Residents in the Aral Sea Region Before 1970
- Residents in the Aral Sea Region Today

Review the four roles—Director, Script Manager, Props Manager, and Stage Manager—listed on Student Handout 26A, and assign each student a role for the activity. Tell students that they will

Geoterms 26

Student Handout 26A

Student Handout 26B

each be responsible for leading their teams through one step in preparing their documentaries, and that everyone will take part in the presentation. Review the remaining steps for creating the documentary.

4 Monitor teams as they prepare for the documentary. Allow teams adequate time (about two class periods) to prepare. Check their work and initial Student Handout 26A as they complete each step.

5 Arrange the classroom for the presentations. Clear a space at the front of the room.

6 Have the first team set up to present their documentary as the rest of the class reads the corresponding section of *Geography Alive! Regions and People.* Have the team assigned to the first group of people, "Farmers in the Aral Sea Region Before 1970," come to the front of the room and begin to arrange their props. As they prepare, have the remaining students read Section 26.3 up to "Salinization Creates a New Desert" and complete the corresponding Reading Notes.

7 Have the first team perform their documentary. Remind actors to speak loudly, clearly, and slowly enough for everyone to hear. After the performance, have students in the audience quickly skim through the section they read prior to the perform-ance and respond to these questions:

- What information from the reading did this team accurately present in their documentary?
- What information, if any, was missing from the documentary?

8 Repeat Steps 6 and 7 for the remaining presentations. Call groups in the order they are listed in Step 3 above. While each successive team prepares to present, have the remaining students read the appropriate part of the text.

9 Conduct a class discussion. After all teams have presented their documentaries, post the graphs they made. (**Note:** The team presenting on "Residents in the Aral Sea Region Before 1970" was not asked to create a graph.) Encourage students to examine the information in these graphs. Then center a discus-sion on these questions:

- What is the most startling information or trend you see in these graphs?
- What are some of the major problems facing people who live near the Aral Sea?

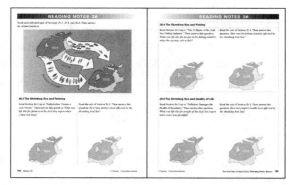

Reading Notes 26

- Whose lives do you think have been most dramatically affected by the changes in the sea?

- What are some things that must be done if these people are going to survive?

Global Connections

1 **Introduce the Global Connections.** Have students read Section 26.6. Tell them that they will now see how some of the issues they encountered in the activity play out on a global scale.

2 **Project** *Transparency 26B: Global Connections.* Help students analyze the map by asking the following questions. Use the additional information to enrich the discussion.

- **What does this map tell us?**
  This map shows how much land in areas around the world is irrigated. Countries with more irrigated land use a greater percentage of their freshwater supply to water crops.

- **Why do societies need to irrigate?**
  Societies need to irrigate if there is not enough rainfall to water their crops naturally. Sometimes this is because of a dry climate. Sometimes it is because the crops being grown require a great deal of water.

- **In what regions do you notice a greater reliance on irrigation?** *Areas with larger populations, like China and India, seem to rely more heavily on irrigation. Areas with dry, hot, desertlike climates also have more irrigated land.*

Transparency 26B

3 **Have students read Section 26.7 and examine the rest of the information in the section.** Then lead a discussion of these questions:

- **What factors might affect how much water a region uses for irrigating crops?**

- **What areas are most likely to experience water stress?**

- **What choices can people make to reduce water stress?**

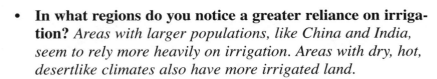

Processing

Have students complete Processing 26 in their Interactive Student Notebooks. You may wish to assign Step 1 as homework and Step 2 in class the following day. Or, complete Step 1 as a class by giving students access to the Internet for exploring where the water they use comes from. Finally, center a discussion on these questions:

- How is your water source being affected by the water use of nearby communities, farming, and industry?

- Is there a potential for water stress in your area in the future? Why or why not?

Processing 26

Online Resources

For more information on the Aral Sea, refer students to Online Resources for *Geography Alive! Regions and People* at www.teachtci.com.

Assessment

Masters for assessment appear on the three pages that follow the next page, followed by answers and scoring rubrics.

Mastering the Content

Shade in the oval by the letter of the best answer for each question.

1. Water stress is **best** defined as which of the following?
   - ○ A. a long-term shortage of water
   - ○ B. the excess use of water supplies
   - ○ C. the poisoning of water by pollution
   - ○ D. a flood of water due to heavy rainfall

2. What is the **main** cause of the shrinking of the Aral Sea?
   - ○ A. the decreased number of fish living in the sea
   - ○ B. the increased use of water from the sea by local towns
   - ○ C. the decreased precipitation in the region around the sea
   - ○ D. the increased use of rivers flowing into the sea for irrigation

3. What happens to water when salinization occurs?
   - ○ A. It evaporates.
   - ○ B. It becomes salty.
   - ○ C. It soaks into the soil.
   - ○ D. It turns green with algae.

4. Which of these is the **most likely** result of environmental degradation?
   - ○ A. extreme weather conditions
   - ○ B. land use conflict
   - ○ C. loss of biodiversity
   - ○ D. spread of nuclear radiation

5. How did salinization affect fish in the Aral Sea?
   - ○ A. It had no effect on many species.
   - ○ B. Many species died out completely.
   - ○ C. Many species increased in number.
   - ○ D. New species replaced many old ones.

6. Which of these crops has contributed **most** to the creation of a new desert in the Aral Sea region?
   - ○ A. cotton
   - ○ B. rice
   - ○ C. sugarcane
   - ○ D. wheat

7. Which statement **best** describes what the graph shows about infant mortality rates in Kazakhstan and Uzbekistan?

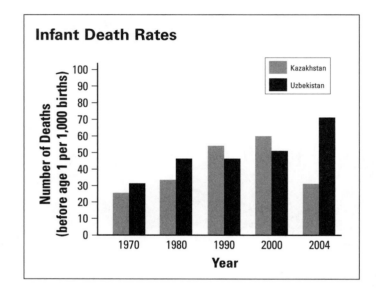

   - ○ A. Rates have remained unchanged since 1980.
   - ○ B. Rates reached their highest point in 1995.
   - ○ C. Rates have dropped since 2004.
   - ○ D. Rates have risen since 1970.

8. What can farmers living around the Aral Sea do to help repair the environmental degradation of the sea itself?
   - ○ A. build more dams
   - ○ B. irrigate more land
   - ○ C. plant less thirsty crops
   - ○ D. increase the use of fertilizer

Applying Geography Skills:
Sequencing Steps in a Process

Use this diagram and your knowledge of geography to complete the tasks below.

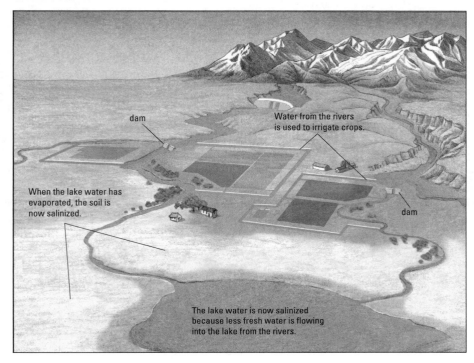

dam

Water from the rivers is used to irrigate crops.

When the lake water has evaporated, the soil is now salinized.

dam

The lake water is now salinized because less fresh water is flowing into the lake from the rivers.

The diagram shows how an inland sea can become salinized.

1. Each statement in the table below describes one step in the salinization process. Sequence the six steps from first to last. Write the number 1 by the first step, 2 by the second, and so on.

Steps in the Salinization Process

	The lake shrinks and becomes saltier.
	Water is taken from rivers to irrigate fields.
	Rivers form from mountain runoff.
	Water flowing into the lake is reduced.
	Rain falls on nearby mountains.
	Runoff washes small amounts of salt out of soil.

2. Write the numbers of the six steps on the diagram where that step takes place.

Test Terms Glossary
To **sequence** means to put things in order.

Exploring the Essential Question

How are humans affected by changes they make in the physical environment?

In Chapter 26, you explored how the shrinking Aral Sea has affected the people that live near it. Now you will use what you learned. Use the information in the table below and your knowledge of geography to complete this task.

Data Table on the Aral Sea Region

	Type of data	1960	1970	1980	1990	1999
	Irrigated Land (in thousands of acres)	11,140	12,720	17,090	18,770	19,510
	Fish Caught (in tons)	47,400	19,200	0	0	0
	Gross Domestic Product (in millions of U.S. dollars)	16	32	48	75	54
	Infant Death Rate in Uzbekistan (before age 1 per 1,000 births)	84	31	47	47	45
	Water for Irrigation (in cubic miles per year)	13	18	26	25	23

The Task: Summarizing Causes and Effects of the Aral Sea Disaster

In 1960, the Aral Sea began to shrink. Your task is to write about the causes and effects of this ecological disaster.

Step 1: Decide whether the data shown in each row of the table is a *cause* of the Aral Sea disaster or an *effect*. Write a C in the space to the left of causes. Write an E in the space to the left of effects.

Step 2: On another sheet of paper, write a two-paragraph essay that summarizes the causes and effects of this disaster. Make sure your essay has these elements:

- a title that tells what your essay is about
- one paragraph that summarizes the causes of the Aral Sea disaster. Include at least two pieces of data from the table in your paragraph.
- one paragraph that summarizes the effects of the Aral Sea disaster. Include at least two pieces of data from the table in your paragraph.

Writing Tips: Linking Causes to Their Effects
Organizing writing into causes and effects helps show a reader the relationship between events and their results. Here are some of the words that writers use to link causes to effects: *because, since, therefore, as a result,* and *due to.*

Example: *The rise in GDP was due to the planting of more cotton.*

Applying Geography Skills: Sample Responses

1. Steps in the Salinization Process

6	The lake shrinks and becomes saltier.
4	Water is taken from rivers to irrigate fields.
3	Rivers form from mountain runoff.
5	Water flowing into the lake is reduced.
1	Rain falls on nearby mountains.
2	Runoff washes small amounts of salt out of soil.

2. Each step should be written on its corresponding part of the diagram.

Exploring the Essential Question: Sample Response

Step 1: Data Table on the Aral Sea Region

	Type of data	1960	1970	1980	1990	1999
C	Irrigated Land (in thousands of acres)	11,140	12,720	17,090	18,770	19,510
E	Fish Caught (in tons)	47,400	19,200	0	0	0
E	Gross Domestic Product (in millions of U.S. dollars)	16	32	48	75	54
E	Infant Death Rate in Uzbekistan (before age 1 per 1,000 births)	84	31	47	47	45
C	Water for Irrigation (in cubic miles per year)	13	18	26	25	23

Step 2: Essays should include the all of the elements listed in the prompt: a title, a paragraph summarizing causes of the Aral Sea disaster, and a paragraph summarizing its effects. Students should support their main ideas with data from the chart.

Mastering the Content Answer Key

1. A	2. D	3. B	4. C
5. B	6. A	7. D	8. C

Applying Geography Skills Scoring Rubric

Score	General Description
2	Student responds to all parts of the task. Response is correct and clear.
1	Student responds to some parts of the task. Response is mostly correct.
0	Response does not match the task or is incorrect.

Exploring the Essential Question Scoring Rubric

Score	General Description
3	Student responds to all parts of the task. Response is correct, clear, and supported by details.
2	Student responds to most or all parts of the task. Response is generally correct but may lack details.
1	Student responds to at least one part of the task. Response may contain errors and lack details.
0	Response does not match the task or is incorrect.

Create a Documentary on the Shrinking of the Aral Sea

The shrinking of the Aral Sea has affected many groups of people living in the region. You will work with your team to prepare a short documentary about the effects on one group in the region. In the documentary, you will interview a person from that group. Circle the group you have been assigned:

- Farmers in the Aral Sea Region Before 1970 (*Section 26.3*)
- Farmers in the Aral Sea Region Today (*Section 26.3*)
- Fishing Industry in the Aral Sea Region Before 1960 (*Section 26.4*)
- Fishing Industry in the Aral Sea Region Today (*Section 26.4*)
- Residents in the Aral Sea Region Before 1970 (*Section 26.5*)
- Residents in the Aral Sea Region Today (*Section 26.5*)

_____ **Step 1: Review the roles.** Your teacher will assign each member of your team a role. Make sure everyone understands his or her responsibilities.

- **Director:** You will lead your team during Step 3 as you gather background information for creating your documentary.
- **Script Manager:** You will lead your team during Step 4 as it prepares the script for your documentary. Make sure everyone writes his or her own dialog and is involved in developing the script.
- **Props Manager:** You will lead your team during Step 5 as you prepare materials for your documentary. Make sure your presentation is as realistic as possible.
- **Stage Manager:** You will lead your team during Step 6 as it rehearses. Make sure your documentary includes all the requirements and that everyone is involved.

_____ **Step 2: Learn how the shrinking of the Aral Sea has affected your assigned group.** With your team, read the section of your book for your group (see above). Complete the matching section of your Reading Notes.

_____ **Step 3: Gather background information for your documentary.** Examine your team's copy of *Student Handout 26B*. On another sheet of paper, your **Director** will take notes on what you might include in your documentary for each of the following three segments. List specific details from the handout. Also record at least two statistics you want to include in your documentary.

- **Segment 1:** A brief introduction that sets the stage for your interview
- **Segment 2:** An interview with someone from your assigned group
- **Segment 3:** Some concluding remarks that summarize what was learned from the interview

_____ **Step 4: Write the script for your documentary.** Your documentary should last 2 to 3 minutes. Your **Script Manager** will now gather ideas from your team about details that should be included in the script for your documentary. The Script Manager will then guide your team through the writing of the script. During this time, your **Props Manager** will use the information in the table on _Student Handout 26B_ to create a large graph to use in your presentation. (The team assigned to "Residents in the Aral Sea Region Before 1970" will not make a graph.)

_____ **Step 5: Brainstorm ideas for costumes and props.** Your documentary should be as realistic as possible. Before you begin creating costumes and props, the **Props Manager** will gather ideas from your team and use them to complete the table below.

List costumes you will include in your documentary and the materials needed to create them.	Who is responsible for each costume?
List props you will include in your documentary and the materials needed to create them.	Who is responsible for each prop?

_____ **Step 6: Rehearse your documentary.** After you have created costumes and props, make sure you can present your documentary in 2 to 3 minutes. As you rehearse, the **Stage Manager** will make sure that

- each team member is actively involved in the documentary.
- the documentary flows smoothly.
- costumes and props are used effectively.
- lines are spoken loudly enough to be heard by the audience.
- all requirements of the documentary are met.

Create a Documentary on Farmers in the Aral Sea Region Before 1970

Use the background information below to help you create a documentary on farmers in the Aral Sea region before 1970. Your documentary should have three segments:

Segment 1: A *brief introduction* that answers these questions:
- *Who* will you be interviewing? (a farmer)
- *Where* does he (or she) live?
- *When* was he a farmer?
- *What* was his life like back then?
- *Why* did his life change?

Segment 2: An *interview* with a farmer that
- takes place "on location," either in the fields where the farmer worked, near his home, or by an irrigation canal.
- includes questions that guide the farmer to explain
  —how the Soviet government helped farmers produce larger cotton crops.
  —how their fields were irrigated.
  —what the environment and daily life were like for him and his family.

Segment 3: Some *concluding remarks* that review what we have learned from the interview. This segment should also include a line or bar graph that summarizes the data in the table on the next page.

Background Information on Farmers in the Aral Sea Region Before 1970

It sounded like a good plan to the farmers around the Aral Sea. They could divert water from two rivers, the Amu Darya and Syr Darya, to irrigate their cotton fields. These rivers, however, fed the Aral Sea. Without them pumping water and life into the sea, the Aral Sea could suffer. But cotton would live.

Cotton was quickly becoming one of Uzbekistan's leading exports. This was odd, since most of Uzbekistan is desert, and cotton is a thirsty crop. It usually needs 30 inches of rainfall a year. Uzbekistan gets only about 8 inches annually. But in the 1960s, demand increased for this "white gold." The government believed that the economic benefits of more cotton would outweigh the damage to the Aral Sea and the fishing industry.

Farmers in the area were thrilled with the idea of growing more cotton. To irrigate the crops, water was diverted from the rivers that fed the sea. At first, cotton harvests were plentiful. Production rose. The economy grew stronger. The population of the region rose as well. More and more people moved into the Aral Sea basin to work in the fields and the cotton mills.

Pesticides were used to help produce the most cotton possible. These chemicals were sprayed from airplanes that flew over villages and fields. The pesticides rained down on the ground below, where workers knelt picking cotton. Pesticides protected the cotton from harmful bugs, resulting in larger harvests. Cotton, indeed, was becoming king in the region.

Resources in the Aral Sea Basin

Resource	1960	1970
Population (in millions)	14	20
Irrigated Land (in thousands of acres)	11,140	12,720
Water for Irrigation (in cubic miles per year)	13	18
Gross Domestic Product (in millions of U.S. dollars)	16	32

Source: *UNEP/GRID-Arendal*, "Water Resources," enrin.grida.no/aral/aralsea/english/water/water.htm.

Create a Documentary on Farmers in the Aral Sea Region Today

Use the background information below to help you create a documentary on farmers in the Aral Sea region today. Your documentary should have three segments:

Segment 1: A *brief introduction* that answers these questions:
- *Who* will you be interviewing? (a farmer)
- *Where* does he (or she) live?
- *What* is his life like?
- *How* has his life been affected by the shrinking of the Aral Sea?

Segment 2: An *interview* with a farmer that
- takes place "on location," either in a field or near the farmer's home.
- includes questions that guide the farmer to explain
  —what he grows.
  —the difficulties of his job.
  —how these difficulties are related to changes in the Aral Sea.

Segment 3: Some *concluding remarks* that review what we have learned from the interview. This segment should also include a line or bar graph that summarizes the data in the table on the next page.

Background Information on Farmers in the Aral Sea Region Today

In the 1960s, Uzbekistan was the second largest producer of cotton in the world. This was odd, since most of Uzbekistan is desert, and cotton is a thirsty crop. It usually needs 30 inches of rainfall a year. Uzbekistan gets only about 8 inches annually. But demand was increasing for this "white gold." The government believed that the economic benefits of producing more cotton would outweigh the damage to the Aral Sea and the fishing industry.

For a while, it worked. From 1965 to 1983, the cotton harvest rose by 70 percent. The population in the Aral Sea region swelled along with the cotton crop. So did the need for irrigated land. In addition, pesticides were sprayed from airplanes. These chemicals were meant to protect the cotton plants from bugs and disease. But the airplanes flew over villages and fields where workers knelt picking cotton. They covered the whole area with pesticides. Cotton, indeed, became king in this region, but at a high cost to people's health.

Today, due to the extreme irrigation practices needed to keep the cotton crop alive, the Aral Sea has lost over half of its water volume. The sea level has dropped more than 45 feet. The land that has been exposed is dry and salty. Winds often sweep through this area. They pick up the salt and sprinkle it everywhere within a 250-mile radius. This salt is slowly destroying what's left of the arable land. (Arable land is land that can be used for farming.) Summer temperatures are blazing hot, and winters have become harsher. The growing season has been shortened by several weeks.

Farmers in Uzbekistan today struggle to survive. Water is harder to come by. Salty air is poisoning the crops, not to mention harming the farmers and their families. The sea is dying. And so is the cotton that the sea was drained to nourish in the first place.

Resources in the Aral Sea Basin

Resource	1960	1970	1980	1990	1999
Population (in millions)	14	20	27	34	40
Irrigated Land (in thousands of acres)	11,140	12,720	17,090	18,770	19,510
Water for Irrigation (in cubic miles per year)	13	18	26	25	23
Gross Domestic Product (in millions of U.S. dollars)	16	32	48	75	54

Source: *UNEP/GRID-Arendal,* "Water Resources," enrin.grida.no/aral/aralsea/english/water/water.htm.

Create a Documentary on the Fishing Industry in the Aral Sea Region Before 1960

Use the background information below to help you create a documentary on the fishing industry in the Aral Sea region before 1960. Your documentary should have three segments:

Segment 1: A *brief introduction* that answers these questions:
- *Who* will you be interviewing? (a member of the fishing industry)
- *Where* does he (or she) live?
- *When* did he work in the fishing industry?
- *What* was his life like?

Segment 2: An *interview* with a fishing-industry worker that
- takes place "on location," either in the fisherman's house or near his boat in Moynaq.
- includes questions that guide the fisherman to explain
  - where he used to fish.
  - how abundant the fish were.
  - what the fishing industry of the Aral Sea was like.

Segment 3: Some *concluding remarks* that review what we have learned from the interview. This segment should also include a line or bar graph that summarizes the data in the table on the next page.

Background Information on the Fishing Industry in the Aral Sea Region Before 1960

The man rose early, before the sun. It was only a short walk to the harbor in Moynaq. There, his boat rested peacefully. Each morning it waited for him and his small crew of three men to rouse it from its slumber. That morning in 1959 was brisk. He pulled the collar of his yellow slicker higher and tugged his knit cap a bit lower to block out the cold air that stung his ears.

There were others walking with him this morning. Each one bent over to ward off the early morning cold. Most were fishermen, beckoned by the clear, blue Aral Sea. They woke before the sun to lure the fish from their beds. Some of the men captained the ferries that glided across the Aral from south to north and back again.

The Aral Sea was fed by two rivers, the Amu Darya and the Syr Darya. In the 1950s, this sea was the fourth largest inland body of water in the world. In 1959, the fishing fleet in the Aral Sea pulled in nearly 50,000 metric tons of fish. Carp, bream, and sturgeon were hauled up from the water's depths. Much of this catch was loaded into refrigerated train cars. The trains rolled off to Moscow, taking tons of fresh fish with them. In Moynaq, fishing boats brought several thousand tons of sturgeon, perch, and carp to canning factories that employed about 35,000 people.

The sea supported other wildlife, too. Thick forests of reed and rush surrounded its shores. Large populations of antelope, wild boar, wolf, fox, muskrat, turkey, goose, and duck lived around the sea and in the river delta.

Yet it was only fish that the man's thoughts turned to that morning. He climbed aboard his boat and began to gather his nets and supplies for the day. It would be a good day of fishing, he knew. Every day spent out on the Aral was a good day of fishing in 1959.

Fish Caught in the Aral Sea

Year	Fish Caught (in tons)
1945	28,700
1950	40,800
1955	47,400
1957	54,000
1960	47,400

Source: T. Petr, "Irrigation Systems and Their Fisheries in the Aral Sea Basin, Central Asia," www.lars2.org/unedited_papers/unedited_paper/Petr.pdf.

Create a Documentary on the Fishing Industry in the Aral Sea Region Today

Use the background information below to help you create a documentary on the fishing industry in the Aral Sea region today. Your documentary should have three segments:

Segment 1: A *brief introduction* that answers these questions:
- *Who* will you be interviewing? (a cannery employee or fishing boat captain)
- *Where* does he or she live?
- *What* is his or her life like?
- *Why* has his or her life changed?

Segment 2: An *interview* with a former employee of a cannery in Moynaq that
- takes place "on location," either in a deserted cannery or on a fishing boat.
- includes questions that guide the employee to explain
  —how his or her environment has been affected by the Aral Sea's decline.
  —how his or her life has been affected by the Aral Sea's decline.

Segment 3: Some *concluding remarks* that review what we have learned from the interview. This segment should also include a line or bar graph that summarizes the data in the table on the next page.

Background Information on the Fishing Industry in the Aral Sea Region Today

The sign welcoming visitors to Moynaq, Uzbekistan, carries a picture of a fish. But ask any fishing boat captain living in Moynaq today about the fish, and he will probably laugh.

"That fish," he might say, stroking his beard, "is a reminder of the way things once were in Moynaq. This city was once built around our harbor. But today it is a dried-out ghost town in the middle of a desert."

He might go on to tell stories of how his life used to be. Before the government decided that cotton growing was more important than fish catching, his life was good. He might talk of his days out on the sea. He'll describe the fishing boat he once captained. He will talk about how he would rise with the sun to lure the fish from their beds in the clear, blue Aral Sea.

A museum in Moynaq tells the story of this city's fishing industry. Greeting visitors at the door is a mural. On it, boats dot the surface of the Aral Sea, and seagulls fly overhead. On display in this museum are 25-year-old tins of fish from Moynaq's cannery. A rusted anchor sits in a display case. Nets and fishing hooks of all sizes hang on the walls.

But today the cannery that produced those tins of fish sits abandoned. The sea is nearly 90 miles away, and there is nothing to can. The jobs of about 35,000 people were washed away with the receding tide of the sea.

Fishing and related activities once provided half this region's income. For a few years, when the Aral Sea began losing its fish, the Soviet government flew in shipments of fish caught elsewhere to be processed at Moynaq's canneries. But even that has ended now.

Fish Caught in the Aral Sea

Year	Fish Caught (in tons)
1960	47,400
1965	34,200
1970	19,200
1975	3,240
1980	0
1985	0
1990	0

Source: T. Petr, "Irrigation Systems and Their Fisheries in the Aral Sea Basin, Central Asia," www.lars2.org/unedited_papers/unedited_paper/Petr.pdf.

Create a Documentary on Residents in the Aral Sea Region Before 1970

Use the background information below to help you create a documentary on residents in the Aral Sea region before 1970. Your documentary should include three segments:

Segment 1: A *brief introduction* that answers these questions:
- *Who* will you be interviewing? (a tourist to the Aral Sea)
- *Where* is he or she vacationing?
- *When* is he or she visiting the Aral Sea?
- *What* attracted him or her to visit this area?

Segment 2: An *interview* with a tourist that
- takes place "on location," either on a beach near the Aral Sea or at a summer camp.
- includes questions that guide the tourist to explain
  —why he or she chose to visit the Aral Sea.
  —what he or she is enjoying most about this vacation.
  —where he or she is from (possibly somewhere in Russia).

Segment 3: Some *concluding remarks* that review what we have learned from the interview.

Background Information on Residents in the Aral Sea Region Before 1970

Moynaq once sat on the southern shores of the Aral Sea. It was an important city for the fishing industry. But it was also once a very popular spa town and vacation resort. Soviet tourists once flocked to Moynaq to escape the dirt and grime of the city. They came to get a break from the cold winters that plagued Russia and the far north.

In Moynaq, tourists swam lazily in the blue Aral Sea. Many people believed that this water could heal skin diseases. Sunbathers gathered on beaches. Families soaked up the warm rays of the desert sun. Children rode buses into Moynaq bound for summer camps. Parents wanted them to breathe the fresh sea air. In Moynaq, people could eat fresh fish, caught only hours before by the many boats that dotted the horizon.

Walking through Moynaq today, it is easy to catch glimpses of the charming seaside village it once was. Pretty fences still surround many homes. The sand underfoot is soft and brings to mind sand castles and sunbathers. The nearby airport used to handle 50 flights a day during the spring and summer months. The planes were filled with vacationers ready for hours of sun-filled fun and relaxation. Tourists were plentiful back then.

Water was plentiful, too. Many people drank directly from the sea. Those that could not received their drinking water through the Aral-Sorbulak water pipeline. This pipeline was connected to an underground water source. The government made plans to construct branches of this pipeline to reach even faraway villages.

The Aral Sea once attracted visitors from thousands of miles away. They came for its beauty. They came for its calm. They came for the warm climate and sandy beaches. But mostly, they came for the water.

Create a Documentary on Residents in the Aral Sea Region Today

Use the background information below to help you create a documentary on residents in the Aral Sea region today. Your documentary should have three segments:

Segment 1: A *brief introduction* that answers these questions:
- *Who* will you be interviewing? (a mother with sick children, or a doctor or nurse)
- *Where* does she (or he) live?
- *What* is her life like?
- *Why* are people getting sick in the Aral Sea region?

Segment 2: An *interview* with a mother, doctor, or nurse in Uzbekistan that
- takes place "on location," either in the woman's home or in a hospital.
- includes questions that guide the person to explain how the changes to the environment have affected residents living near the Aral Sea.

Segment 3: Some **concluding remarks** that review what we have learned from the interview. This segment should also include a line or bar graph that summarizes the data in the first table on the next page. Use the numbers for the Russian Federation and the United States as a comparison. Also include a table of the major diseases and their causes in this segment.

Background Information on Residents in the Aral Sea Region Today

Ask any doctor who practices in the Aral Sea region what kinds of diseases he most often treats. He may ask you to sit down before he begins his long list.

"Well," he might say slowly, raising his hand to count them off on his fingers. "There is kidney and liver disease. Asthma and throat cancer. Arthritis has increased. Nine out of 10 pregnant women suffer from anemia. Our child mortality rate is one of the highest in the world. Nearly one in every 10 children will die before their first birthday."

He may pause then, but he is not done. Cancer, tuberculosis, allergies, typhoid fever… the list is endless. "Why?" you might ask. "What is going on here?"

There are as many causes as there are diseases. But nearly all lead back to one thing: the shrinking of the Aral Sea. The water is contaminated with pesticides. Underground water supplies have been poisoned by salt and chemicals. Sewage systems are rare. Those that do exist are in poor repair. Many towns simply dump their sewage back into the rivers. This pollutes the water supply even more.

The tuberculosis ward at the hospital in Moynaq is extremely crowded. The beds are filled with women. Children, and a few men, are found here and there. Tuberculosis cases have increased in this region. And though there are more hospitals than there used to be, they are often in poor condition. It is hard to find good nurses when nurses here make only about $8.50 per month. And the Aral Sea continues to shrink. This situation does not seem likely to improve any time soon.

Women have forgotten what it is like to serve fresh vegetables, fish, or salad to their children. Instead they prepare meals of bread, tea, and pasta. They cannot properly clean their homes because they don't have sufficient water. Schools and kindergartens often have no water for children to wash their hands.

The United Nations has reported that reported that restoring the Aral Sea to its original level could cause more damage to the environment. So, what can be done to bring life back to the region?

Infant Death Rates (deaths before age 1 per 1,000 births)

Country or Republic	1970	1980	1990	2000	2004
Russian Federation	23	22	21	18	17
United States	20	13	9	7	7
Uzbekistan	31	47	47	51	71
Kazakhstan	26	33	54	60	31

Source: *Central Intelligence Agency*, "CIA World Factbook," www.cia.gov/cia/publications/factbook/. *United Nations Statistics Division*, unstats.un.org.

Common Diseases in the Aral Sea Region

Disease	Major Causes
Breathing problems	blowing salt and dust
Hepatitis	polluted water
Typhoid fever	polluted water
Stomach problems	blowing salt and dust, contaminants
Cancer	polluted water, blowing salt and dust
Birth defects	contaminants
Plague	huge rat population where the sea used to be

Read each indicated part of Sections 26.3, 26.4, and 26.5. Then answer the related question.

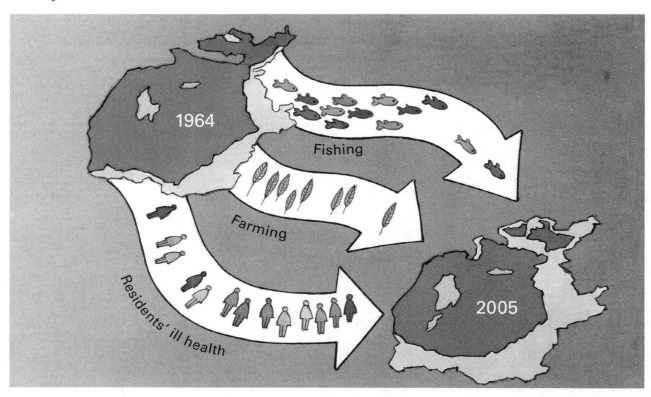

26.3 The Shrinking Sea and Farming

Read Section 26.3 up to "Salinization Creates a New Desert." Then answer this question: *What was life like for farmers in the Aral Sea region when cotton was king?* Farmers' crop production increased when the Soviet government built dams on the Amu and Syr rivers to irrigate their cotton. They were also helped by an increase in the use of pesticides. These farmers were proud of their cotton, and even named a local soccer team the Cotton Pickers.

Read the rest of Section 26.3. Then answer this question: *How have farmers been affected by the shrinking Aral Sea?*
A shrinking Aral Sea meant increasingly less water for irrigation and increasingly salty soil. Cotton production fell as the land around the sea became less suitable for agriculture. The growing season shortened as well, and some farmers started growing rice instead of cotton.

26.4 The Shrinking Sea and Fishing

Read Section 26.4 up to "The Collapse of the Aral Sea Fishing Industry." Then answer this question: *What was life like for people in the fishing industry when the sea was rich in fish?*

Until about 1980, people who worked in the fishing industry had plenty of work. Fishermen caught 95 million pounds of fish annually. People who worked in canneries produced over 20 million cans of seafood a year. In all, about 35,000 people had jobs because of the plentiful fish in the Aral Sea.

Read the rest of Section 26.4. Then answer this question: *How was the fishing industry affected by the shrinking Aral Sea?*

As the sea shrank, fisheries were left without water nearby. Fish died off because of the increasing salinity of the water. Fishing crews and cannery workers found themselves without jobs. Thousands of people have left Moynaq to find other work. Only 3,000 of the 40,000 people who used to live in Moynaq remain.

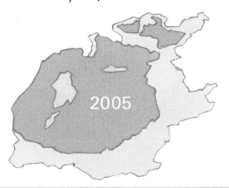

26.5 The Shrinking Sea and Quality of Life

Read Section 26.5 up to "Pollution Damages the Health of Residents." Then answer this question: *What was life like for people of the Aral Sea region when water was plentiful?*

Before the 1960s, the Aral Sea provided water for nearby towns. There was enough water for people to use both in their households and for their crops.

Read the rest of Section 26.5. Then answer this question: *How has people's health been affected by the shrinking Aral Sea?*

Many people have stomach problems and liver disease from drinking polluted water. Air pollution causes tuberculosis and throat cancer. Poverty is also causing health problems, like anemia in pregnant women and sick babies.

UNIT 7 Monsoon Asia

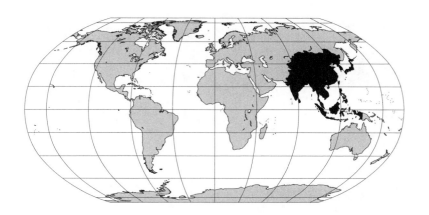

Waiting for the Rains: The Effects of Monsoons in South Asia

Overview

In this lesson, students learn how monsoons influence the climate of South Asia and affect the lives of the people who live there. In a **Social Studies Skill Builder,** students work in pairs to complete puzzles by correctly matching a climagraph, a climate map, a photograph, and a list of effects of and adaptations to that climate for four cities in South Asia. After assembling their puzzles and discovering how monsoons affect life in South Asia, students determine how the climate where they live influences human activity.

Objectives

Students will

- define and explain the importance of these key geographic terms: *atmospheric pressure, monsoon, orographic effect, rain shadow.*
- discover what monsoons are, why they occur, and how they influence climate.
- examine the effects of climate and how it shapes life in four climate zones in South Asia.
- investigate how climate affects other parts of the world.

Materials

- *Geography Alive! Regions and People*
- Interactive Student Notebooks
- Transparencies 27A and 27B
- Information Master 27 (1 transparency)
- Student Handout 27 (1 per student)
- scissors
- gluesticks (1 per pair)

Preview

1 Project the climagraph at the top of *Transparency 27A: The Climate of Mumbai, India.* Cover the photograph at the bottom. Have students analyze the climagraph by asking,

- What are some details you notice?
- What information does the bar graph tell us? *the average monthly precipitation for this city*
- What information does the line graph tell us? *the average monthly temperatures for this city*
- What does a climagraph give information about? *the average temperature and precipitation in a place over a year*

Transparency 27A

2 Have students complete Preview 27 in their Interactive Student Notebooks. Then discuss their responses to these questions in the Preview:

- What is the wettest month or months in Mumbai?
- What is the driest month or months in Mumbai?
- What effects might this city's climate have on the people who live here? *Possible answers: People must adapt to periods of heavy rain as well as periods of no rain. They might experience flooding. They must wear clothing and build housing suited for warm weather.*
- Which of these climate zones do you think Mumbai might be in? Why? *tropical wet and dry; It's hot all year, with rainy and dry seasons.*

Preview 27

3 Uncover the photograph so that students now see both it and the climagraph. Explain that this image was taken in India during the wet monsoon months. Then ask,

- What might be some of the challenges of living in a city that receives this much rainfall in such a short period of time? *Possible answers: flooding, mudslides, contaminated drinking water, difficult transportation, difficult farming*
- What might be some of the adaptations people make to survive in this climate? *Possible answers: They might build structures that can withstand heavy rain, plant crops to correspond with seasonal rain, or find alternative modes of transportation when streets are flooded (such as walking, bikes, and elevated railways).*

4 Explain the connection between the Preview and the upcoming activity. Tell students that they will now will examine climagraphs, photographs, and climate maps to learn how climate affects people's lives in four cities in South Asia. They will discover how the people of South Asia have adapted to the various climates in this region, and especially to the yearly monsoon season.

Essential Question and Geoterms

1 **Introduce Chapter 27 in** *Geography Alive! Regions and People.* Explain that in this chapter, students will learn about South Asia and, specifically, about the monsoons that shape climate and human activity in this region. Have students read Section 27.1. Then have them examine the photograph of a street flooded due to a summer monsoon and ask,

- What details do you notice?
- What aspects of life might be affected by conditions like this?

2 **Introduce the Graphic Organizer and the Essential Question.** Have students examine the climagraph. Ask,

- What does this climagraph tell us?
- How might climagraphs be useful for comparing the climates of various cities around the globe?

Have students read the accompanying text. Make sure they understand the Essential Question, *How does climate influence human activity in a region?* You may want to post the Essential Question in the room or write it on the board for the duration of the activity.

3 **Have students read Section 27.2.** Then have them complete Geoterms 27 in their Interactive Student Notebooks, individually or in pairs. Have them share their answers with another student, or have volunteers share their answers with the class. In addition, take a few minutes to discuss the diagram of the orographic effect and the answers to these questions:

- How are monsoons created? *Monsoons are created when the air over South Asia warms up. As this hot air rises, it creates a low-pressure area. When this happens, cool, moist air from the Indian Ocean flows into the area of low pressure. This movement of air creates the monsoon winds.*

- Why are monsoons important in South Asia? *The monsoons in South Asia occur in the summer and can bring up to 90 percent of the year's rainfall.*

- How might cities on the eastern side of the Western Ghats be *less* affected by summer monsoons? *These cities sit in the rain shadow of the Ghats. Rain shadows occur when moist breezes come up against a mountain range. As the air rises up the Ghats, it releases all its moisture in the form of rain. The dry air continues over the mountain as wind. Cities on this side of the mountains receive far less rain than those on the side nearest the Arabian Sea.*

Geoterms 27

Social Studies Skill Builder

1 Place students in mixed-ability pairs. You may want to create a seating chart on a transparency to show them who their partners are and where to sit.

2 Explain the activity. Tell students that they will work with their partners to assemble four puzzles by correctly matching a climagraph, a climate map, a photograph, and a list of effects of and adaptations to that climate for four cities in South Asia. They will use clues about each city's climate to assemble each puzzle correctly.

3 Project *Information Master 27: Puzzle Assembly*. Review the steps for this activity with students, and answer any questions they have. Information Master 27 also directs students when to complete Reading Notes 27 for each section. (**Note:** You may want to give each pair of students a copy of the master.)

4 Conduct the Social Studies Skill Builder. Distribute all three pages of *Student Handout 27: Puzzle Pieces* to each student, and have students cut out the 16 puzzle pieces (maps, climagraphs, photographs, and lists) from the handout. (**Note:** Consider cutting Student Handout 27 apart prior to the activity to save time in class. For best viewing of the climate maps on Student Handout 27, consider projecting this page from your Digital Teacher Resource CD.) Remind students that they must verify with you that each puzzle is correctly assembled before gluing down the pieces and reading the corresponding section of *Geography Alive! Regions and People*. Project Information Master 27 during the activity as a reference.

5 Conduct a wrap-up activity. After all students have correctly assembled all four puzzles, have students create a human bar graph. Follow these steps:

- Write the names of the four cities from this lesson—Dhaka, Bangladesh; Jodhpur, India; Calcutta, India; and Pune, India—along the chalkboard. Clear a space in front of the board.

- Ask students to work in their pairs to analyze which of the four cities they believe is the most different from their own city. Tell them to consider carefully each city's climate, the effects of the monsoons, and the adaptations each city has made to its particular climate.

- Have one student from each pair stand in front of their chosen city. As students come forward, guide them to stand in single-file lines—like the bars on a graph—in front of the four city names.

Information Master 27

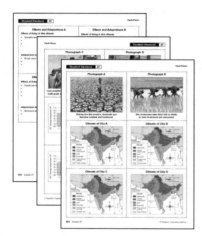

Student Handout 27

Reading Notes 27

- Ask the remaining students these questions: *According to our human bar graph, which city do most pairs believe is most different from their own? Why do you think most pairs chose this city? If you were to move to this city, how might you adapt your clothing, recreational activities, and lifestyle to this climate?*

- If time allows, consider creating human bar graphs for these questions as well: *In which city would you most like to live? Which city's climate would be most difficult to adjust to?*

Global Connections

1 Introduce the Global Connections. Have students read Section 27.7. Then explain that they will now examine some of the adaptations people make to climates in various parts of the world.

2 Project *Transparency 27B: Global Connections.* Have students analyze the map and climagraphs by discussing and sharing their answers to the questions below. Use the additional information given to enrich the discussion.

- **What information does this map tell you?** *It shows the various climate zones around the world.*

- **What are some things you notice about these climagraphs?**

- **How would you describe the climate of Barrow, Alaska?** *Barrow has a tundra climate. For nine months of the year, temperatures average below freezing. In addition, it has relatively low precipitation, usually less than 10 inches annually.*

- **How would you describe the climate of London, England?** *London has a marine west coast climate. It experiences mild summers and mild winters, due to the moderating effect of ocean currents. It often has heavy cloud cover and high humidity. Rain and drizzle are frequent.*

- **How would you describe the climate of Tindouf, Algeria?** *Tindouf has a tropical desert climate. It is one of the driest places on Earth. It experiences irregular and unreliable rainfall and high temperatures. It also has a very large range of temperatures during the course of a day.*

3 Have students turn to Section 27.8. Have them take a moment to read the three postcards. Then have them read the section. Finally, ask them for examples of the kinds of adaptations people make to life in various climates.

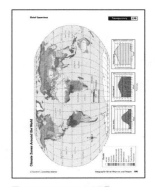

Transparency 27B

Processing

Have students complete Processing 27 in their Interactive Student Notebooks. You may wish to direct them to the Internet (such as www.usatoday.com/weather/resources/climate/wusaclim.htm or www.worldclimate.com) or the library to research average rainfall and temperature information needed to construct their climagraphs. Or you may choose to make a transparency of Processing 27, locate your city or the nearest large city on either of these sites, and fill in the table in Step 1 for students to copy and use to complete their climagraphs. You might also model how to plot the data for the first month.

Processing 27

Online Resources

For more information on monsoons and South Asia, refer students to Online Resources for *Geography Alive! Regions and People* at www.teachtci.com.

Assessment

Masters for assessment appear on the next three pages followed by answers and scoring rubrics.

Mastering the Content

Shade in the oval by the letter of the best answer for each question.

1. The term *monsoon* means
   - A. extreme weather.
   - B. prolonged drought.
   - C. seasonal wind.
   - D. storm surge.

2. Atmospheric pressure is a measure of which of the following?
   - A. the total solar energy received by Earth
   - B. the weight of air pushing down on Earth
   - C. the speed of prevailing winds circling Earth
   - D. the amount of water vapor in the air around Earth

3. Which of these **best** explains why cities on opposite sides of a mountain receive different amounts of rain?
   - A. cloud seeding
   - B. the water cycle
   - C. altitudinal zonation
   - D. the orographic effect

4. Based on this climagraph, Mumbai lies in which of these climate zones?

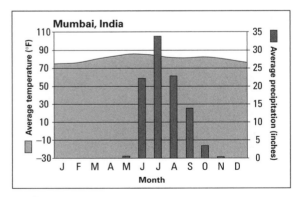

   - A. tropical wet and dry
   - B. marine west coast
   - C. humid continental
   - D. tropical wet

5. What is one way that people adapt to the semiarid climate of Jodhpur?
   - A. They grow thirsty crops.
   - B. They use drip irrigation.
   - C. They build houses on stilts.
   - D. They drive rickshaws to work.

6. Based on this climagraph, which of these would be the **most** pleasant month for an outdoor festival in Calcutta?

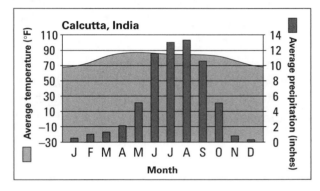

   - A. July
   - B. August
   - C. September
   - D. October

7. Because Pune, India, lies in a rain shadow, its people have learned to live with
   - A. frequent droughts.
   - B. tropical cyclones.
   - C. water salinization.
   - D. widespread flooding.

8. Which of these South Asian cities is known as one of the world's wettest capitals?
   - A. Abuja
   - B. Ankara
   - C. Dhaka
   - D. Ottawa

Assessment | **27**

Applying Geography Skills: Analyzing Climagraphs

Use the climagraphs and your knowledge of geography to complete the tasks below.

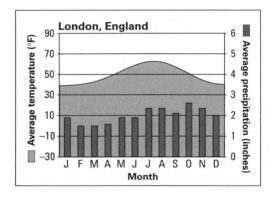 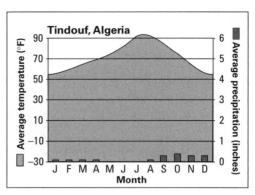

These climagraphs provide information about two cities.

1. Tell what the bar graphs on the climagraphs show. Also tell what the line graphs show.

2. On each climagraph, circle the two months with the highest average temperature.

3. Compare London's highest average monthly temperature with that of Tindouf.

4. Compare London's average monthly rainfall with that of Tindouf.

5. Use the table below to help you identify the climate zone of London. Also identify the climate zone of Tindouf.

Five Climate Zones

ice cap	very cold all year
marine west coast	warm, wet summers and cool, wet winters
Mediterranean	warm all year, dry summers
semiarid	hot, dry summers and cool, dry winters
tropical wet	hot and rainy all year

Exploring the Essential Question

How does climate influence human activity in a region?

In Chapter 27, you examined how monsoons influence life in South Asia. Now you will use what you learned. Use the information on the climagraph and the table below to complete this task.

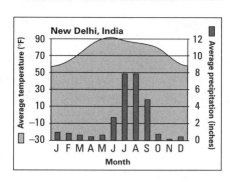

New Delhi Festivals and Holidays

Festival	Month	Description
Republic Day	January	This holiday marks the day India became a nation. It is celebrated in New Delhi with a huge parade, bands, fireworks, and folk dancing.
Holi	March	This festival welcomes spring. The night before, bonfires burn all over New Delhi. The next day, people celebrate the arrival of spring by spraying each other with paint.
Rakhi	August	This festival celebrates the bond between brothers and sisters. Sisters tie colorful threads on their brothers' wrists. Brothers promise to protect their sisters and give them gifts.
Children's Day	November	On this special day for children, schools have special programs and competitions. Students don't have to wear uniforms, and they receive special treats. Television stations feature children's shows all day.

The Task: Planning a Trip to India

The table has information about festivals and holidays celebrated in New Delhi, the capital of India. The climagraph shows information about the city's climate. Your task is to plan a trip to New Delhi using this information.

Step 1: Decide which festival or holiday you would most like to celebrate in New Delhi. Circle your choice. Also circle the month of that holiday on the climagraph.

Step 2: Briefly describe the weather you would be likely to find in New Delhi during the month of the holiday you chose.

Step 3: On a separate sheet of paper, describe the trip you are planning to New Delhi. Include the following information:
A. the name of the festival you plan to attend and the reason you chose it
B. the time of year you will be visiting India
C. the weather you expect to find in New Delhi
D. four things you plan to take with you to be prepared for these weather conditions

Applying Geography Skills: Sample Responses

1. The bar graphs show the average amount of rainfall for each month. The line graphs show the average temperatures for each month.
2. Students should have circled July and August on both climagraphs.
3. London's highest average temperature is about 65°F compared to above 90°F in Tindouf.
4. London has an average of about 2 inches of rain each month all year. Tindouf receives very little rain year round.
5. London is in a marine west coast climate zone. Tindouf is in a semiarid climate zone.

Exploring the Essential Question: Sample Response

Step 1: Students should circle one festival on the table. They should also circle the month of that festival on the climagraph.

Step 2: Answers will depend on the festival chosen. January, March, and November will be relatively cool and dry. August will be hot and rainy.

Step 3: Answers will depend on the festival chosen but should have all of the elements listed in the prompt.

I would like to visit New Delhi during the Rakhi festival. During this festival, Indians celebrate the bond between brothers and sisters. I chose this festival because I have two younger sisters, and I like the idea of going to India with them. This festival takes place in August. It will be hot and rainy in New Delhi at that time of year. I plan to take sunscreen to protect my skin from the hot sun. I will take an umbrella to help keep me dry in the rain. I will pack waterproof shoes so I can walk around in wet streets. I will also take quick-drying shorts and shirts. I know it will be hot, but I expect to have a good time.

Mastering the Content Answer Key

1. C	2. B	3. D	4. A
5. B	6. D	7. A	8. C

Applying Geography Skills Scoring Rubric

Score	General Description
2	Student responds to all parts of the task. Response is correct and clear.
1	Student responds to some parts of the task. Response is mostly correct.
0	Response does not match the task or is incorrect.

Exploring the Essential Question Scoring Rubric

Score	General Description
3	Student responds to all parts of the task. Response is correct, clear, and supported by details.
2	Student responds to most or all parts of the task. Response is generally correct but may lack details.
1	Student responds to at least one part of the task. Response may contain errors and lack details.
0	Response does not match the task or is incorrect.

Directions for Assembling the Puzzles

Step 1: Cut out the 16 puzzle pieces from Student Handout 27.

Step 2: Work with your partner to assemble your first puzzle.
Follow these steps:

- Turn to Reading Notes 27. Identify the city for Section 27.3.

- Look at your four climate maps. Using the coordinates given for this city, find the map with the star that matches those coordinates. Place this puzzle piece in the correct location in your Reading Notes. (Don't glue it down yet.)

- Using what you learn from the climate map about the climate zone of this city, find what you think is the climagraph for this city. Place it in the correct location on the page.

- Choose which of the four photographs and which list of effects and adaptations you think match this city, and place them on the page.

Step 3: Have your teacher check your puzzle. One of you should take the completed puzzle to your teacher. If you have assembled it correctly, your teacher will instruct you to glue in the pieces. If any pieces are incorrect, you will be asked to return to your seat and reassemble it. Recheck your work with your teacher before gluing in the pieces.

Step 4: Read the corresponding section of *Geography Alive! Regions and People*. Complete the Reading Notes for that section by writing a caption for the climagraph and completing the list of effects and adaptations.

Step 5: Repeat Steps 2 to 4 for the other three puzzles.

Photograph A

During the dry months, riverbeds can become cracked and hardened.

Photograph B

Dry monsoons take their toll on fields, so wet monsoons are welcomed.

Climate of City A

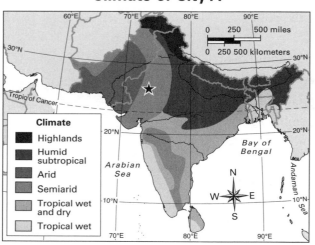

Climate of City B

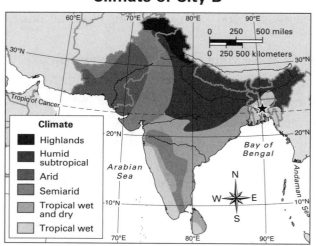

Climate of City C

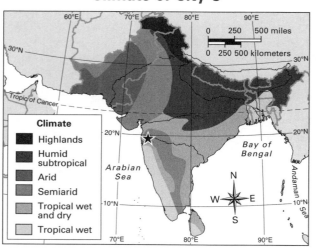

Climate of City D

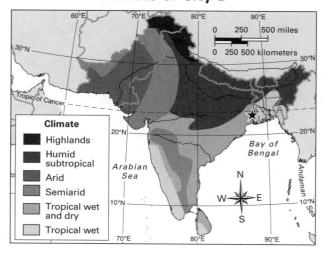

Photograph C

Less moisture means that people must sometimes walk great distances to the nearest water source.

Photograph D

Finding uncontaminated water after monsoon flooding can be a challenge.

Climagraph A

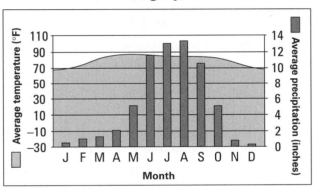

Climagraph B

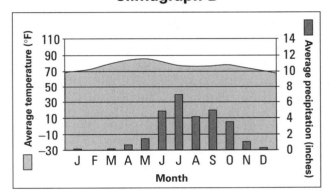

Climagraph C

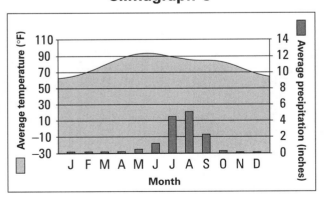

Climagraph D

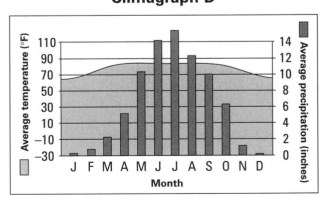

Effects and Adaptations A

Effects of living in this climate:

- Droughts are common.
-
-

Adaptations to living in this climate:

- People raise livestock in addition to crops.
-
-

Effects and Adaptations B

Effects of living in this climate:

- Only 29 inches of rain falls in a year.
-

Adaptations to living in this climate:

- Cloud seeding is used to help bring rain.
-

Effects and Adaptations C

Effects of living in this climate:

- Floods can destroy property and take lives.
-
-
-

Adaptations to living in this climate:

- Structures are built on stilts to prevent flood damage.
-

Effects and Adaptations D

Effects of living in this climate:

- Farmers get needed water for dry fields.
-
-
-
-

Adaptations to living in this climate:

- Rickshaws carry passengers through flooded streets.
-
-

27.3 The Wet Months in Dhaka, Bangladesh (24°N, 90°E)

Follow these steps to complete the Reading Notes for Section 27.3:

1. When you have assembled your puzzle for Dhaka correctly, read Section 27.3.

2. As you read the subsection "One of the World's Wettest Capitals," look for details about Dhaka's climate. Write a caption below your climagraph that summarizes that climate.

3. As you read "Life Depends on the Rain," look for more *effects of* and *adaptations to* this climate. Add them to the list below.

Climate of City B

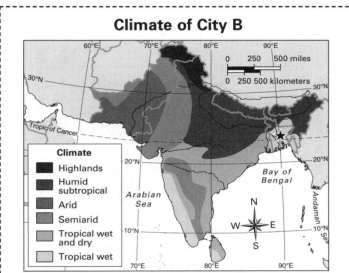

Climagraph D

Dhaka has one of the wettest climates on Earth. It can receive up to 80 inches of rain in a year, mostly in the summer months.

Photograph D

Finding uncontaminated water after monsoon flooding can be a challenge.

Effects and Adaptations C

Effects of living in this climate: Possible answers:

- Floods can destroy property and take lives.
- Crops can be destroyed if fields flood.
- Flooded streets hurt transportation.
- Drinking water can be polluted.
- Schools and businesses might close.
- Diseases spread.

Adaptations to living in this climate:

- Structures are built on stilts to prevent flood damage.
- Farmers often grow rice, which requires a lot of water.

27.4 The Dry Months of Jodhpur, India (26°N, 73°E)

Follow these steps to complete the Reading Notes for Section 27.4:

1. When you have assembled your puzzle for Jodhpur correctly, read Section 27.4.

2. As you read the subsection "A City on the Edge of a Desert," look for details about Jodhpur's climate. Write a caption below your climagraph that summarizes that climate.

3. As you read "Water Is a Critical Resource," look for more effects of and adaptations to this climate. Add them to the list below.

Climate of City A

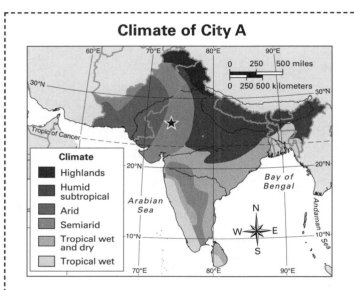

Climagraph C

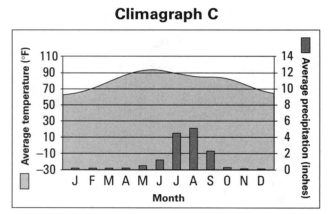

Jodhpur has a semiarid climate and usually receives about 14 inches of rain yearly. Average temperatures do not drop below 60°F. Summer monsoons bring rains from June to September.

Photograph A

During the dry months, riverbeds can become cracked and hardened.

Effects and Adaptations A

Effects of living in this climate: Possible answers:

- Droughts are common.
- Less than 14 inches of rain falls per year.
- Growing crops is difficult.
- When crops fail, people grow weak from hunger.
- Drinking water can become scarce.
- Diseases spread.

Adaptations to living in this climate:

- People raise livestock in addition to crops.
- Farmers use drip irrigation.
- Families survive by eating samas, a wild grass.

27.5 Waiting for the Rains in Calcutta, India (23°N, 88°E)

Follow these steps to complete the Reading Notes for Section 27.5:

1. When you have assembled your puzzle for Calcutta correctly, read Section 27.5.

2. As you read the subsection "Wet Summers and Dry Winters," look for details about Calcutta's climate. Write a caption below your climagraph that summarizes that climate.

3. As you read "Monsoon Rains Begin and End Life," look for more effects of and adaptations to this climate. Add them to the list below.

Climate of City D

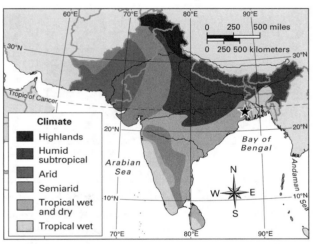

Climagraph A

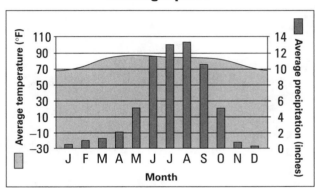

Calcutta's winters are dry and pleasant. But from June to September, monsoons can dump nearly 50 inches of rain on the city. Temperatures can soar to 100°F.

Photograph B

Dry monsoons take their toll on fields, so wet monsoons are welcomed.

Effects and Adaptations D

Effects of living in this climate: Possible answers:

- Farmers get needed water for dry fields.
- Flooding is common.
- Transportation suffers.
- City's sewer system backs up quickly.
- 50 inches of rain can fall in 4 months.
- Children wade through flooded streets to get to school.
- Mosquitoes breed and diseases spread.

Adaptations to living in this climate:

- Rickshaws carry passengers through flooded streets.
- Canals might be rebuilt to help with flooding.
- Sewer lines are being repaired.
- Rivers are kept clear of garbage to prevent flooding.

27.6 Living in the Rain Shadow: Pune, India (19°N, 74°E)

Follow these steps to complete the Reading Notes for Section 27.6:

1. When you have assembled your puzzle for Pune correctly, read Section 27.6.

2. As you read the subsection "A Year-Round Dry Climate," look for details about Pune's climate. Write a caption below your climagraph that summarizes that climate.

3. As you read "Limited Rainfall Makes Water Precious," look for more effects of and adaptations to this climate. Add them to the list below.

Climate of City C

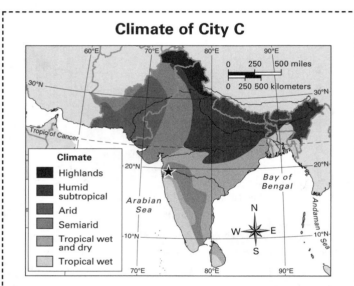

Climagraph B

Pune sits in a rain shadow. For most of the year, the air is hot and dry. The monsoon brings rains from June to September. Pune's rainfall totals only 29 inches for the entire year.

Photograph C

Less moisture means that people must sometimes walk great distances to the nearest water source.

Effects and Adaptations B

Effects of living in this climate: Possible answers:

- Only 29 inches of rain falls in a year.
- Crops are hard to grow.
- There is no flooding.

Adaptations to living in this climate:

- Cloud seeding is used to help bring rain.
- Farmers plant drought-resistant crops, like sugar beets.

Tech Workers and Time Zones: India's Comparative Advantage

Overview

In this lesson, students read about the global revolution in information technology (IT) and explore the factors that give countries such as India a comparative advantage in attracting IT jobs. In a **Writing for Understanding** activity, students participate in simulated Internet searches and online meetings with three people from Bangalore, India: a call center agent, an auto-rickshaw driver, and a software engineer. Students use their notes from these experiences to write a feature article about the impact of the IT revolution on India.

Objectives

Students will

- define and explain the importance of these key geographic terms: *comparative advantage, information technology (IT), outsource, time zone.*

- examine the factors that give India a comparative advantage in the global IT revolution.

- investigate the impact of the global IT revolution (outsourcing) on Bangalore, India.

- discover factors that cause foreign companies to invest in the United States and the effects of such investment.

Materials

- *Geography Alive! Regions and People*
- Interactive Student Notebooks
- Transparencies 28A–28D
- Student Handouts 28A–28C (1 set for every 2 students)
- Information Master 28 (1 transparency)
- CD Tracks 20–22
- colored markers or pencils (2 colors for every 2 students)

Preview

1 Introduce the Preview. Tell students that they will now take on the role of magazine reporters. First they will learn about several countries where jobs in information technology (IT) are increasing. Explain that these jobs involve such activities as answering customer calls, fixing computer problems, writing software programs, and developing technology systems for businesses. Students will color and analyze three choropleth maps to help them learn more about IT jobs. Later, they will write an article about one of the countries heavily involved in information technology.

2 Have students work in pairs to complete Preview 28 in their Interactive Student Notebooks. Put students in mixed-ability pairs. Give each pair two colors of markers or pencils. Review the directions for Preview 28, and answer any questions students have. Here are some additional tips for conducting the activity:

- If possible, give all pairs the same two colors of markers or pencils (for example, one blue and one red), and have the class create the map key together.

- Have students consult the world political map in the back of their books, if necessary, to identify the locations of specific countries.

- You may want to complete and make transparencies of the three maps beforehand. Once students have finished their own maps, project each map and have students check their work.

3 Explain the connection between the Preview and the upcoming activity. Tell students that India, as well as other countries, have one or more factors that help them attract new information technology jobs. In the upcoming activity, students will learn more about the factors that have allowed India to become a leader in attracting IT jobs. They will also write an article about the effects these jobs have had upon some of India's people.

Essential Question and Geoterms

1 Introduce Chapter 28 in *Geography Alive! Regions and People*. Explain that in this chapter, students will learn about the factors that have helped India to become a leader in attracting IT jobs. Have students read Section 28.1. Then ask them to identify at least four details in the photograph that represent ideas in the text they just read.

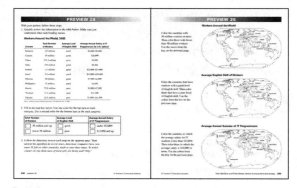

Preview 28

2 Introduce the Graphic Organizer and the Essential Question. Have students examine the illustration of the two workers. Ask,

- What do you see?
- In which regions of the world are these two people located?
- How might the person on the right be using information technology to communicate with the person in the United States?

Have students read the accompanying text. Make sure they understand the Essential Question, *What factors give some countries a comparative advantage in the global IT revolution?* You may want to post the Essential Question in the room or write it on the board for the duration of the activity.

3 Have students read Section 28.2. Then have them complete Geoterms 28 in their Interactive Student Notebooks, individually or in pairs. Have them share their answers with another student, or have volunteers share their answers with the class.

Geoterms 28

Writing for Understanding

1 Before class, prepare for the activity.

- Set up the room according to the diagram. Students will work in their pairs from the Preview. You may want to prepare a transparency that shows student pairs where to sit.
- Create "Internet search stations," one for every pair of students, by posting copies of *Student Handouts 28A–28C: Internet Searches* on the walls three or four feet apart. Tape the pages on top of one another, with Student Handout 28A on top. Students will examine one handout each time they are instructed to conduct an Internet search. They can remove the top handout when they conduct each subsequent search.

Student Handouts 28A–28C

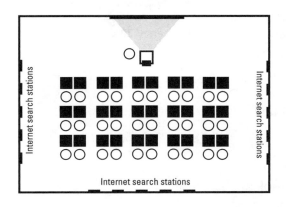

2 Introduce the activity. Explain that students will now, in their role as magazine reporters, research and write a feature article about factors that give India a comparative advantage in the global IT revolution and how this has affected people in Bangalore, India. In their pairs, students will gather information for their articles by reading and taking notes from Chapter 28, conducting "Internet searches," and participating in "online meetings" in which they interview three people from Bangalore, India. Explain that an online meeting is a form of global communication. People in various locations link up through a telephone conference call. Callers can talk to one another, and the meeting's leader can direct a visual presentation through the Internet.

3 Have students prepare for their first online meeting. Have them read Section 28.3 and follow the directions for taking notes on the reading in their Interactive Student Notebooks.

4 Have students conduct an "Internet search" of their first interviewee. Explain that this will allow them to get to know a bit about the person before the meeting. Have pairs bring their Interactive Student Notebooks to an Internet search station and conduct the Internet search (read the handout posted at the station). Have them complete their notes for the Internet search and then return to their desks.

Reading Notes 28

5 Have students participate in their first online meeting. Begin the first meeting by playing CD Track 20, "Online Meeting with Call Center Agent Meena Kumar." Have *Transparency 28A: Meena Kumar's Photographs* ready to project. Instruct students to listen carefully and to record key information in their Reading Notes. (**Note:** Your role is to facilitate the online meetings by projecting transparencies and pausing and playing the CD when prompted by the recording.) Here are some tips for running the meeting smoothly:

- When Meena tells what time it is in India and asks what time it is in your state, pause the CD and have students use the time zone map in Section 28.2 to calculate the time difference. Have them record the "current" time in their time zone in their Reading Notes.

- When Meena is ready for the question, pause the CD and have a volunteer stand and read the interview question for Meena from the Reading Notes.

- Transparency 28A serves as Meena's graphic presentation for the student reporters. When Meena cues them to look at her first photograph, project the top half of the transparency. When she mentions the second photograph, project the bottom half.

Transparency 28A

- After the online meeting, consider reviewing the Reading Notes as a class to make sure all students have accurately recorded the key information.

6 Repeat Steps 3 to 5 for two more online meetings. Make these modifications:

- *Online Meeting 2:* Have students read Section 28.4. To conduct the meeting, play CD Track 21, "Online Meeting with Auto-Rickshaw Driver Nareesh Patel," and show the three images on *Transparency 28B: Nareesh Patel's Photographs* when they are referred to in the dialogue.

- *Online Meeting 3:* Have students read Section 28.5. To conduct the meeting, play CD Track 22, "Online Meeting with Software Engineer Varun Joshi," and show the two images on *Transparency 28C: Varun Joshi's Photographs* when they are referred to in the dialogue.

7 Hold a class discussion. Center the discussion on these questions:

- What factors give India a comparative advantage in the global IT revolution?

- What positive effects has the global IT revolution had upon people from Bangalore?

- What negative or neutral effects has the global IT revolution had upon people from Bangalore?

8 Have students draft their articles about the global IT revolution in India. Return the classroom to its regular configuration, and project a transparency of *Information Master 28: Writing a Feature Article.* (**Note:** You may want to supply each student with a copy.) Review the directions, and answer any questions. Give students time in class or as homework to write their first drafts.

9 Review students' work and have them write their final drafts. Consider using a technique such as peer-checking or peer read-around to give students feedback on their writing before they prepare their final drafts.

Transparency 28B   **Transparency 28C**

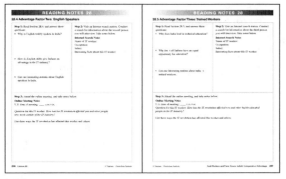

Reading Notes 28

Information Master 28

Global Connections

1 Introduce the Global Connections. Have students read Section 28.6. Then explain that they will now learn about another country that attracts foreign business by having comparative advantage: the United States.

2 Project *Transparency 28D: Global Connections.* Have students analyze the map by discussing the questions below. Use the additional information given to enrich the discussion.

Transparency 28D

- **What interesting details do you see?**

  This map shows which states have attracted the most foreign-company jobs.

- **What do the various colors represent?**

  Red states have attracted the most foreign-company jobs, orange the second most, and yellow the least.

- **Which parts of the United States attract the fewest jobs from foreign companies? Why might this be so?**

  Western and Midwestern states like Idaho, Montana, Wyoming, North Dakota, South Dakota, Nebraska, Kansas, and Oklahoma attract the fewest jobs because of their landlocked locations, which makes the transportation of goods more expensive. Also, there are fewer available workers because the populations of these states are lower.

- **Which states attract the most jobs from foreign companies? What do they have in common?**

  States near oceans or other major bodies of water—like California, Texas, Florida, Michigan, and Ohio—offer foreign businesses access to transportation as well as large working populations.

- **What factors might give some states a comparative advantage in attracting foreign-company jobs?**

  Having highly educated and productive workforces give states like Massachusetts and Ohio a comparative advantage. Having a growing population gives states like Texas a comparative advantage.

3 Have students read Section 28.7 and examine the rest of the information in the section. You may want to read this section as a class so you can facilitate a discussion of these questions:

- **Is the number of Americans working for foreign companies rising or falling?**

- **What kinds of jobs are created by foreign-owned companies in the U.S.?**

- **What gives the U.S. a comparative advantage in attracting foreign businesses?**

Processing

The magazine article serves as a Processing assignment for this lesson.

Online Resources

For more information on the global IT revolution and India, refer students to Online Resources for *Geography Alive! Regions and People* at www.teachtci.com.

Assessment

Masters for assessment appear on the next three pages followed by answers and scoring rubrics.

Assessment 28

Mastering the Content

Shade in the oval by the letter of the best answer for each question.

1. Which of these inventions is **not** part of the global revolution in information technology?
   - ○ A. cell phones
   - ○ B. personal computers
   - ○ C. multifunctional platforms
   - ○ D. communication satellites

2. Which term **best** describes hiring someone outside a company to do work that was once done by the company's own workers?
   - ○ A. recycling
   - ○ B outsourcing
   - ○ C. smart growth
   - ○ D. division of labor

3. India today is the world's largest
   - ○ A. democracy.
   - ○ B. nation-state.
   - ○ C. cultural region.
   - ○ D. developed country.

4. Which city on the map below is the main hub of IT work in India?

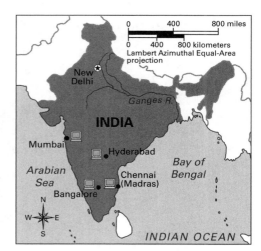

   - ○ A. Bangalore   ○ C. Hyderabad
   - ○ B. Chennai   ○ D. Mumbai

5. How many standard time zones are there in the world today?
   - ○ A. 12
   - ○ B. 24
   - ○ C. 30
   - ○ D. 60

6. What comparative advantage does India have over many other countries in attracting IT jobs from the United States?
   - ○ A. India's brain drain
   - ○ B. India's caste system
   - ○ C. many Hindi speakers
   - ○ D. many English speakers

7. According to this graph, how did technical and IT programs in India change between 1997 and 2004?

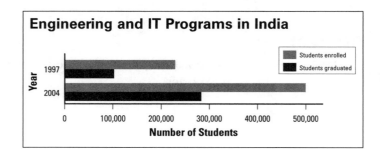

   - ○ A. Twice as many programs offered IT classes.
   - ○ B. The number of women graduated from IT programs about doubled.
   - ○ C. The number of students enrolled in IT programs about doubled.
   - ○ D. Twice as many IT students went to other countries to study.

8. Which of these is a comparative advantage that attracts foreign companies to the United States?
   - ○ A. low living costs
   - ○ B. long life expectancies
   - ○ C. many linguistic groups
   - ○ D. highly educated workers

Applying Geography Skills:
Analyzing a Time Zone Map

Use this map and your knowledge of geography to complete the task below.

Time Zones Around the World

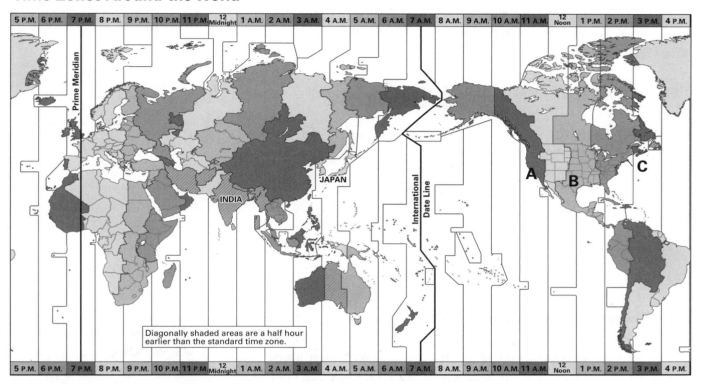

This map shows standard time zones around the world. India has a nonstandard time zone. It is a half-hour off standard time. On this map, the time in India would be 11:30 P.M. These three states are marked on the map with letters: A, California; B, Texas; C, New York.

1. Find India and California (A) on the map. When it is 11:30 P.M. in India, what time is it in California?

2. Find Texas (B) on the map. How many hours difference are there between Texas and California?

3. Find New York (C) on the map. When it is 5:00 P.M. in New York, what time is it in Texas?

4. Find the International Date Line and Japan on the map. Suppose that you are flying across the Pacific from the United States to Japan. You leave California at 11:00 A.M. on Monday, March 1. Your flight lasts 12 hours. What time, day, and date is it in Japan when you arrive?

Exploring the Essential Question

What factors give some countries a comparative advantage in the global IT revolution?

In Chapter 28, you explored India's comparative advantage in the global IT revolution. Now you will use what you learned. Use these graphics and your knowledge of geography to complete the task below.

Salaries of Call Center Workers, 2003

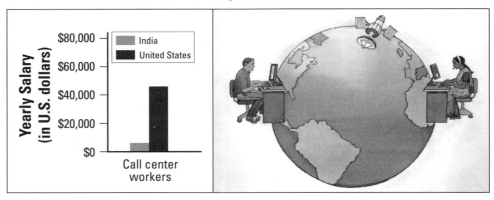

The Task: Framing Questions for an Outsourcing Interview

You are president of a new company that provides tutoring services to students in the United States. Students who need help with their homework can phone your call center to talk with a tutor. Or, they can contact a tutor in the call center by e-mail.

You have decided to outsource late-night calls and e-mails to a call center in India. You have found several IT companies that would like to do this work. Your task is to write five questions to ask when you visit each company. The answers to your questions should help you decide which company to use. Complete these steps on another piece of paper.

Step 1: Think about the kinds of questions and requests for help that a homework-help call center in India might receive. List some of the subjects that workers would need to know to answer such questions.

Step 2: Think about the students who might contact the call center. List the skills call center workers in India might need to work with these students.

Step 3: Think about things that a company can do to make its business successful. List the most important ones.

Step 4: Write five questions you plan to ask the companies you visit in your outsourcing search. Use your notes to help you decide which questions to ask.

Writing Tips: Framing Good Questions

A good question is clearly worded. It asks for information about the topic you are most interested in. To get that information, try to ask questions that need more than a yes or no answer.

Example of a yes or no question: *Does your company pay your call center workers well?*

Example of a question calling for more information: *How much does a call center worker in your company earn each month?*

Applying Geography Skills: Sample Responses

1. 11:00 A.M.
2. 2 hours difference
3. 4:00 P.M.
4. 4:00 P.M., Tuesday, March 2

1. C	2. B	3. A	4. A
5. B	6. D	7. C	8. D

Exploring the Essential Question: Sample Response

Step 1: Answers will vary. Call center workers should be familiar with subjects taught in American schools, such as language arts, social studies, science, and math.

Step 2: Answers will vary. Call center workers will need to speak clear American English. They will need to be able to explain complex ideas in simple terms. They will need to be friendly and patient with callers.

Step 3: Answers might include paying workers well, providing training for workers, using up-to-date technology, and treating customers well.

Step 4: Answers will vary. Accept any reasonable question.
Examples:
- What kind of training do you give to call center workers?
- What hours does your call center operate?
- How many hours do your workers work each day?
- How much do you pay your call center workers?
- How well do your call center workers speak and understand American English?
- How much education have your call center workers completed?
- What kind of teaching experience do your call center workers have?
- How do you train your workers to make young callers feel comfortable?

Applying Geography Skills Scoring Rubric

Score	General Description
2	Student responds to all parts of the task. Response is correct and clear.
1	Student responds to some parts of the task. Response is mostly correct.
0	Response does not match the task or is incorrect.

Exploring the Essential Question Scoring Rubric

Score	General Description
3	Student responds to all parts of the task. Response is correct, clear, and supported by details.
2	Student responds to most or all parts of the task. Response is generally correct but may lack details.
1	Student responds to at least one part of the task. Response may contain errors and lack details.
0	Response does not match the task or is incorrect.

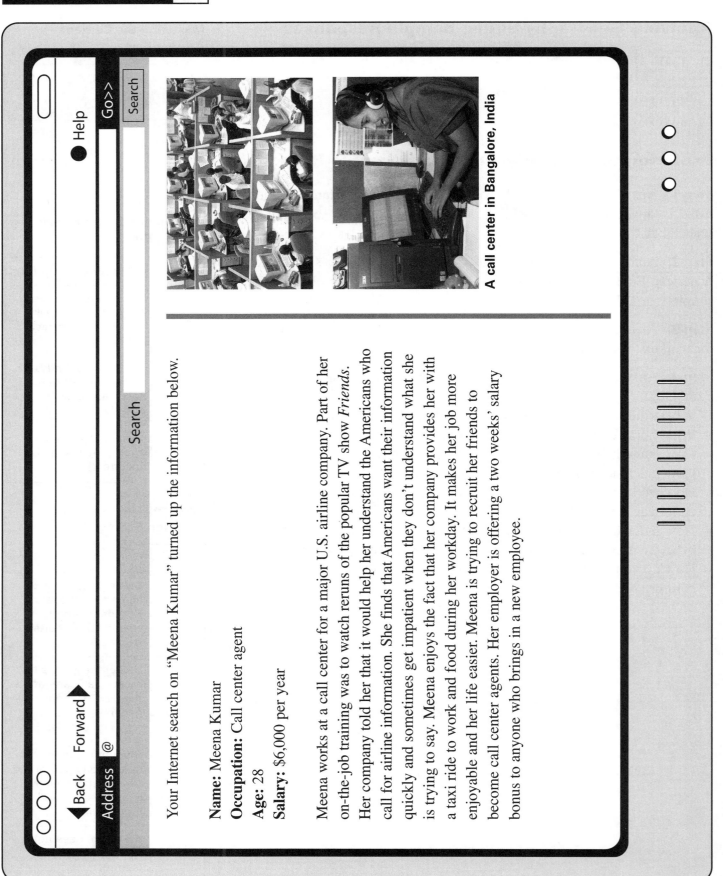

A call center in Bangalore, India

Your Internet search on "Meena Kumar" turned up the information below.

Name: Meena Kumar
Occupation: Call center agent
Age: 28
Salary: $6,000 per year

Meena works at a call center for a major U.S. airline company. Part of her on-the-job training was to watch reruns of the popular TV show *Friends*. Her company told her that it would help her understand the Americans who call for airline information. She finds that Americans want their information quickly and sometimes get impatient when they don't understand what she is trying to say. Meena enjoys the fact that her company provides her with a taxi ride to work and food during her workday. It makes her job more enjoyable and her life easier. Meena is trying to recruit her friends to become call center agents. Her employer is offering a two weeks' salary bonus to anyone who brings in a new employee.

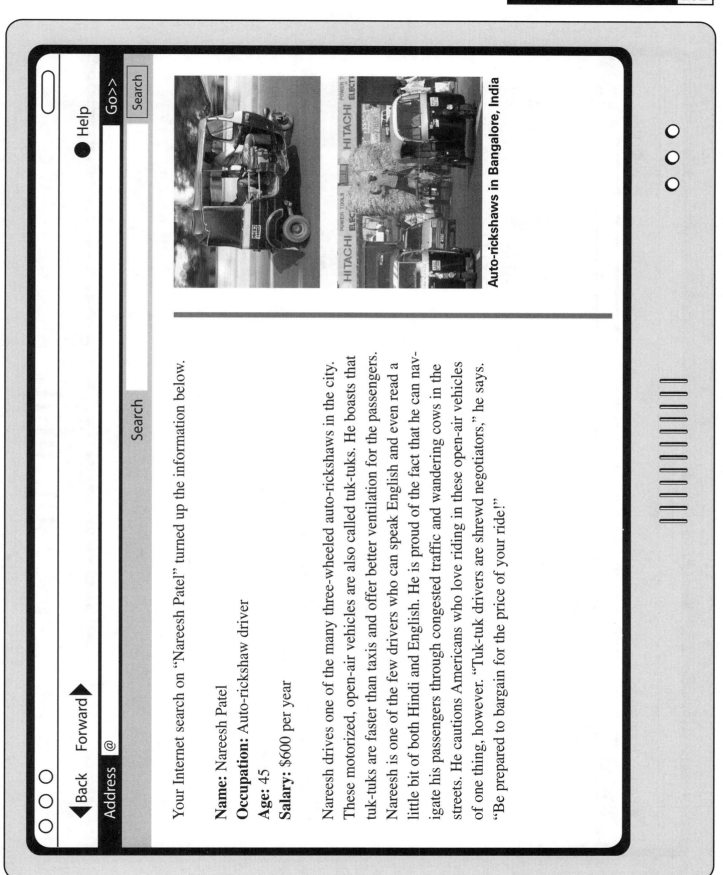

Your Internet search on "Nareesh Patel" turned up the information below.

Name: Nareesh Patel
Occupation: Auto-rickshaw driver
Age: 45
Salary: $600 per year

Nareesh drives one of the many three-wheeled auto-rickshaws in the city. These motorized, open-air vehicles are also called tuk-tuks. He boasts that tuk-tuks are faster than taxis and offer better ventilation for the passengers. Nareesh is one of the few drivers who can speak English and even read a little bit of both Hindi and English. He is proud of the fact that he can navigate his passengers through congested traffic and wandering cows in the streets. He cautions Americans who love riding in these open-air vehicles of one thing, however. "Tuk-tuk drivers are shrewd negotiators," he says. "Be prepared to bargain for the price of your ride!"

Auto-rickshaws in Bangalore, India

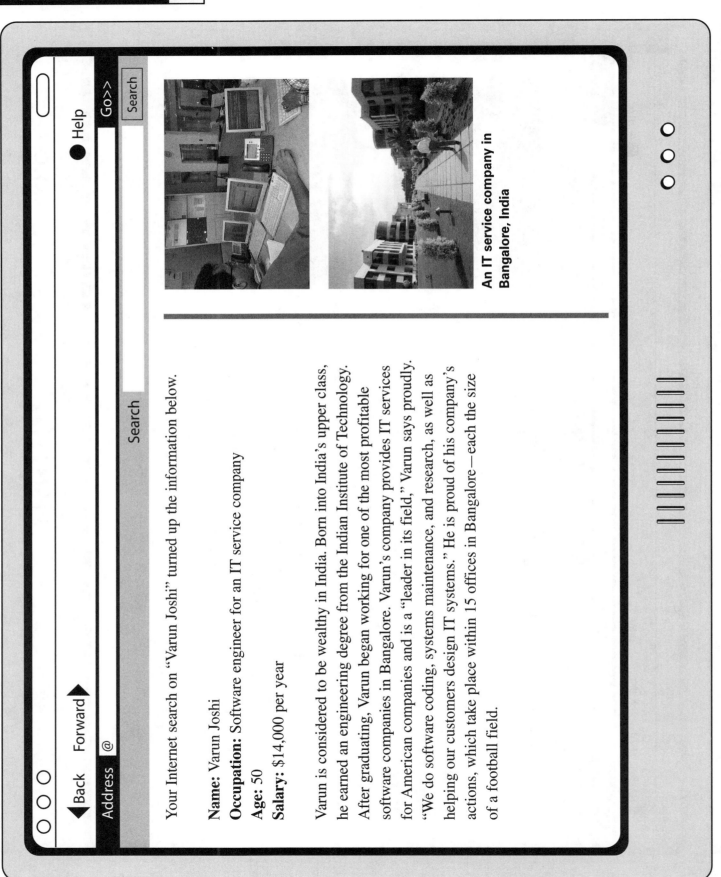

Your Internet search on "Varun Joshi" turned up the information below.

Name: Varun Joshi
Occupation: Software engineer for an IT service company
Age: 50
Salary: $14,000 per year

Varun is considered to be wealthy in India. Born into India's upper class, he earned an engineering degree from the Indian Institute of Technology. After graduating, Varun began working for one of the most profitable software companies in Bangalore. Varun's company provides IT services for American companies and is a "leader in its field," Varun says proudly. "We do software coding, systems maintenance, and research, as well as helping our customers design IT systems." He is proud of his company's actions, which take place within 15 offices in Bangalore—each the size of a football field.

An IT service company in Bangalore, India

Write an Article About India's Global IT Revolution

Write a feature article for a magazine that highlights India and the global IT revolution. Your article should address these questions:

- What factors give India a comparative advantage in the global IT revolution?
- How have people in Bangalore been affected by the IT revolution?

Use information from your reading, Internet searches, and online meetings. Your article must have these things:

- A short, catchy title.
- An introductory paragraph that tells about India's geography and history. It should also state your purpose for writing.
- A second paragraph that explains why India has become a leader in the IT revolution. Include at least two factors.
- A third paragraph that describes how the IT revolution has affected people from Bangalore. Give at least two examples.
- Two images (photographs, maps, or graphs) that show something you wrote about. These can be drawings you make or images from a book or the Internet. For Internet searches, use any of these key phrases: *Bangalore India, information technology, India outsourcing.* Give each image a short caption.
- Correct grammar and spelling.

Use these terms in your article: *comparative advantage, information technology, outsource,* and *time zone.* Add clever and creative touches to make your article more realistic.

28.3 Advantage Factor One: Low Wages

Step 1: Read Section 28.3, and answer these questions:

- What are two reasons why wages for workers in India are lower than in many other countries?

With so many people competing for jobs, Indians will often accept lower pay than workers in less populated countries. Indians also have a lower cost of living.

- Why do Indian workers want IT jobs?

IT jobs offer some of the best pay and working conditions in India.

- List one interesting statistic about low wages in India.

Possible answer: In 2003, a U.S. call center worker earned $46,000 while one in India earned $6,000.

Step 2: Visit an Internet search station. Conduct a search for information about the first person you will interview (read the handout on the wall). Take notes below.

Internet Search Notes

Name of IT worker: Meena Kumar
Occupation: call center agent
Salary: $6,000 per year
Interesting facts about this IT worker:
Possible answers:

- Part of her on-the-job training was to watch reruns of the TV show "Friends."

- Her company provides her with a taxi ride to work and food during her workday.

- Meena is trying to recruit friends to become call center agents to earn a bonus of two weeks' salary.

Step 3: Attend the online meeting, and take notes below.

Online Meeting Notes

U.S. time of meeting: _____ A.M./P.M. Answers will vary.
Question for this IT worker: *How has the IT revolution affected you and other people who work in the IT industry?*

List three ways the IT revolution has affected Meena and other Indian workers.
Possible answers:

- IT workers earn a decent salary and have money to spend on entertainment and fun.
- Internet cafes are located in many cities, and people of all ages and both sexes are welcome.
- Women in the IT field have more job opportunities.
- Many women are becoming more independent, and their parents are learning to accept that.

28.4 Advantage Factor Two: English Speakers

Step 1: Read Section 28.4, and answer these questions:

• Why is English widely spoken in India?

When Britain made India a colony, officials set up schools where Indians were taught in English. By the time India gained independence in 1947, English was widely spoken. Today English serves as the main language of business and government.

• How do English skills give Indians an advantage in the IT industry?

India can provide IT services in English better than countries where little English is spoken.

• List one interesting statistic about English speakers in India.

Possible answer: About a third of all Indians speak some English.

Step 2: Visit an Internet search station. Conduct a search for information about the second person you will interview. Take notes below.

Internet Search Notes

Name of IT worker: Nareesh Patel
Occupation: auto-rickshaw driver
Salary: $600 per year
Interesting facts about this IT worker:
Possible answers:

• Auto-rickshaws, or tuk-tuks, are faster than taxis and offer better ventilation for the passengers.

• Nareesh can navigate his passengers through congested traffic and wandering cows.

• Nareesh is willing to negotiate the price of a tuk-tuk ride.

Step 3: Attend the online meeting, and take notes below.

Online Meeting Notes

U.S. time of meeting: _____ A.M./P.M. Answers will vary.

Question for this IT worker: *How has the IT revolution affected you and other people who work outside of the IT industry?*

List three ways the IT revolution has affected this worker and others.
Possible answers:

• Traffic is bad because many people come to Bangalore to find work and many IT workers can now afford cars or scooters.

• Office complexes, highways, and cellular towers are popping up everywhere.

• New jobs have been created, like janitors, security guards, and construction workers.

• Bangalore is growing too fast and the government can't keep up with the needs of the city. Sidewalks are in poor repair, power outages are common, roads in the poor sections are unpaved, and families live in shacks without water or electricity.

• There is a large economic gap between those who work in the IT industry and those who do not.

28.5 Advantage Factor Three: Trained Workers

Step 1: Read Section 28.5, and answer these questions:

• Why does India lead in technical education?
India has made efforts to promote technical education. The Indian Institute of Technology, founded in 1951, now has seven campuses.

• Why don't all Indians have an equal opportunity for education?
Many poor children have to work to support their families. Also, children born into lower castes are not expected to be well educated.

• List one interesting statistic about India's trained workers.
Possible answer: In 2003, more than 3 million Indians graduated from college.

Step 2: Visit an Internet search station. Conduct a search for information about the third person you will interview. Take notes below.

Internet Search Notes
Name of IT worker: Varun Joshi
Occupation: software engineer
Salary: $14,000 per year
Interesting facts about this IT worker:
Possible answers:

• Varun's company provides IT services for American companies and is a leader in its field.

• Varun's company occupies 15 enormous offices.

Step 3: Attend the online meeting, and take notes below.

Online Meeting Notes
U.S. time of meeting: _____ A.M./P.M. Answers will vary.
Question for this IT worker: *How has the IT revolution affected you and other highly educated people in the IT industry?*

List three ways the IT revolution has affected this worker and others.
Possible answers:

• The IT revolution has allowed some men who own their own companies to become billionaires.

• IT campuses have swimming pools, recreation centers, golf courses, gyms, and stores for workers' enjoyment and convenience.

• Bangalore is now being called "the Silicon Valley of India," as many top computer and software corporations base their companies there.

• Engineers must keep innovating to keep India the global leader it has become.

Mount Everest: Climbing the World's Tallest Physical Feature

Overview

In this lesson, students learn about the physical characteristics of Mount Everest—the world's tallest mountain—and the reasons people are working to protect it. In an **Experiential Exercise,** teams of students assume the role of climbers on Mount Everest, discovering some of the challenges presented by this physical feature as they "ascend" the mountain. After discussing their experience, students read about the challenges faced by real climbers and the impact of climbing expeditions. They record their discoveries in illustrated journal entries that commemorate their experience.

Objectives

Students will

- define and explain the importance of these key geographic terms: *acclimatize, carrying capacity, exposure, World Heritage site.*

- identify the physical characteristics of Mount Everest and the challenges presented by climbing the world's tallest physical feature.

- understand the impact of Everest expeditions on people and the environment.

- explain the reasons people want to protect World Heritage sites.

Materials

- *Geography Alive! Regions and People*
- Interactive Student Notebooks
- Transparencies 29A–29E
- Student Handouts 29A–29D (1 of each for every 4 students)
- masking tape
- string (8 feet for every 4 students)
- empty plastic bottles
- painter's masks (or folded pieces of paper; 1 per student)
- sticky notes (1 per student)
- dice (1 or more)

Preview

1 Have students complete Preview 29 in their Interactive Student Notebooks. Ask several to share their responses. Consider asking what attracts them to the places they chose: human geography, physical geography, or both.

2 Explain the connection between the Preview and the upcoming activity. Tell students that just as they would like to visit different places for a variety of reasons, some people travel to cities or towns that are important to their families, others journey to museums and historical sites to learn about other cultures or the past, and still others trek to national parks and the wilderness to enjoy the physical beauty of those places. In this lesson, students will discover why people attempt the challenging climb up Mount Everest, the world's tallest mountain. They will also learn about its physical characteristics and why people want to protect this special place. (**Note:** There is continuing debate on the exact height of Mount Everest. In the 1950s, its height was estimated at 29,028 feet. A survey in 2005 measured it to be 29,017 feet. Whatever its exact height, the mountain remains the tallest in the world.)

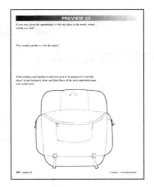

Preview 29

Essential Question and Geoterms

1 Introduce Chapter 29 in *Geography Alive! Regions and People*. Explain that in this chapter, students will learn about the physical characteristics of Mount Everest and the reasons people are working to protect it. Have students read Section 29.1. Then ask them to identify at least four details in the photograph of Mount Everest that represent ideas in the text they just read.

2 Introduce the Graphic Organizer and the Essential Question. Have students examine the illustration of Mount Everest. Ask,

- What do you see?
- What has been drawn on this mountain?
- Why do you think there are several camps on the way to the summit?
- What are some of the challenges people might face as they climb this mountain?
- Why might people want to climb this physical feature?

Have students read the accompanying text. Make sure they understand the Essential Question, *How can people both experience and protect the world's special places?* You may want to post the Essential Question in the room or write it on the board for the duration of the activity.

3 Have students read Section 29.2. Then have them complete Geoterms 29 in their Interactive Student Notebooks, individually or in pairs. Have them share their answers with another student, or have volunteers share their answers with the class.

Geoterms 29

Experiential Exercise

1 Prepare students for the Experiential Exercise. The day before, explain that they will be participating in an activity that will require them to have their coats with them. (**Note:** If school regulations prohibit bringing coats to class, you might instead ask students to bring in an extra sweatshirt or sweater.)

2 Arrange students in mixed-ability groups of four.

3 Explain the activity. Tell students that in this activity, they will assume the role of climbers who are trying to reach the summit of Mount Everest. In groups of four, they will experience some of the challenges presented by the mountain's physical geography. They will then read about the challenges real climbers face and the impact of climbing expeditions. (**Note:** This activity has four phases. In each phase, students experience a different portion of the climb up Everest. You may choose to skip or modify the steps in one or two of the phases to accommodate the needs of your classroom.)

Phase 1: From Lukla to Base Camp

1 Prepare the classroom. Move chairs and desks to the edges of the room to create a large open space in the center. You may want to ask several volunteers to help you set up the room. (**Note:** Alternatively, conduct this phase of the activity in a large open space, such as a gymnasium.) Project *Transparency 29A: From Lukla to Base Camp.*

2 Introduce the "climb." Give each team a copy of *Student Handout 29A: Directions for Climbing from Lukla to Base Camp.* Review the steps with students.

Transparency 29A   **Student Handout 29A**

"Climb" from Lukla to Base Camp.

Teams line up here.

3 Conduct the climb from Lukla to Base Camp. Here are some tips for executing the steps on Student Handout 29A:

- *Step 1:* Allow students to use backpacks or book bags to carry their belongings. (**Note:** If backpacks aren't allowed in the classroom, consider supplying teams with boxes or heavy-duty trash bags.)

- *Step 2:* If necessary, reduce the porter's load by having two students carry each team's belongings.

- *Step 3:* Remind students that this phase of the climb is not a race. It is more important that they take the time to acclimatize than to be the first team to reach Base Camp.

4 Debrief the activity. Ask students,

- How did it feel to climb from Lukla to Base Camp? Why might people want to make this climb?

- Who do you think carries all of the equipment and supplies on climbing expeditions?

- What positive effects might these expeditions have on the local community? What might be some negative effects?

5 Have students read Section 29.3. Then have them complete the Reading Notes for Section 29.3 in their Interactive Student Notebooks. Use Guide to Reading Notes 29 to review their answers.

Reading Notes 29

Phase 2: From Base Camp to Camp I

1 Prepare the classroom. You may want to ask several volunteers to help you.

- Arrange two rows of desks across the room to represent seracs (giant chunks of ice). Leave an open space between the rows. (**Note:** Alternatively, use strips of masking tape to represent the seracs. When students reach the tape, have them pantomime climbing over the ice.)

- Create "trails" by placing six to eight sheets of paper between the two rows of desks for each team of students. Mark at least one sheet of paper along each trail with an X. Place the sheets face down, and tape them along one side to keep students from looking at them.

- Dim the lights to represent that this section of the hike usually begins before dawn.

- Project *Transparency 29B: From Base Camp to Camp I.*

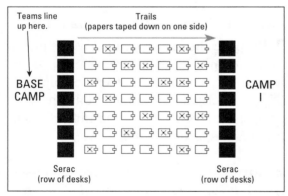

⊠ Crevasses ('X' marked on underside of paper)

Transparency 29B

2 Introduce the climb. Give each team a copy of *Student Handout 29B: Directions for Climbing from Base Camp to Camp I,* and review the steps with them.

3 Conduct the climb from Base Camp to Camp I. Here are some tips for executing the steps on Student Handout 29B:

- *Step 2:* To avoid crowding, assign one desk in the first serac (row of desks) to each team.

- *Step 3:* Yell "Freeze!" only when all teams have successfully climbed over the first serac and all climbers are standing on a trail (sheets of paper).

4 Debrief the activity. Ask,

- How did it feel to climb from Base Camp to Camp I? Why might people want to make this climb?

- Why do you think this part of the climb is considered the most dangerous?

- Who or what might help the climbing expeditions reach Camp I safely?

5 Have students read and complete the Reading Notes for Section 29.4. Use the Guide to Reading Notes to review their answers.

Phase 3: From Camp I to Camp IV

1 Prepare the classroom. You may want to ask several volunteers to help you.

- Move desks and chairs to the edges to create a large open space in the center.

- Use masking tape to create a trail across the floor for each team. The strips of tape represent the steep, icy walls and narrow ledges of the trail from Camp I to Camp IV.

- At the end of the trails, place several empty plastic bottles and crumpled sheets of paper to represent the trash found at Camp IV.

- Project *Transparency 29C: From Camp I to Camp IV.*

2 Introduce the climb. Give each team a copy of *Student Handout 29C: Directions for Climbing from Camp I to Camp IV,* and review the steps with them.

Student Handout 29B

Reading Notes 29

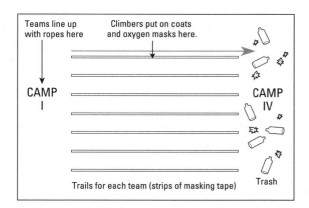

Transparency 29C

Student Handout 29C

3 Conduct the climb from Camp I to Camp IV. Here are some tips for executing the steps on Student Handout 29C:

- *Step 1:* Use your discretion in allowing students who were injured in the previous phase to rejoin their teams. Make it clear that injured people would not typically rejoin their teams but instead recuperate at Base Camp or at a hospital much farther away. Give each student an "oxygen mask" (painter's mask). Remind students that they should not put on their masks until they are halfway up the trail to Camp IV.

- *Step 2:* Give each team an 8-foot length of string.

- *Step 3:* Remind students that halfway up the trail, they must put on their coats and oxygen masks. When they reach Camp IV, use your discretion in allowing them to move the "trash" to set up their camps. Make it clear that, in reality, climbers may not be able to move the trash they discover at the camp.

4 Debrief the activity. Ask,
- How did it feel to climb from Camp I to Camp IV? Why might people want to make this climb?
- What is unique about the geography of Mount Everest from Camp I to Camp IV?
- What impact might humans have had on the mountain's physical geography?

5 Have students read and complete the Reading Notes for Section 29.5. Use the Guide to Reading Notes to review their answers.

Reading Notes 29

Phase 4: From Camp IV to the Summit

1 Prepare the classroom. You may want to ask several volunteers to help you.
- Project *Transparency 29D: From Camp IV to the Summit.*
- Place a sturdy table directly in front the image to represent the summit.
- Immediately to the right of the summit, place three chairs in a row to represent the Hillary Step. (**Note:** Alternatively, use masking tape to mark off two 3-foot-by-4-foot rectangles on the floor to represent the summit and the Hillary Step. When students step into each rectangle, have them pantomime climbing to a higher elevation.)

Transparency 29D

- To the right of the Hillary Step, create a trail on the floor with two strips of masking tape, placed about two and a half feet apart.
- Turn off the lights to represent that this part of the climb usually begins before midnight.

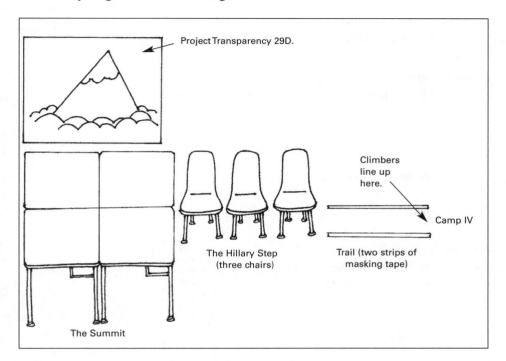

Project Transparency 29D.

Climbers line up here.

Camp IV

The Hillary Step (three chairs)

Trail (two strips of masking tape)

The Summit

2 Introduce the climb. Give each team a copy of *Student Handout 29D: Directions for Climbing from Camp IV to the Summit,* and review the steps with them.

3 Conduct the climb from Camp IV to the Summit. Here are some tips for executing the steps on Student Handout 29D:

- *Step 1:* Give each student a sticky note and have them quickly create their tokens. Use your discretion in allowing injured students to continue the ascent. Make it clear that injured people would typically recuperate at Base Camp or at a hospital much farther away.
- *Step 2:* Have each team roll the die once. If a team rolls for good weather, have its members line up on the trail (but not start climbing). (**Note:** Alternatively, you may want to give one die to each team and allow all teams to roll at once, but make sure they roll only once.)
- *Step 3:* Allow approximately five minutes for students to attempt to climb to the summit. Then announce that those students still on the Hillary Step or the summit have taken too long and have "died" from exposure. Any students who have not yet reached the summit will not be able to finish the climb.

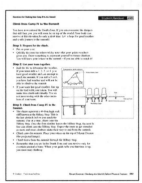

Student Handout 29D

4 Debrief the activity. Ask,

- How many of you made it to the summit? How many of you did not make it? Why not?

- How did it feel to climb to the summit? Why might people want to make this climb?

- What might be the greatest challenges in reaching the summit?

- What do you think it is like to be "on top of the world"?

5 Have students read and complete the Reading Notes for Section 29.6. Use the Guide to Reading Notes to review their answers.

Global Connections

1 Introduce the Global Connections. Have students read Section 29.7. Then explain that they will now look at other sites around the world that draw people to explore.

2 Project *Transparency 27E: Global Connections.* Have students analyze the map by discussing and sharing their answers to the questions below. Use the additional information given to enrich the discussion.

Transparency 29E

- **What interesting details do you see on this map?**

- **What types of World Heritage sites are there?**

- **Where are World Heritage sites located?**
  As of September 2005, there were 812 World Heritage sites in 134 countries around the world. Of these, 160 are natural sites, 628 are cultural sites, and 24 are mixed sites. There are 20 World Heritage sites in the United States; Everglades National Park in Florida is 1 of 12 natural sites, and the Statue of Liberty and Independence Hall are 2 of 8 cultural sites.

3 Have students read Section 29.8, including the captions. Then ask,

- **How does a place become a World Heritage site?**

- **What risks do World Heritage sites face today?**
  Many are at risk of being damaged or lost for various reasons, such as war, pollution, commercial development, and uncontrolled tourism. Earthquakes, hurricanes, and other natural disasters also put World Heritage sites at risk. The mission of the World Heritage Committee is to protect these sites, which reflect the natural and cultural heritage of the world. The committee encourages countries to nominate

new sites and helps countries set up management plans and monitor conservation efforts. Technology, training, public-awareness campaigns, and emergency funding are available to help countries protect these sites.

If there are immediate and serious threats to a site's well-being, it can be put on a list of World Heritage sites in danger. After an earthquake in December 2003, the Iranian city of Bam was placed on this special list. This ancient city was an important stop along the ancient Silk Road trade routes. Everglades National Park in Florida was placed on the list in 1993 after Hurricane Andrew devastated the region the year before.

• **Why should World Heritage sites be protected?**

Processing

Have students complete Processing 29 in their Interactive Student Notebooks.

Online Resources

For more information on Mount Everest, refer students to Online Resources for *Geography Alive! Regions and People* at www.teachtci.com.

Assessment

Masters for assessment appear on the next three pages followed by answers and scoring rubrics.

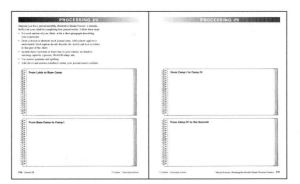

Processing 29

Mastering the Content

Shade in the oval by the letter of the best answer for each question.

1. In which of these mountain ranges is Mount Everest located?
   ○ A. Andes
   ○ B. Caucasus
   ○ C. Himalayas
   ○ D. Urals

2. What is the **main** reason people want to climb to the top of Mount Everest?
   ○ A. It is the world's oldest mountain.
   ○ B. It is the world's tallest mountain.
   ○ C. It is the world's most beautiful mountain.
   ○ D. It is the world's most dangerous mountain.

3. Based on the information in this table, about how much does it cost a guide service to take seven climbers to the top of Everest?

What Does It Cost to Climb Everest?

Item	Cost for a Team of Seven Climbers
Crew (includes guides, cooks, and doctor)	$98,000
Transportation and lodging en route to Base Camp	$41,000
Permits and fees	$79,000
Supplies (includes fuel, oxygen, batteries, tents, medical supplies, and climbing gear)	$49,000

   ○ A. under $150,000
   ○ B. around $500,000
   ○ C. less than $200,000
   ○ D. more than $250,000

4. Climbers on Everest stop from time to time to acclimatize to
   ○ A. crowded trails.
   ○ B. elevation changes.
   ○ C. extreme cold.
   ○ D. windy weather.

5. The carrying capacity of a place is a measure of which of the following?
   ○ A. the plants and animals it can support
   ○ B. the replacement rate of its population
   ○ C. the renewable resources it can produce
   ○ D. the environmental degradation it has suffered

6. What is the **main** cause of Acute Mountain Sickness among mountain climbers?
   ○ A. bad water
   ○ B. rugged climbs
   ○ C. strange foods
   ○ D. thin air

7. What caused the problem described by a climber in this excerpt?

   The wind kicked up huge swirling waves of powder snow. Ice formed over my goggles, making it difficult to see. I began to lose feeling in my feet. My fingers turned to wood.

   ○ A. exposure
   ○ B. salinization
   ○ C. storm surge
   ○ D. altitude sickness

8. On their way up Mount Everest, climbers enter the Death Zone. What makes this zone so challenging?
   ○ A. lack of sleep
   ○ B. lack of shelter
   ○ C. lack of oxygen
   ○ D. lack of daylight

Applying Geography Skills:
Matching Descriptions to Places

Use this diagram and your knowledge of geography to complete the tasks below

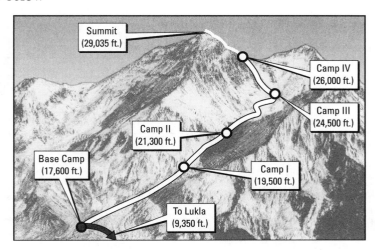

The diagram shows a popular route to the top of Mount Everest. You have read many descriptions of the climb along this route. Read those that appear below. Match what you read to the part of the climb that is being described. Write the number of the description on the diagram of Mount Everest where you think it belongs.

1. Climbing in the Death Zone is a real physical test. "You take a step and you breathe six to eight times and then you take another step and then you breathe six or eight times," a climber recalled.

2. Climbers reach the Khumbu Icefall on the second stage of their journey. "Imagine trying to hopscotch uphill through a field of ice boulders the size of houses and weighing some 30 tons, each of which could shift at any moment without warning," wrote a climber about the icefall.

3. "My first sensation was one of relief—relief that the long grind was over," Edmund Hillary wrote. "I turned and looked at Tenzing. Even beneath his oxygen mask and the icicles hanging from his hair, I could see his infectious grin of sheer delight."

4. Once climbers go beyond 19,600 feet, they enter a long valley called Western Cwm, or "Valley of Silence." On a sunny day, the valley gets quite hot. This comes as a surprise to climbers who expect freezing conditions. "You literally pray for a puff of wind or a cloud to cover the sun," one climber said.

5. This "tent city" is made up of dozens or even hundreds of tents. It has kitchens, dining halls, and even solar-powered lights. Most climbers spend weeks here to get used to the thin air.

Test Terms Glossary
To **match** means to bring things together that share the same features.

Exploring the Essential Question

How can people both experience and protect the world's special places?

In Chapter 29, you explored how people experience and protect Mt. Everest. Now you will use what you learned.

The Task: To Nominate a Place as a World Heritage Site

World Heritage sites are places of great natural or cultural value to the world. The table lists World Heritage sites in the United States. Your task is to nominate another place in this country to become a World Heritage site.

Step 1: Some places on the World Heritage list are natural sites. These sites have special natural features, unique ecosystems, or great biodiversity. Write an N beside four sites that you think are natural sites.

Step 2: Some places on the World Heritage list are cultural sites. These sites have great historic, artistic, or scientific value. Write a C beside four sites that you think are cultural sites.

Step 3: Identify a place in the United States that you

C or N	World Heritage Sites in the United States	Location
	Cahokia Mounds State Historic Site	Illinois
	Carlsbad Caverns National Park	New Mexico
	Chaco Culture National Historic Park	New Mexico
	Everglades National Park	Florida
	Grand Canyon National Park	Arizona
	Great Smoky Mountains National Park	North Carolina, Tennessee
	Hawaii Volcanoes National Park	Hawaii
	Independence Hall Historic Park	Pennsylvania
	Kluane/Wrangell—St Elias/Glacier Bay/Tatshenshini—Alsek	Alaska and Canada
	La Fortaleza and San Juan Historic Site	Puerto Rico
	Mammoth Cave National Park	Kentucky
	Mesa Verde National Park	Colorado
	Monticello and the University of Virginia in Charlottesville	Virginia
	Olympic National Park	Washington
	Pueblo de Taos	New Mexico
	Redwood National Park	California
	Statue of Liberty National Monument	New Jersey, New York
	Waterton-Glacier International Peace Park	Montana and Canada
	Yellowstone National Park	Idaho, Montana, Wyoming
	Yosemite National Park	California

think could become a new World Heritage site. On another sheet of paper, write a brief statement nominating your place for this honor. Your statement should include the following:

A   an introduction that tells the name of the place and whether it is a cultural or natural site

B.   a description of the place that tells why it is special

C.   a conclusion telling why the place should be a World Heritage site

Applying Geography Skills: Sample Responses

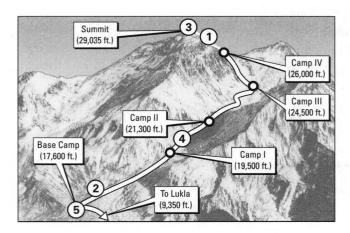

Exploring the Essential Question: Sample Response

Steps 1 and 2: Four sites on the list should be labeled N, and four should be labeled C.

Step 3: Accept any reasonable site in the United States not already a World Heritage site. The nomination statement should include the elements listed in the prompt.

C or N	World Heritage Sites in the United States
C	Cahokia Mounds State Historic Site
N	Carlsbad Caverns National Park
C	Chaco Culture National Historic Park
N	Everglades National Park
N	Grand Canyon National Park
N	Great Smoky Mountains National Park
N or C	Hawaii Volcanoes National Park
C	Independence Hall Historic Park
N	Kluane/Wrangell—St Elias/Glacier Bay/ Tatshenshini—Alsek
C	La Fortaleza and San Juan Historic Site
N	Mammoth Cave National Park
C	Mesa Verde National Park
C	Monticello and the University of Virginia in Charlottesville
N	Olympic National Park
C	Pueblo de Taos
N	Redwood National Park
C	Statue of Liberty National Monument
N	Waterton-Glacier International Peace Park
N	Yellowstone National Park
N	Yosemite National Park

Mastering the Content Answer Key

1. C	2. B	3. D	4. B
5. A	6. D	7. A	8. C

Applying Geography Skills Scoring Rubric

Score	General Description
2	Student responds to all parts of the task. Response is correct and clear.
1	Student responds to some parts of the task. Response is mostly correct.
0	Response does not match the task or is incorrect.

Exploring the Essential Question Scoring Rubric

Score	General Description
3	Student responds to all parts of the task. Response is correct, clear, and supported by details.
2	Student responds to most or all parts of the task. Response is generally correct but may lack details.
1	Student responds to at least one part of the task. Response may contain errors and lack details.
0	Response does not match the task or is incorrect.

Climb from Lukla to Base Camp

Welcome to Lukla, Nepal! You are about to begin your ascent of Mount Everest. First you will climb to Base Camp. During this phase of the climb, you will transport all of your equipment and supplies with the help of your team's porter. Don't forget to take this time to allow your body to acclimatize!

Step 1: Prepare for the climb.

- Put on your coat.
- Take all of your belongings with you. They represent your climbing equipment and supplies.

Step 2: Get your team together.

- With your team, form a line along one side of the room.
- Give all of your belongings to the first person in line for your team. He or she will act as the porter for your team.

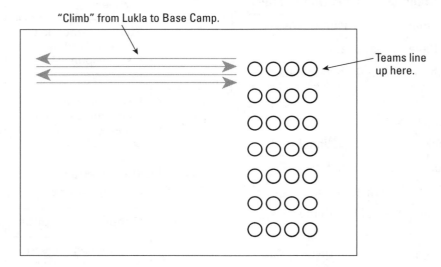

"Climb" from Lukla to Base Camp.

Teams line up here.

Step 3: Climb from Lukla to Base Camp.

- As a team, walk in a line across the room to the opposite wall. Walk slowly and take deep breaths as if your body is trying to acclimatize to the high elevation.
- When your team reaches the opposite wall, switch all of the team's equipment and supplies to the next person in line. This person will now be your team's porter.
- Continue "climbing" back and forth across the room until all members of your team have had a chance to act as the porter.

Climb from Base Camp to Camp I

You have been waiting patiently at Base Camp to acclimatize. While you've waited, supplies have been brought up, and the trail ahead has been made for you. Now you face one of the most challenging parts of the climb: up the Khumbu Icefall to Camp I. It's finally time to start— but watch out for those crevasses!

Step 1: Prepare for the climb.
- Put on your coat.
- Leave your belongings.

Step 2: Get your team together.
- With your team, form a line at Base Camp. Line up perpendicular to the two rows of desks.
- In your line, stay no more than one arm's length away from one another. This way, you can help each other during the challenging parts of the climb.

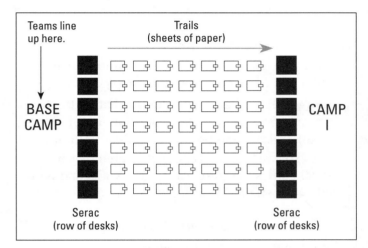

Step 3: Climb from Base Camp to Camp I.
- The rows of desks represent enormous chunks of ice called *seracs*. You must climb over the seracs to reach Camp I. One by one, have members of your team climb over the first serac to the other side.
- Once you are over the first serac, you must stay on the "trail" (path of papers) that has been made for you.
- When you hear your guide (teacher) yell "Freeze!" you must stand still. Turn over the paper you are standing on. If you see an X, it means you have fallen through one of the deep crevasses in the ice. You must sit down outside the climbing area to show that you have been injured.
- With the remaining members of your team, arrive at Camp I by climbing one at a time over the second serac.

Climb from Camp I to Camp IV

Congratulations! You have made it through the dangers of the Khumbu Icefall. But there are many more challenges to face as you climb from Camp I to Camp IV. You'll encounter temperatures up to 100°F, steep icy walls, and narrow ledges. Are you ready?

Step 1: Prepare for the climb.

- Tie your coat around your waist to show how hot this section of this climb can be.

- Carry with you only the oxygen mask given to you by your guide (teacher). Don't put it on until you are halfway up the trail to Camp IV. Otherwise, you will waste precious oxygen that you will need later.

Step 2: Get your team together.

- With your team, form a line at Camp I. Line up at the end of one trail (strip of masking tape).

- Your guide will give your team a length of string. The string represents the ropes that the Sherpas have fixed for you on the trail. Take hold of the rope, spacing yourselves evenly along it. To safely travel across the trail's steep, icy walls and narrow ledges, keep one hand on the string at all times.

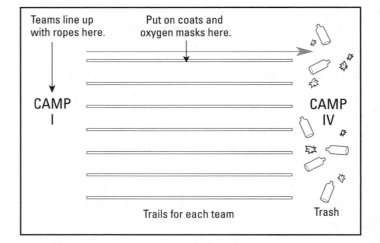

Step 3: Climb from Camp I to Camp IV.

- Climb along the trail to Camp IV.

- Stay on the trail by walking on the masking tape. If you lose your balance and step off the tape, you have fallen off the trail. If you fall off the trail, you must sit down outside the climbing area to show that you have been injured.

- About halfway up the trail, put on your coat and oxygen mask. Remember to stay connected to the rope and remain on the trail. If you don't, you have fallen off the trail and become injured.

- Once your team arrives at Camp IV, you may discard the rope and find a clear spot to set up camp. Do this by sitting in a circle on the floor. There should be no trash inside your circle.

Climb from Camp IV to the Summit

You have now entered the Death Zone. If you can overcome the dangers that still face you, you will soon be on top of the world! Your body can survive at this elevation for only a short time. Let's hope for good weather and a safe journey to the summit!

Step 1: Prepare for the climb.
- Put on your coat.
- Quickly decorate the token (sticky note) that your guide (teacher) gives you. Draw something to represent yourself to future climbers. You will leave your token on the summit—if you are able to reach it!

Step 2: Get your team together.
- Roll the die to determine the weather. If your team rolls a 1, 2, 3, or 4, you have good weather and can attempt to reach the summit. If you roll a 5 or 6, you have bad weather and will not be able to climb to the summit.
- If your team has good weather, line up on the trail with your token. You will make this climb individually. You do not have to stay with the other members of your team.

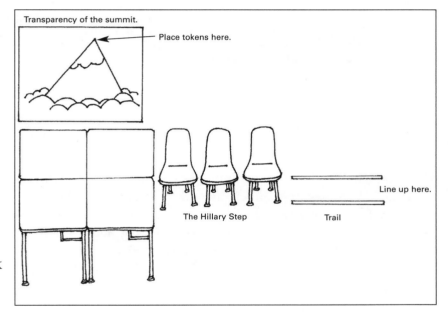

Step 3: Climb from Camp IV to the Summit.
- The chairs represent a 40-foot-high rock cliff known as the Hillary Step. This is the last obstacle before you reach the summit. One at a time, climb onto the Hillary Step. Once the first climber leaves the Hillary Step, the next in line can climb onto the Hillary Step. Expect the route to get crowded as more and more climbers make their way to and from the summit.
- Climb onto the summit. Place your token on the top of Mount Everest (the projected image).
- Climb down from the summit through the Hillary Step.
- Remember that you are in the Death Zone and can survive only for a certain amount of time. When your guide tells you that time is up, you must stop climbing.

29.3 From Lukla to Base Camp

1. On the map, color the route from Lukla to Base Camp. Also fill in the elevations.

   Starting elevation: __9,350__ feet

   Ending elevation: __17,600__ feet

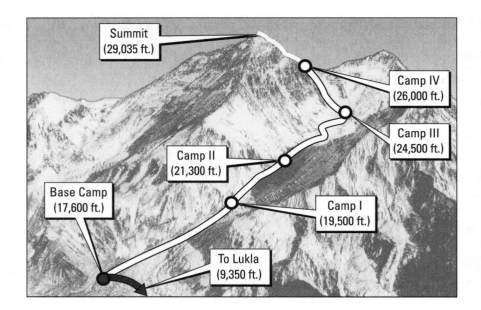

Summit
(29,035 ft.)

Camp IV
(26,000 ft.)

Camp III
(24,500 ft.)

Camp II
(21,300 ft.)

Base Camp
(17,600 ft.)

Camp I
(19,500 ft.)

To Lukla
(9,350 ft.)

2. Why is it important for climbers to acclimatize? Climbers who don't acclimatize may show signs of altitude sickness, such as nausea and headaches. In severe cases, this can cause fluid in the lungs, brain swelling, and even death.

3. What positive effects have climbing expeditions and tourism had on Nepal? What negative effects have they had? Tourism brings in money as tourists pay for food, lodging, supplies, and porters. But some porters are overworked and mistreated. And cutting down trees for building and fuel has led to deforestation and erosion.

4. Compare what you just read to your classroom experience. List at least two similarities and two differences.

Similarities	Differences
Answers will vary.	

29.4 From Base Camp to Camp I

1. Color the route from Base Camp to Camp I, and fill in the elevations.

   Starting elevation: 17,600 feet

   Ending elevation: 19,500 feet

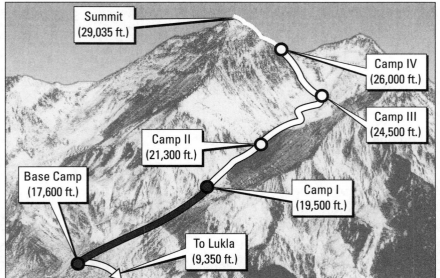

2. Why is the Khumbu Icefall the most dangerous part of the climb up Everest? More climbers have died on the Khumbu Icefall than on any other part of the mountain. Some people have been crushed by shifting seracs, some have fallen into crevasses, and some have been swept down the mountain by avalanches.

3. What role do Sherpas play on Everest expeditions? Sherpas act as guides, cooks, and porters. They set up camp and carry supplies. They go through the icefall first to set up ladders and ropes.

4. Compare what you just read to your classroom experience. List at least two similarities and two differences.

Similarities	Differences
Answers will vary.	

29.5 From Camp I to Camp IV

1. Color the route from Camp I to Camp IV, and fill in the elevations.

   Starting elevation: **19,500** feet

   Ending elevation: **26,000** feet

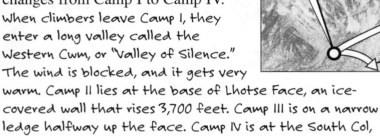

2. Describe how the physical geography changes from Camp I to Camp IV. When climbers leave Camp I, they enter a long valley called the Western Cwm, or "Valley of Silence." The wind is blocked, and it gets very warm. Camp II lies at the base of Lhotse Face, an ice-covered wall that rises 3,700 feet. Camp III is on a narrow ledge halfway up the face. Camp IV is at the South Col, a saddle between the face and the summit.

3. What is being done to clean up Mount Everest? Groups of climbers have scaled the mountain to bring down trash. Nepal's government charges climbers a fee to use the mountain, part of which goes to cleanup. Climbing groups must also leave a $4,000 garbage deposit, which they lose if they don't carry their trash off the mountain. Nepal is also working to reduce deforestation.

4. Compare what you just read to your classroom experience. List at least two similarities and two differences.

Similarities	Differences
Answers will vary.	

29.6 From Camp IV to Summit

1. Color the route from Camp IV to the summit, and fill in the elevations.

   Starting elevation: 26,000   feet

   Ending elevation: 29,035   feet

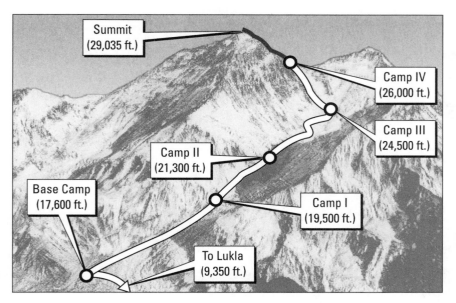

Summit (29,035 ft.)

Camp IV (26,000 ft.)

Camp III (24,500 ft.)

Camp II (21,300 ft.)

Camp I (19,500 ft.)

Base Camp (17,600 ft.)

To Lukla (9,350 ft.)

2. What difficulties do climbers face in trying to reach the summit?
   Climbers are now in the Death Zone, the most grueling stage of the climb because it's hard to breathe at this elevation. Deep snow, steep drop-offs, and harsh weather make it more difficult.

3. Over the years, how have climbers sought new challenges?
   Some climbers make the ascent without oxygen or do it very rapidly. Some come down the mountain on skis or snowboards. Others climb Everest as part of the Seven Summits Challenge, which involves scaling the tallest mountains on all seven continents.

4. Compare what you just read to your classroom experience. List at least two similarities and two differences.

Similarities	Differences
Answers will vary.	

China: The World's Most Populous Country

Overview

In this lesson, students learn about the ways China has tried to address the challenges created by its large and increasing population. In a **Response Group** activity, students assume the roles of demographers attending a conference on population. They learn about and analyze three plans implemented by the Chinese government to meet the challenges presented by its growing population and then explore whether they would recommend each plan for countries facing similar challenges.

Objectives

Students will

- define and explain the importance of these key geographic terms: *doubling time, famine, rate of natural increase, zero population growth*.
- examine the challenges created by a large and growing population.
- analyze the steps taken by China to meet its challenges as the world's most populous country.
- investigate ways in which rapidly growing countries around the world might address the challenges created by their expanding populations.

Materials

- *Geography Alive! Regions and People*
- Interactive Student Notebooks
- Transparencies 30A–30E
- Information Master 30 (1 transparency)
- transparency pens

Preview

1 Conduct a quick activity to demonstrate the size of China's population. Have all students stand up. Explain that they now represent the population of the world, which in 2005 was 6.5 billion people. (**Note:** You may want to ask them to calculate approximately how many people each of them represents.) Have students count off from 1 to 5, and then ask all but the 1s to sit down. Explain that those who remain standing represent the population of China. In 2005, the population of China was 1.3 billion, or one of every five people in the world.

2 Project *Transparency 30A: Preview 30*. Have students analyze the circle graph of world population by asking,

- What percent of the world's population lives in China?
- What is the next most populous country? What percent of the world's population lives there?
- What other countries are listed? What percent of the world's population lives in each of those countries?
- What percent of the world's population lives in the rest of the world?
- What are some challenges the five most populated countries might face? (**Note:** As an example, consider mentioning that China has only 7% of all the land in the world suitable for growing crops yet must feed 20% of the world's population.)
- What additional challenges might these countries face if their large populations were also growing at a fast rate? (**Note:** You may want to use the Global Databank to share the annual population growth from births and deaths for China, India, the United States, Indonesia, and Brazil.)

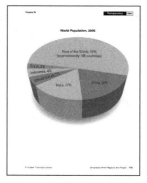

Transparency 30A

3 Explain the connection between the Preview and the upcoming activity. Explain that just as students predicted, it is not easy to support a large and growing population. People need food, clean water, a place to live, jobs, education, health care, and much more. It is a difficulty familiar to China—a country that saw its already large population double between 1950 and 1990. In the upcoming activity, students will examine the challenges created by a large and growing population. They will also learn about the steps that China, as the world's most populous country, has taken to address such challenges.

Essential Question and Geoterms

1 Introduce Chapter 30 in *Geography Alive! Regions and People*. Explain that in this chapter, students will learn how China has tried to meet the challenges created by its large and growing population. Have students read Section 30.1. Then ask them to identify details in the photograph that represent ideas in the text they just read.

2 Introduce the Graphic Organizer and the Essential Question. Have students examine the bar graph. Ask,

- What do you see?
- What does the graph show?
- Over what time periods did China's population grow most quickly?
- What is the approximate size of China's population today?
- What challenges might China face as the world's most populous country?

Have students read the accompanying text. Make sure they understand the Essential Question, *How does a country meet the challenges created by a large and growing population?* You may want to post the Essential Question in the room or write it on the board for the duration of the activity.

3 Have students read Section 30.2. Then have them complete Geoterms 30 in their Interactive Student Notebooks, individually or in pairs. Have them share their answers with another student, or have volunteers share their answers with the class.

Geoterms 30

Response Group

1 Place students in mixed-ability groups of three. You may want to prepare a transparency that shows them with whom they will work and where they will sit. Have them arrange their desks so that group members can both talk among themselves and clearly see the board.

2 Introduce the activity. Explain to students that in this activity, they will take on the role of demographers. Demographers study human populations, looking for trends and how populations change over time. As demographers, they will attend a "conference" to learn about the challenges China has faced with its large and growing population and about the plans China has implemented to try to address those challenges. After reading about the impact of each plan, students discuss whether they would recommend these plans for countries facing similar challenges.

3 Begin the conference by projecting *Transparency 30B: Plan One*. Have students analyze the image by asking,

- What do you see?
- What is the size of the family pictured here?
- How might you describe this family's living standard?
- How might that living standard change if the size of this family increased?
- This photograph represents the Chinese government's response to a challenge it faced. What challenge do you think this is? What steps might China have taken to address this challenge?

Transparency 30B

4 Have students read and take notes on Section 30.3 to learn about China's plan to slow population growth. Have students open their Interactive Student Notebooks to Reading Notes 30. Review the directions with them. Here are some tips for helping them complete the Reading Notes for Section 30.3:

- *Step 1:* After students draw and label a vertical line on the graph to represent the year the one-child policy began, you might ask them to estimate China's population at the time.
- *Step 3:* When each group finishes their lists, use Guide to Reading Notes 30 to check that they have included all the important benefits and costs. (**Note:** Alternatively, review these answers as a class.)
- *Step 4:* Groups should discuss whether they would recommend this plan for meeting the challenges created by a large and growing population. They should be prepared to defend why they marked the spectrum as they did by explaining the benefits and the costs of the one-child policy.

Reading Notes 30

5 Appoint a Presenter for each group. Explain that the role of Presenter will rotate with each plan.

6 Assign each group a number, and have students share their decisions on a transparency of *Information Master 30: Conference Spectrum*. Place the transparency on the projector. Before turning the projector on, have each Presenter come up and write the group's number on the appropriate place along the spectrum. Then turn on the projector and reveal the opinions of the various groups.

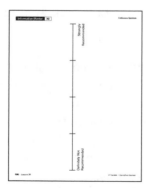

Information Master 30

7 Call on Presenters to explain their spectrum placement to the other demographers at the conference. Remind them to support their group's placement by pointing out the benefits and costs of the one-child policy in China.

8 Repeat Steps 3–7 for the remaining two plans. Make these modifications:

- *Plan Two:* Display *Transparency 30C: Plan Two* and ask, *What do you see? Along what type of body of water is this structure located? What do you think is being built here? What purposes do hydroelectric dams serve? What challenge do you think this photograph represents? What steps might China have taken to address this challenge?* Then have students read and complete the Reading Notes for Section 30.4 to learn about the plan to increase the supply of clean energy.

- *Plan Three:* Project *Transparency 30D: Plan Three* and ask, *What do you see? What is this worker making? Where might this product be sold? What benefits do factories like this one bring to a country? What challenge do you think this photograph represents? What steps might China have taken to address this challenge?* Then have students read and complete the Reading Notes for Section 30.5 to learn about the plan to promote economic development.

Transparency 30C   **Transparency 30D**

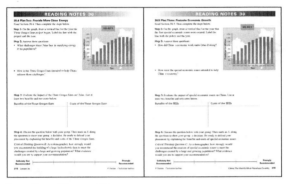

Reading Notes 30

9 Debrief the activity by asking the questions that follow. (**Note:** Alternatively, create a "conference evaluation form" using these questions, and have students complete it individually. You might also use this opportunity to have students evaluate their presentation skills.)

- What challenges were created by China's large and growing population?

- In what ways has China tried to address those challenges?

- Which of these plans has been the most effective? Why?

- Which of these plans has been the least effective? Why?

- How might China's experience help other countries with large and growing populations to meet their challenges?

Global Connections

1 Introduce the Global Connections. Have students read Section 30.6. Then explain that they will now learn about how countries around the world address the challenges created by their population size and rate of growth.

2 Project *Transparency 30E: Global Connections.* Have students analyze the map by discussing and sharing their answers to the questions below. Use the additional information to enrich the discussion.

- **What interesting details do you see on this map?**

- **Which areas of the world are experiencing a high rate of natural increase? A low rate of natural increase?**

Transparency 30E

China: The World's Most Populous Country   **673**

- **What are some challenges that countries with a high rate of natural increase might face?**

  At a 2% rate of natural increase, a country's population will double in 35 years. At a 2.5% rate, it doubles in 28 years. At a 3% rate, the doubling time is only 23 years. Niger, for example, is growing so quickly that its population of 12 million (2004) is expected to reach 53 million people by the year 2050. Once a population doubles, there will be twice as many people to feed, provide jobs for, and educate. Twice as many people will use the country's water and natural resources and need access to health care. This is just a sampling of the challenges that might face countries with a rapid rate of natural increase.

3 Have students read Section 30.7 and analyze the additional information in the section. Then ask these questions:

- **How might money spent on health care affect a country's rate of natural increase?**

  With better health care, infant mortality rate drops. Costa Rica, for example, spent $743 per person on health care in 2002. From 1995 to 2003, 98% of births there were attended by a skilled health professional. In 2003, the infant mortality rate in Costa Rica was 8 per 1,000 live births. Guatemala, by contrast, spent $199 per person on health care in 2002. Only 41% of births from 1995 to 2003 were attended by a skilled health professional. And the 2005 estimated infant mortality rate in Guatemala was 36 per 1,000 live births.

  Life expectancy rises with better care, and parents worry less that their children won't survive childhood. In Guatemala from 1995 to 2003, 23% of children under age 5 were underweight for their age, and 49% were underheight. In Costa Rica, on the other hand, only 5% of children under age 5 were underweight, and only 6% were underheight. When children are more likely to survive, parents may decide to have fewer of them. In Guatemala, the rate of natural increase in 2004 was 2.8%. In Costa Rica, it was 1.4%.

- **How might money spent on educating women affect a country's rate of natural increase?**

  Women who are educated generally have more control over the number of children they have. Educated women often marry later. They may put off having children to focus on a career. A 2003 study of Nigeria is revealing. Of women age 20 to 24 living in the country's southeastern region, 87.5% had seven or more years of education. Only 22.4% of these women married before the age of 20, and 9.3% gave birth before age 20. The northwestern region of Nigeria tells a different story. Only 19.7% of women age 20 to 24 had seven or more years of education. Some 89.1% married before the age of 20, and 71.7% gave birth before age 20.

When educated women do have children, they usually have fewer than do women who lack education. In Cambodia, 19% of eligible females were enrolled in secondary school for the 2002–2003 school year. In 2003, the literacy rate of women over age 15 was 64.1%. The total fertility rate (births per woman) from 2000 to 2005 was 4.1. Indonesia, on the other hand, saw 54% of its eligible females enrolled in secondary school for the 2002–2003 school year. The 2003 literacy rate of women over age 15 was 83.4%. The total fertility rate in Indonesia from 2000 to 2005 was 2.4. Indonesia had a 1.6% rate of natural increase in 2004, while Cambodia had a 2.2% rate.

- **How might a country with rapid population growth benefit by slowing its rate of natural increase?**

Processing

Have students complete Processing 30 in their Interactive Student Notebooks. Review the directions with them, and answer any questions they have.

Online Resources

For more information on China and population growth, refer students to Online Resources for *Geography Alive! Regions and People* at www.teachtci.com.

Assessment

Masters for assessment appear on the next three pages followed by answers and scoring rubrics.

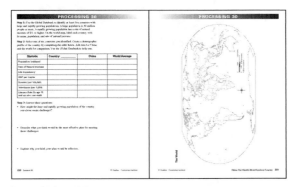

Processing 30

Assessment ▌30▐

Mastering the Content

Shade in the oval by the letter of the best answer for each question.

1. What does a country's rate of natural increase indicate?
   - ○ A. how much energy it uses each year
   - ○ B. how many babies are born there each year
   - ○ C. how fast its population is growing each year
   - ○ D. how many businesses start there each year

2. Which statement about China is **best** supported by the bar graph below?

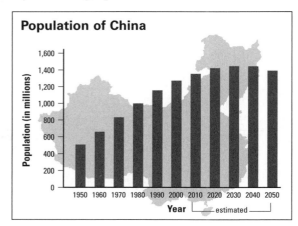

   - ○ A. Its population peaked between 1990 and 2000.
   - ○ B. Its population will begin to decline after 2010.
   - ○ C. Its population will continue to grow until 2050.
   - ○ D. Its population doubled between 1950 and 1990.

3. According to the bar graph above, when did China's population first reach 1 billion?
   - ○ A. in the 1970s   ○ C. in the 1990s
   - ○ B. in the 1980s   ○ D. in the 2000s

4. The Three Gorges Dam is expected to provide all of these benefits **except**
   - ○ A. clean energy.   ○ C. safer river shipping.
   - ○ B. flood control.   ○ D. more steel production.

5. What is the **main** goal of China's one-child policy?
   - ○ A. less spatial inequality
   - ○ B. lower infant mortality
   - ○ C. zero population growth
   - ○ D. increased life expectancy

6. Which of these policies has been **most** successful in increasing China's gross domestic product?
   - ○ A. the Cultural Revolution
   - ○ B. special economic zones
   - ○ C. the Great Leap Forward
   - ○ D. zero population growth

7. Which conclusion is best supported by this population pyramid?

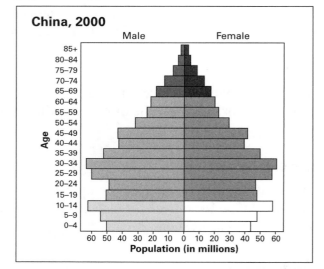

   - ○ A. There were more boys under age 5 than girls.
   - ○ B. There were more people over 70 than under 20.
   - ○ C. There were more children under age 14 than adults.
   - ○ D. There were more retired people than working people.

8. Special economic zones attract more foreign business than other parts of China because they offer companies that locate there
   - ○ A. cleaner air.   ○ C. cheaper energy.
   - ○ B. greater freedom.   ○ D. warmer weather.

Applying Geography Skills:
Drawing Conclusions from Multiple Maps

Use these maps and your knowledge of geography to complete the tasks below.

HDI Rank by Province

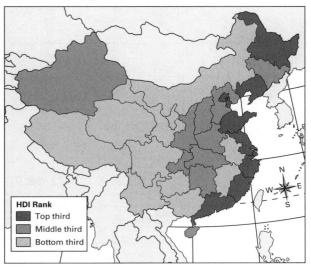

Special Economic Zones

These maps show special economic zones (SEZs) and the Human Development Index (HDI) rankings of China's provinces. Remember, the HDI ranking of a place is based on per capita GDP, life expectancy, and education level of its people.

1. Examine the map that shows the HDI ranking of China's provinces. Draw an outline around the top-rated provinces to create a high HDI-ranking region.

2. Examine the map that shows the location of some of China's SEZs. Draw an outline around the SEZs on the map to create an SEZ region.

3. Compare your SEZ region to your high HDI-ranking region. Draw a conclusion about the relationship of SEZs and HDI rankings based on what you see.

> **Test Terms Glossary**
> A **conclusion** is a judgment reached after looking at the facts.

Exploring the Essential Question

How does a country meet the challenges created by a large and growing population?

In Chapter 30, you explored how China is dealing with a very large population. Now you will use what you learned to analyze the information below.

Health Care Spending and GDP in Eight Countries, 2004

	Rate of Natural Increase							
	Rapid		Moderate		Slow		Negative	
Country, Rate	Laos, 2.4%	Uganda, 3.0%	Algeria, 1.5%	Panama, 1.8%	South Korea, 0.5%	Uruguay, 0.6%	Czech Republic, −0.2%	Germany, −0.2%
Per Person Spending on Health Care*	$49	$57	$169	$458	$948	$948	$1,129	$2,820
Per Capita GDP*	$1,759	$1,390	$5,740	$6,170	$16,950	$7,830	$15,780	$27,100

*Data computed in U.S. dollars.

The Task: Comparing Countries with Different Rates of Natural Increase

The tables above and to the right present information about eight countries. Your task is to compare data about two of these countries.

Step 1: Choose two countries in the top table to compare. One should have a rapid or moderate rate of natural increase. The other should have a slow or negative rate. Circle the two countries on both tables.

Step 2: Use the table at the lower right to estimate the doubling time for the two countries you chose.

Step 3: On another sheet of paper, write a short essay comparing the two countries you chose. Your essay should include the following:

- a topic sentence that identifies your two countries
- the rate of natural increase and estimated doubling time of the two countries
- a comparison of wealth, heath care spending, and female education in the two countries
- a conclusion that summarizes what your comparison shows about population growth and living standard

Females Enrolled in Secondary Schools, 2004

Laos	32%
Uganda	13%
Algeria	64%
Panama	65%
South Korea	89%
Uruguay	76%
Czech Republic	90%
Germany	88%

Natural Increase and Doubling Time

Rate of Natural Increase	Doubling Time (years)
3%	23
2%	35
1%	70
0%	no doubling time

Applying Geography Skills: Sample Responses

1. HDI Rank by Province

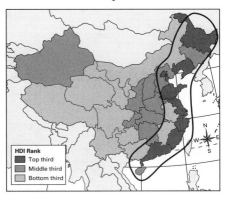

2. Special Economic Zones

3. Many of the areas with the highest HDI rankings are areas where SEZs have created new jobs and wealth in China.

Exploring the Essential Question: Sample Response

Step 1: Students should circle the same two countries on both tables. The two countries should have different rates of natural increase.

Step 2: Answers will depend on choice of countries but should fall in these ranges:

- Rapid growth: less than 35 years
- Moderate growth: 35–70 years
- Slow growth: more than 70 years
- Negative growth: no doubling time

Step 3: Essays should include all the elements listed in the prompt.

> Uganda and Germany are about as different as any two countries could be. Uganda has a rapid rate of natural increase and a doubling time of 23 years. Germany, in contrast, has a negative rate of natural increase and is not growing at all. Uganda is a poor country. Incomes are low. The government does not spend much money on health care or education for women. Compared to Uganda, Germany is a wealthy country with good health care and educational opportunities for women. These differences point to a strong relationship between population growth and the wealth of a country. The lower the rate of natural increase, the better off a country and its people are likely to be.

Applying Geography Skills Scoring Rubric

Score	General Description
2	Student responds to all parts of the task. Response is correct and clear.
1	Student responds to some parts of the task. Response is mostly correct.
0	Response does not match the task or is incorrect.

Exploring the Essential Question Scoring Rubric

Score	General Description
3	Student responds to all parts of the task. Response is correct, clear, and supported by details.
2	Student responds to most or all parts of the task. Response is generally correct but may lack details.
1	Student responds to at least one part of the task. Response may contain errors and lack details.
0	Response does not match the task or is incorrect.

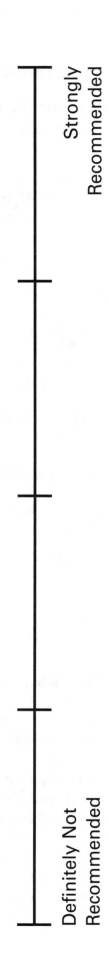

Strongly Recommended

Definitely Not Recommended

30.3 Plan One: Slow Population Growth

Read Section 30.3. Then complete the steps below.

Step 1: On the graph, draw a vertical line for the year the one-child policy began. Label the line with the policy and the year.

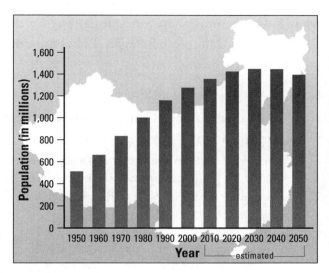

Step 2: Answer these questions:

• What was the Great Leap Forward? What challenges did it create for China?

In 1958, Mao launched the Great Leap Forward to change China into a modern industrial country. Two of its goals were to increase steel and food production. Unfortunately, there was little increase in production, and there were severe droughts across China. More than 30 million people died between 1958 and 1962 during a famine. These deaths were a reminder that China could not continue to support its rapidly growing population.

• How does the one-child policy try to address the challenges created by China's large and growing population?

The one-child policy limits parents to or encourages parents to have only one child. This moves China toward zero population growth.

Step 3: Evaluate the impact of the one-child policy on China. List at least two benefits and two costs below.

Benefits of the One-Child Policy	Costs of the One-Child Policy
Possible answers: • The policy slowed population growth. • The policy reduced strain on food and water supplies. • Mothers and babies tend to be healthier in smaller families.	Possible answers: • People don't want to be told how many children they can have. • Many people want a son if they can have only one child. • There are fewer children to care for older family members.

Step 4: Discuss the question below with your group. Then mark an X along the spectrum to show your group's decision. Be ready to defend your placement by explaining the benefits and costs of the one-child policy.

Critical Thinking Question A: As a demographer, how strongly would you recommend the use of the one-child policy to meet the challenges created by a large and growing population? What evidence would you use to support your recommendation?

Definitely Not Recommended |————————————————————————————| Strongly Recommended

30.4 Plan Two: Provide More Clean Energy

Read Section 30.4. Then complete the steps below.

Step 1: On the graph, draw a vertical line for the year the Three Gorges Dam project began. Label the line with the project and the year.

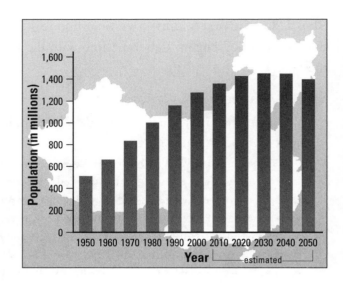

Step 2: Answer these questions:

• What challenges does China face in supplying energy to its population?

China is the second-largest consumer of energy in the world. As its population grows, its energy needs will grow. The country has large deposits of coal, but coal is not a clean energy source.

• How is the Three Gorges Dam intended to help China address those challenges?

The Three Gorges Dam will provide hydroelectric power, a clean energy source. When it is finished in 2009, it will provide up to one ninth of China's electricity.

Step 3: Evaluate the impact of the Three Gorges Dam on China. List at least two benefits and two costs below.

Benefits of the Three Gorges Dam	Costs of the Three Gorges Dam
Possible answers: • The dam will provide energy without polluting the air. • The dam will provide flood control. • River shipping will be safer. • The dam will provide safer boat travel and shipping.	Possible answers: • Hundreds of archeological sites will be lost. • Cities and towns will be submerged. • The dam will change the river's ecosystem. • The dam sits on an earthquake fault, creating the risk of a catastrophic flood if it fails.

Step 4: Discuss the question below with your group. Then mark an X along the spectrum to show your group's decision. Be ready to defend your placement by explaining the benefits and costs of the Three Gorges Dam.

Critical Thinking Question B: As a demographer, how strongly would you recommend the building of a large hydroelectric dam to meet the challenges created by a large and growing population? What evidence would you use to support your recommendation?

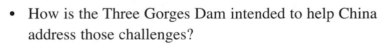

Definitely Not Recommended   Strongly Recommended

30.5 Plan Three: Promote Economic Growth

Read Section 30.5. Then complete the steps below.

Step 1: On the graph, draw a vertical line for the year that the first special economic zones were created. Label the line with the policy and the year.

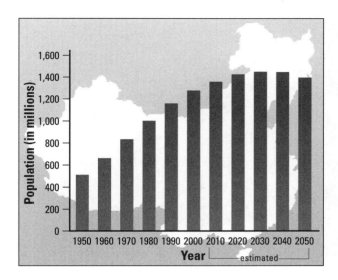

Step 2: Answer these questions:

- How did China's economy work under Mao Zedong?

    Mao's goal was to make China self-sufficient. His government controlled the economy. Government officials decided what should be produced and at what price. They controlled who should do what job and for what pay.

- How were the special economic zones intended to help China's economy?

    After Mao's death, China's leaders wanted to open the country's economy to the rest of the world. They hoped foreign companies would set up businesses there, creating jobs and economic growth. SEZs have laws that differ from those in the rest of the country. Businesses there can decide what to produce and at what price.

Step 3: Evaluate the impact of special economic zones on China. List at least two benefits and two costs below.

Benefits of the SEZs	Costs of the SEZs
Possible answers: • SEZs have brought economic growth. • SEZs have created millions of new jobs. • Extra money means people enjoy a higher standard of living.	Possible answers: • SEZs have widened the income gap between rich and poor. • SEZs have created a "floating population" of migrant workers.

Step 4: Discuss the question below with your group. Then mark an X along the spectrum to show your group's decision. Be ready to defend your placement by explaining the benefits and costs of special economic zones.

Critical Thinking Question C: As a demographer, how strongly would you recommend the creation of special economic zones to meet the challenges created by a large and growing population? What evidence would you use to support your recommendation?

Definitely Not Recommended |———————|———————|———————|———————| **Strongly Recommended**

Population Density in Japan: Life in a Crowded Country

Overview

In this lesson, students learn about the effects of population density. In an **Experiential Exercise,** they use their bodies and varying amounts of floor space to simulate the population densities of Australia, the United States, and Japan. They then read about and analyze the effects of population density on life in Japan and around the world.

Objectives

Students will

- define and explain the importance of these key geographic terms: *arable land, arithmetic population density, physiologic population density, population distribution.*
- describe how population density affects various aspects of life in Japan.
- analyze how population density affects life in their own community and around the world.

Materials

- *Geography Alive! Regions and People*
- Interactive Student Notebooks
- Transparencies 31A–31D
- Information Master 31 (1 transparency)
- $8\frac{1}{2}''$ x 11" sheets of scrap paper
- masking tape

Preview

1 Project *Transparency 31A: Map of Japan.* Have students turn to Preview 31 in their Interactive Student Notebooks and work in pairs to complete Step 1.

2 Discuss students' facts about Japan. Ask volunteers to step forward to share their facts and to point to the part of the map that supports their ideas. Students might share such facts as these:
- Japan is relatively small.
- Japan is a very mountainous country.
- Japan is an island nation.

3 Have students complete Steps 2 and 3 of the Preview. Then lead a discussion about their predictions for the locations of Japan's largest cities and the reasoning behind their predictions.

4 Project *Transparency 31B: Japan at Night.* Discuss these questions:
- From where and at what time of day was this image taken? *from a satellite above Earth at night*
- What countries can be seen in this image? (Have students consult a physical map, if necessary, to identify the countries shown.) *Japan, China, North Korea, South Korea, Vietnam, Laos, Thailand, Cambodia, and the Philippines*
- What do the bright areas represent? *areas where more people live* The dark areas? *areas where fewer people live*
- What major city or cities in China can be seen on the map? *Beijing* In Korea? *Seoul* In Japan? *Tokyo, Osaka, Nagoya, Yokohama, and Sapporo*
- What do you notice about Japan's mountainous areas? Are they heavily populated? *Mountainous areas show far less settlement than lowland areas.*
- Are Japan's lowlands heavily populated? *Much of Japan's lowlands show great concentrations of people.*
- The five most populated cities in Japan are Tokyo, Osaka, Nagoya, Yokohama, and Sapporo. How do their locations match your predictions? *Answers will vary. You may want students to label their maps with these major cities.*
- Generally, where is most of the settlement in Japan? *in the lowlands, near bays and inlets*
- Why might settlement have occurred in this pattern? *It is harder to build or farm in Japan's mountainous areas. Ocean resources and trade have been strong magnets for settlement in the country. Agriculture, especially cultivated rice, is also more productive in lowland areas.*

Transparency 31A

Preview 31

Transparency 31B

5 **Make a connection between the Preview and the upcoming activity.** Tell students that Japan is a country with a high population density. *Population density* is a term geographers use to talk about where on Earth's surface people live. Some places, like Japan, are densely populated. Millions of people live there. Other places, such as Antarctica, are sparsely populated. Few people live there.

Japan is one of the most densely populated places in the world. The country is slightly smaller than California, but its population is roughly half that of the United States. In addition, the vast majority of people who live in Japan are settled in only about 16% of the country, in the lowlands. Japan is a crowded place.

Tell students that in this activity they will learn how population density affects life in Japan and around the world.

Essential Question and Geoterms

1 **Introduce Chapter 31 in** *Geography Alive! Regions and People.* Explain that in this chapter, students will learn how population density affects life in Japan and ways geographers measure how crowded a country is by its arable land, population distribution, and arithmetic and physiologic population densities. Have students read Section 31.1. Then ask them to examine the photograph (which shows a swimming park in Tokyo), and ask,

- What do you see in this picture?
- What can this image tell us about life in Japan?

2 **Introduce the Graphic Organizer and the Essential Question.** Have students examine the diagram. Ask,

- What do you see?
- What do the red dots on the map represent?
- According to this diagram, what areas of life does population density influence?
- What other aspects of life might be affected by population density?

Have students read the accompanying text. Make sure they understand the Essential Question, *How does population density affect the way people live?* You may want to post the Essential Question in the classroom or write it on the board for the duration of the activity.

3 **Have students read Section 31.2.** Then have them work individually or in pairs to complete Geoterms 31 in their Interactive Student Notebooks. Have them share their answers with another student, or have volunteers share their answers with the class.

Geoterms 31

Experiential Exercise

1 Explain the purpose of the activity. Tell students that this activity is designed to allow them to discover how Japan's population distribution and physical geography influence life there. (**Note:** During the activity, help students understand that the unique aspects of Japanese culture are only partially a by-product of the country's population density; religion, climate, historical events, topography, and proximity to China and Korea are some of the many other factors influencing Japanese life.)

2 Have students move the desks to the periphery of the classroom.

3 Project a transparency of *Information Master 31: Population Density Table* **and ask students to simulate the population density of Australia.** Follow these steps:

Information Master 31

- Reveal the portion of the table that shows Australia's total land area only. (**Note:** Use sticky notes or paper to cover and then reveal specific pieces of data throughout this activity.)

- Reveal the population of Australia, and have students use calculators to compute the arithmetic population density of Australia. Then reveal the answer.

- Spread out 29 sheets of paper on the floor. Explain that they represent Australia's total land area, 2,941,283 square miles. (Each sheet represents approximately 100,000 square miles.)

- Ask two students to stand "in Australia." Ask, *How does it feel to have so much space to yourselves? What three words or phrases would you use to describe this situation? Why did you choose to stand in that particular spot?*

- Quickly reveal this information about Australia: *Australia is an island continent lying between the Indian and Pacific oceans. Covering an area of nearly 3 million square miles, Australia is primarily a flat, low-lying plateau with about 95 percent of its land standing less than 1,970 feet above sea level. About 85 percent of Australia's 20 million people live in urban areas located on a coastal plain, which extends along most of Australia's coast. The population density of Australia is about 6.7 people per square mile.*

4 Have students simulate the population density of the United States.

- Reveal the portion of the table that shows the United States' total land area.

- Reveal the population of the United States, and have students calculate the arithmetic density of the United States. Then reveal the answer.

- Add 6 sheets of paper to those in the center of the room. Tell students that the paper now represents the total land area in the United States, 3.5 million square miles.

- Ask 29 students to stand "in the United States." Ask, *How do you feel? What three words or phrases would you use to describe this situation? Why are you standing where you are? In terms of population, what is it like in the United States compared to Australia?*

- Quickly reveal this information about the United States: *The land area of the United States is 3,537,418 square miles, making it the fourth largest nation in the world. The most salient feature of the physical geography of the United States is probably its great variety—its environment ranges from moist rainforest to arid desert, from mountain peaks to flat prairie. Of the 293 million people who live in the United States, about 75% live in urban areas, and the overall population density is about 84 inhabitants per square mile.*

5 Have students simulate the population density of Japan.

- Reveal the portion of the table that shows Japan's total land area.

- Reveal the population of the Japan, and have students calculate the arithmetic density of the Japan. Then reveal the answer.

- Dramatically remove all but one of the sheets of paper from the floor.

- Ask 13 students to stand "in Japan." (They won't all be able to stand on the paper, so ask that all of them put at least some part of their bodies "in Japan.") Ask, *How do you feel? What three words or phrases would you use to describe this situation? Why are you standing where you are? What is it like in Japan compared to Australia? Compared to the United States? What geography terminology have you learned that will help describe this situation?*

- Remind students that they simulated arithmetic density, not physiologic density. Use the table to review the difference by uncovering "Percentage of Arable Land," "Arable Land Area," and "Physiologic Population Density" for Australia, the United States, and Japan.

- Pick up the sheet of paper and fold it to create eight equal-size rectangles. Tear off one rectangle, hold it up, and explain that this represents the physiographic density of Japan, one of the most densely populated countries on earth. Place it the center of the room, and ask students to gather around it. Then ask them to discuss adaptations people might make to live in such relatively small areas.

6 Have students simulate a tightly packed subway car in Tokyo at rush hour. Tell students that population density affects life in Japan in a variety of ways. One interesting example is subway crowding. Then follow these steps:

- Use masking tape to mark off one square meter in a corner of the room.

- Project *Transparency 31C: Subway Crowding*. Reveal the first row of the diagram, which shows the typical number of passengers in one square meter of a subway car at rush hour in Hamburg, Germany. Ask three students to step into the square on the floor. Explain that this represents how crowded a subway car is at rush hour in Hamburg.

- One at a time, reveal the information about the other four cities, each time inviting the appropriate number of students to step into the taped-off area until there are nine students crammed into the one square meter. This represents the crowding on a Tokyo subway car at rush hour.

- Have students return to their seats, and reveal the photograph at the bottom of Transparency 31C. Explain that this is a scene from a Tokyo subway station. Ask, *What is the man outside the subway car doing? Why might he do this?* Explain that Tokyo subways are so crowded at certain times of the day that people are hired to push passengers into the cars. Then ask, *How might it feel to board a subway at rush hour in Tokyo? What qualities might help the Japanese deal with this sort of crowding?* Tell students that social etiquette and manners are stressed more in Japan than in Australia or the United States. The Japanese have developed a social structure, with systematic ways of interacting, that minimizes interpersonal strife and makes it possible for people to live in crowded conditions while minimizing serious conflict.

Tell students that overcrowded subways are just one way in which population density affects life there. In the next segment of the activity, they will learn how population density affects other areas of life in Japan.

7 Have students read Sections 31.3 to 31.6 and complete the corresponding Reading Notes. For each section, students make predictions about the effects of population density on life in Japan. They then read to discover whether their predictions hold up. Consider one of these three ways to complete this reading:

- Have students complete all of the readings on their own or with a partner.

- Complete the readings one at a time as a class. Have students make predictions, and then discuss the information after they have completed each reading section.

Transparency 31C

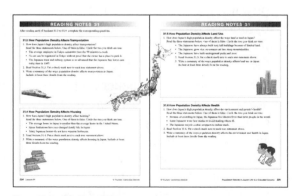

Reading Notes 31

- Have students complete predictions for all four sections of the Reading Notes. Then jigsaw the reading so that one fourth of the class completes each of the four sections and is prepared to report. Then put students into mixed groups and have them assist one another in completing the Reading Notes.

Global Connections

1 Introduce the Global Connections. Tell students that population density affects life not only in Japan but in every other nation around the world. Explain that now they will examine ways that population density affects other areas of the world. Have students read Section 31.7.

2 Project *Transparency 31D: Global Connections* **and lead a class discussion.** Help students analyze the information by asking the questions below. Use the additional information given to enrich the discussion.

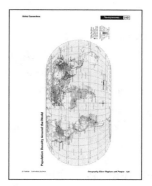

Transparency 31D

- **What are five things you can learn from this map?**

- **Which places on the map are most densely populated? Least densely populated?**
  Some of the most densely populated areas of the world are in Asia. China, India, Japan, and other Asian countries are densely populated—especially in regions rich in agricultural production and industry. Industrialized Western Europe is also densely populated. Two famous areas of high population density in the United States can be observed. One stretches from Washington to Boston and is called the BosWash megalopolis. A megalopolis is a concentration of connected or nearly connected cities. Another area stretches across the southern shore of the Great Lakes from Detroit to Chicago. More and more, Americans are moving to locations with mild climates, such as Nevada, Arizona, and California. Sparsely populated areas can be observed at extreme northern or southern latitudes. Also, desert regions like those seen in Northern Africa, the Arabian Peninsula, and parts of the American West have lower population densities. The hot, dry Australian outback is also a place where few people live.

- **What might explain why one place has high population density while another has low population density?**
  The map shows that most people are concentrated on a small percentage of land. Population is concentrated in locations that are most friendly to human inhabitants. People tend to avoid more difficult environments such as tropical rainforests, deserts, and arctic regions. Interesting facts: Many people live on the shores of lakes and rivers, and most live

within 300 miles of the ocean. People often settle in lowland plains and valleys. The Eastern Hemisphere has more people than the Western Hemisphere. And almost 90% of people reside in the Northern Hemisphere.

3 **Continue the discussion of global population density.**
Place students in mixed-ability pairs, and have them turn to Section 31.8. Ask them to read the information on the left and to examine the rest of the information in this section. Then lead a discussion by asking,

- **What do the tables show?**
  The tables relate population density to two important measures of well-being: life expectancy and per capita income.

- **Can population density affect a nation's well-being?**
  This is difficult to answer. There are places where resources and the environment are heavily stressed by the sheer numbers of people living there. However, some of the most densely populated places are also extremely wealthy. Consider Tokyo, New York, Paris, and Hong Kong. The tables reveal some of these contradictions.

- **Besides population density, what other factors might contribute to a country's well-being?**
  Population density does not tell how rich or how poor an area will be. New York City, in the United States, and New Delhi, in India, are both densely populated cities. One is a wealthy city; the other is a much poorer city. The difference depends on many factors, including availability of resources—such as minerals, oil, water, fertile land, location, climate, economic opportunities, and political stability.

Processing

Have students complete Processing 31 in their Interactive Student Notebooks. (**Note:** Before students complete Processing 31, you may choose to research the total land area and population for your state [see www.census.gov] and fill in those figures on the transparency of the population density table on Information Master 31. With the class, calculate the arithmetic population density of your state and the number of papers and students needed to simulate it. Compare these numbers with those for Australia, the United States, and Japan.)

Processing 31

Online Resources

For more information on population density, refer students to Online Resources for *Geography Alive! Regions and People* at www.teachtci.com.

Assessment

Masters for assessment appear on the next three pages followed by answers and scoring rubrics.

Assessment **31**

Mastering the Content

Shade in the oval by the letter of the best answer for each question.

1. Which of the following physical features has **most** affected Japan's population distribution?
   ○ A. rivers
   ○ B. deltas
   ○ C. deserts
   ○ D. mountains

2. Less than a fifth of Japan is arable land. Which of the following is the **best** definition of *arable land*?
   ○ A. land that is flat
   ○ B. land that is forested
   ○ C. land that can be mined
   ○ D. land that can be farmed

3. The photograph shows a capsule hotel in Japan. Which factor **best** explains the appearance of capsule hotels in Japan?
   ○ A. the filling in of wetlands
   ○ B. the scarcity of land for building
   ○ C. the development of bullet trains
   ○ D. the decrease of extended families

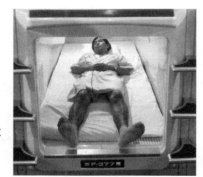

4. The way to calculate a country's physiologic population density is to divide the population by the
   ○ A. total land area.
   ○ B. arable land area.
   ○ C. average family size.
   ○ D. average life expectancy.

5. Which statement **best** describes the impact of high population density on Japan's public transportation system?
   ○ A. Subways and trains seldom run on time.
   ○ B. Subways and trains are overcrowded at rush hour.
   ○ C. Subways and trains are dirty and unpleasant to ride.
   ○ D. Subways and trains do not go where people want to go.

6. The photograph below shows one kind of land use in Japan.

   The fields in this photograph were created by
   ○ A. recycling trash.
   ○ B. filling in wetlands.
   ○ C. terracing hillsides.
   ○ D. building underground.

7. Which of the following statements is true about life expectancy in Japan?
   ○ A. It is among the highest in the world.
   ○ B. It has fallen far behind that of India.
   ○ C. It has dropped as Japan's population has grown.
   ○ D. It is about average among the world's countries.

8. In which of these ways is Japan's population distribution similar to that of the rest of the world?
   ○ A. Most people live in small towns.
   ○ B. Most people live near a coastline.
   ○ C. Most people live near the equator.
   ○ D. Most people live at high elevations.

Applying Geography Skills: Analyzing Tables

Use the tables and your knowledge of geography to complete the tasks below. Write your answers in complete sentences.

Arithmetic Population Density

Country	People per Square Mile of Land
Australia	7
Bangladesh	2,734
Colombia	103
Egypt	198
Japan	880
Netherlands	1,247
Nigeria	390
Singapore	16,492
United States	83

Life Expectancy

Country	Average Life Expectancy (years)
Australia	80
Bangladesh	62
Colombia	71
Egypt	71
Japan	81
Netherlands	79
Nigeria	50
Singapore	82
United States	77

Per Capita Income

Country	Average Income per Person*
Australia	$21,650
Bangladesh	400
Colombia	1,810
Egypt	1,390
Japan	34,510
Netherlands	26,310
Nigeria	320
Singapore	21,230
United States	37,610

*Amounts are in U.S. dollars.

1. Compare Japan and the Netherlands. Identify two ways that these nations are similar to each other.

2. Compare Bangladesh and Nigeria. Identify one way these nations are alike and one way they are different.

3. Decide which factor seems to be most closely related to a nation's life expectancy: its population density or its per capita income. Explain your answer using examples from the tables.

Test Terms Glossary

To **compare** means to consider how two things are similar or different.

To **decide** means to make a choice or come to a conclusion about something.

To **explain** means to make the relationship between two things clear.

Exploring the Essential Question

How does population density affect the way people live?

In Chapter 31, you explored how population density affects life in Japan. Now you will use what you learned. Use the information in the table below and your knowledge of geography to complete this task.

U.S. Census Data, 2000

Type of Data	Alaska	Washington, D.C.
Population to nearest thousand	627,000	572,000
Area (in square miles)	571,951	61
Arithmetic population density	1.1	9,377
Percent of people who own their own homes	62%	41%
Average daily commute time	40 minutes	60 minutes

Source: *U.S. Census Bureau*, "State and County QuickFacts," quickfacts.census.gov.

The Task: Contrasting Places with Different Population Densities

The table contains data on two parts of the United States—Alaska and Washington, D.C. Your task is to write an article contrasting these two places.

Step 1: Examine the table carefully. Circle the two rows that show the greatest differences between Alaska and Washington, D.C.

Step 2: On another sheet of paper, write a three-paragraph article contrasting these two places. Organize your article as follows:

A. In paragraph 1, contrast the population density of Alaska and Washington, D.C. Discuss why the difference is so great.
B. In paragraph 2, contrast homeownership in Alaska and Washington, D.C. Discuss how population density might explain the difference you see in the table.
C. In paragraph 3, contrast commute times in Alaska and Washington, D.C. Discuss how population density might explain the difference you see in the table.

**Writing Tips:
Using Words That
Signal Contrast**

Writers use special signal words when contrasting things. These words tell the reader that two things are different in some way. Words that signal contrast include *but, however, in contrast, compared to, unlike, whereas,* and *on the other hand.*

For example: *Whereas Alaska is thinly populated, Washington, D.C., has a high population density.*

Test Terms Glossary

To **discuss** means to examine a subject in detail.

Applying Geography Skills: Sample Responses

Accurate comparisons not based on the tables should also be accepted.

1. Ways that Japan and the Netherlands are alike:
   • Both have a high population density.
   • Both have a high life expectancy.
   • Both have a high per capita income.

2. Ways that Bangladesh and Nigeria are alike:
   • Both have a low life expectancy.
   • Both have a low per capita income.
   Ways that Bangladesh and Nigeria are different:
   • Bangladesh has a higher population density than Nigeria.
   • Bangladesh is located in Asia; Nigeria is located in Africa.

3. Per capita income seems to be more closely related to life expectancy than population density is. The five nations with life expectancies of 77 or higher also have the highest per capita income, but their population densities vary greatly.

Exploring the Essential Question: Sample Response

Step 1: Students should have circled the "Area" and "Arithmetic population density" rows.

Step 2: The article should include all of the elements listed in the prompt.

The population density of Alaska is very small compared to that of Washington, D.C. The difference is so great because Alaska has a huge area and a relatively small population. As a result, its population density is just over 1 person per square mile. In contrast, Washington, D.C., has a small area of just 61 square miles. Yet more than half a million people are squeezed into this small area. The result is a very high population density.

A greater percentage of people own their own homes in Alaska than in Washington, D.C. Because Alaska has a lot of land, land prices are probably low. This would keep the cost of homes low. Low home prices make it easier for people to buy homes. On the other hand, land in Washington, D.C., is limited. Land costs may be very high. This would drive up home prices and make it harder for people there to buy homes.

The average daily commute time in Alaska is 40 minutes compared to an hour in Washington, D.C. Commute times in Alaska may be shorter because people live near their jobs. Also, the roads may not be as busy. In Washington, D.C., roads are likely to be very crowded during commute times.

Mastering the Content Answer Key

1. D	2. D	3. B	4. B
5. B	6. C	7. A	8. B

Applying Geography Skills Scoring Rubric

Score	General Description
2	Student responds to all parts of the task. Response is correct and clear.
1	Student responds to some parts of the task. Response is mostly correct.
0	Response does not match the task or is incorrect.

Exploring the Essential Question Scoring Rubric

Score	General Description
3	Student responds to all parts of the task. Response is correct, clear, and supported by details.
2	Student responds to most or all parts of the task. Response is generally correct but may lack details.
1	Student responds to at least one part of the task. Response may contain errors and lack details.
0	Response does not match the task or is incorrect.

Population Density Around the World

	Australia	United States	Japan	Your State
Total Land Area (square miles)	2,941,283	3,537,418	144,689	
Papers	29	35	1	
Population	19,913,144	293,027,571	127,333,002	
Students	2	29	13	
Arithmetic Population Density (people per square mile)	6.8	83	880	
Percentage of Arable Land	6.55%	19.13%	12.19%	
Arable Land Area (square miles)	192,654	676,708	17,638	
Physiologic Population Density (people per square mile)	103	433	7,219	

Source: *The World Factbook 2004*, Central Intelligence Agency.

Notes: Each sheet of paper in the "Papers" column represents 100,000 square miles. Each student in the "Students" column represents 10 million people. The arithmetic population density is calculated by dividing the population by the total land area. The physiologic population density is calculated by dividing the population by the arable land area.

After reading each of Sections 31.3 to 31.6, complete the corresponding questions.

31.3 How Population Density Affects Transportation

1. How does Japan's high population density affect transportation?
   Read the three statements below. One of them is false. Circle the two you think are true.

   ✓ • The average employee in Tokyo commutes (travels) 90 minutes to work.

   ✓ • No car can be registered in Tokyo without proof that the owner has a place to park it.

   • The Japanese train and subway system is so advanced that the Japanese buy fewer cars today than in 1960.

2. Read Section 31.3. Put a check mark next to each true statement above.

3. Write a summary of the ways population density affects transportation in Japan.
   Include at least three details from the reading.

   Crowding results in a very long commute time. Crowded rush hours led to the creation of an efficient public transportation system with some of the fastest trains in the world. Parking garages stack cars on top of one another to use less space.

31.4 How Population Density Affects Housing

1. How does Japan's high population density affect housing?
   Read the three statements below. One of them is false. Circle the two you think are true.

   ✓ • The average home in Japan is smaller than the average home in the United States.

   • Space limitations have not changed family life in Japan.

   ✓ • Many Japanese homes do not have separate bedrooms.

2. Read Section 31.4. Put a check mark next to each true statement above.

3. Write a summary of the ways population density affects housing in Japan. Include at least three details from the reading.

Japanese homes are smaller than U.S. homes. People use rooms for more than one purpose. They make things smaller to fit in small spaces. They cremate the dead to save space in cemeteries.

31.5 How Population Density Affects Land Use

1. How does Japan's high population density affect the ways land is used in Japan?
Read the three statements below. One of them is false. Circle the two you think are true.

- The Japanese have always built very tall buildings because of limited land.
✓ • The Japanese grow rice on terraces cut into steep mountainsides.
✓ • The Japanese have built underground parks and zoos.

2. Read Section 31.5. Put a check mark next to each true statement above.

3. Write a summary of the ways population density affects land use in Japan. Include at least three details from the reading.

There is not enough land for everybody's needs in Japan. The Japanese have learned to build taller buildings that are earthquake resistant. They also build underground public spaces, such as shopping malls and museums. Farmers create new farmland by cutting terraces into the sides of mountains.

31.6 How Population Density Affects Health

1. How does Japan's high population density affect the environment and people's health?
Read the three statements below. One of them is false. Circle the two you think are true.

- Because of crowding in Japan, the Japanese live shorter lives than most people in the world.
✓ • Some Japanese wear face masks to avoid making others ill.
✓ • The Japanese recycle cookie wrappers to reduce trash.

2. Read Section 31.6. Put a check mark next to each true statement above.

3. Write a summary of the ways population density affects the environment and health in Japan. Include at least three details from the reading.

Where there are lots of people, there's a lot of trash and pollution. Japan has strict laws for cleaning up the air and water. People recycle a lot in Japan to reduce the amount of garbage in dumps.

The Global Sneaker: From Asia to Everywhere

Overview

In this lesson, students learn about globalization by investigating the athletic shoe industry. In a **Visual Discovery** activity, students analyze images that represent key stages in the production of a sneaker: designing, locating materials, manufacturing, and distributing. Students bring one of the images to life using information from their reading. They apply their new knowledge by creating a choropleth map of the globalization of various products from their homes.

Objectives

Students will

- define and explain the importance of these key geographic terms: *economic interdependence, free trade, globalization, multinational corporation.*
- identify the components and steps of manufacturing a global product.
- explain the impact of globalization on people and places.
- analyze the global efforts needed to design, manufacture, and distribute a particular product.

Materials

- *Geography Alive! Regions and People*
- Interactive Student Notebooks
- Transparencies 32A–32E
- Student Handout 32 (1 role card for every 4 students)
- red, green, and blue markers (1 set per student)

Preview

1 Have students complete Preview 32 in pairs. Put students into pairs, and review the directions to Preview 32 with them. Give pairs five minutes to record as many items and countries as they can. Then have one pair at a time share an item or two from their list. List each country students name on the board, adding a tally mark for each time it is mentioned.

2 Debrief the Preview. Ask,

- What countries were mentioned most often?
- In which regions of the world are these countries located?
- Why do so many of the items we wear and use come from these countries?
- What might be some of the effects on the people who live and work in the countries where these items are made?

3 Explain the connection between the Preview and the upcoming activity. Tell students that in the upcoming activity, they will learn about the places and people in Asia and other areas of the world involved in producing athletic shoes.

Preview 32

Essential Question and Geoterms

1 Introduce Chapter 32 in *Geography Alive! Regions and People*. Explain that in this chapter, students will learn how the globalization of one manufactured product affects people and places around the world. Have students read Section 32.1. Then ask them to identify a detail or details in the photograph that represent ideas in the text they just read.

2 Introduce the Graphic Organizer and the Essential Question. Have students examine the world map. Ask,

- What do you see?
- What regions of the world do the different lines go to?
- How might each region be involved in making a sneaker?
- What effects might producing a "global sneaker" have upon places and people around the world?

Have students read the accompanying text. Make sure they understand the Essential Question, *What is globalization, and how does it affect people and places?* You may want to post it in the room or write it on the board for the duration of the activity.

3 Have students read Section 32.2. Then have them complete Geoterms 32 in their Interactive Student Notebooks, individually or in pairs. Have them share their answers with another student, or have volunteers share their answers with the class.

Geoterms 32

Visual Discovery

1 Introduce the activity. Tell students that in this activity they will analyze images that represent key stages in the production of a sneaker: designing, locating materials, manufacturing, and distributing.

2 Project the black and white photograph on *Transparency 32A: Designing a Global Sneaker* and have students analyze the image. Ask,

- What do you see?
- When might this have been taken? Give evidence to support your idea. *Explain that the photograph is from the 1950s. Evidence: short haircuts; style of shoes, socks, and uniforms; percentage of white players; fans dressed in suits, style of floor*
- What differences might you see between this and a basketball scene today?

Transparency 32A

3 Project both images on Transparency 32A and have students analyze them. Explain that the color photograph was taken in the early 2000s. Ask,

- How has the design of a sneaker changed from the 1950s to the early 2000s? *Explain that, in the 1950s, there were few choices in brands, styles, and colors, and shoes were made of cotton canvas and rubber. In the early 2000s, shoes were more complex, with various colors and styles, new technology in heels, and different materials for the top of the shoes.*
- In which countries do you think sneakers were designed in the 1950s? In the early 2000s? Why do you think so?

4 Have students read Section 32.3 and work with their partners to complete the corresponding Reading Notes. Use Guide to Reading Notes 32 to review their answers. Encourage students to add to their notes key information they hear from other students. Project Transparency 32A and have students apply what they have learned to reanalyze the images.

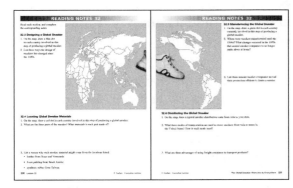

Reading Notes 32

5 Project *Transparency 32B: Locating Global Sneaker Materials.* Help students analyze the image by asking,

- What do you see?
- What are the three main parts of a sneaker? *upper, midsole, and outer sole*
- What might the arrows represent? *They represent the countries that produce the materials used to make each part of a sneaker.*
- What kinds of materials might the upper consist of? The midsole? The outer sole?

Transparency 32B

- What do you notice about where sneaker materials come from? *Most materials come from Asian countries. Some also come from Latin America, the Middle East, and the United States.*

- Why might materials for producing a sneaker come from all over the world? *Resources are not evenly distributed around the world.*

6 **Have students read Section 32.4 and work with their partners to complete the corresponding Reading Notes.** Review the answers with them, encouraging them to add any missing key information. Project Transparency 32B and have students apply what they have learned to reanalyze the image.

7 **Project the photograph at the top of** *Transparency 32C: Manufacturing the Global Sneaker* **and have students analyze the image.** Ask,

- What interesting details do you see?

- What do most of the workers in this factory appear to have in common? *They are young Asian women wearing western-style clothing, with their heads down and actively working.*

- What part of the sneaker are these workers putting together? *the upper*

Transparency 32C

8 **Project the photograph at the bottom of Transparency 32C and have students analyze it.** Ask,

- What parts of the sneaker are these workers putting together? *the outer sole and the upper*

- Why might the manufacturing of sneakers be done in Asia? *Asia has low-wage labor, factories that can make shoes, and ports for shipping.*

- How might the workers in this factory describe their working conditions?

9 **Have students read Section 32.5 and work with their partners to complete the corresponding Reading Notes.** Review the answers with the class, encouraging students to add any missing key information to their notes.

10 **Place students into groups of four to prepare for an act-it-out.** Give each group one role card cut from *Student Handout 32: Act-It-Out Role Cards.* Follow these steps:

- Identify for students which characters in the photographs on Transparency 32C correspond to which role cards. Have them pretend that the supervisor is standing off to the side.

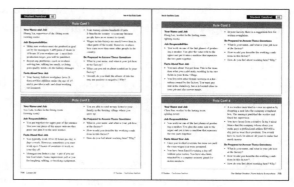

Student Handout 32

- Tell groups to review their role cards as well as their Reading Notes to generate ideas for how to accurately present their characters. Explain that actors will be asked the questions on the role cards and must be prepared to show and demonstrate their answers as accurately as possible.

- Have groups collect props, such as sneakers, and brainstorm ways the person who is chosen to perform can make the character come alive. For example, the supervisor might shout out a command to the workers to work faster.

- Give groups several minutes to prepare.

(**Note:** Alternatively, assign half the groups to become reporters. Give them each one of the role cards and ask them to write one or two additional questions for the character. Their questions must be related to information on the role card.)

11 Conduct the act-it-out. Select at least four actors to come up and step into the image in front of their characters. Have each actor, one at a time, bring the character to life by following the directions on the role card. Then, acting as a reporter, ask the questions the actor has prepared to answer. If you have assigned some groups to act as reporters, have them ask their questions as well.

12 Project *Transparency 32D: Distributing the Global Sneaker.* Help students analyze the map by asking,

Transparency 32D

- What do you see?
- What do the colored arrows on the map represent? *They represent typical routes of sneakers from Asia to stores in the United States and the transportation methods used.*
- About how many miles will sneakers travel along one of these routes?
- Why might sneakers that arrive in Long Beach, California, be shipped to a distribution center in Memphis, Tennessee? *Memphis is located near many population centers.*
- What do the ship, train, and truck have in common? How might this contribute to lower costs and greater efficiency in transporting products like sneakers? *They all carry the same freight containers. The products have to be packed only once, and the same container can travel on ship, train, and truck.*

13 Have students read Section 32.6 and work with their partners to complete the corresponding Reading Notes. Review the answers with the class, encouraging students to add any missing key information. Project Transparency 32D and have students apply what they have learned to reanalyze the image.

Global Connections

1 **Introduce the Global Connections.** Have students read
Section 32.7. Then explain that they will now look at the flow
of foreign investment around the world.

2 **Project** *Transparency 32E: Global Connections.* Have students analyze the map by discussing and sharing their answers
to the questions below. Use the additional information given to
enrich the discussion.

Transparency 32E

• **What interesting details do you see?**

• **According to its title, what does the map focus on?**
  *The map focuses on the foreign investment money that flows
  into developing countries. (**Note:** Developed countries also
  receive foreign investment, but they are not the focus of
  this map.)*

• **What do the colors represent?**
  *Darker colors represent developing countries that receive the
  most foreign investment. Lighter colors represent developing
  countries that receive less foreign investment.*

• **Why might there be no data for some regions?**
  *Some countries are not developed enough for comprehensive
  and accurate data to be accumulated. Nonetheless, these
  countries may have received foreign investment.*

3 **Have students read Section 32.8 and analyze the additional
information in the section.** Then facilitate a class discussion of
these questions:

• **How has foreign investment changed since 1914?**

• **Which developing country attracted the most investment
  money in 2002? How might this investment have affected
  life there?**

• **Which parts of the world attracted the least investment
  money? How might this affect the people living there?**

Processing

Have students complete Processing 32 in their Interactive Student Notebooks. For Step 3, you might present them with this sample question and answer: *Why are most of the shoes in my closet made in Asia? Because low wages and lower environmental standards influence many corporations to manufacture their products in Asian countries.* Have volunteers share their maps and questions with the class.

Online Resources

For more information on globalization and the athletic shoe industry, refer students to Online Resources for *Geography Alive! Regions and People* at www.teachtci.com.

Assessment

Masters for assessment appear on the next three pages followed by answers and scoring rubrics.

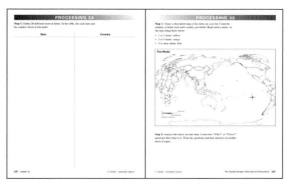

Processing 32

Mastering the Content

Shade in the oval by the letter of the best answer for each question.

1. Globalization has led to a rapid increase in which of the following?
   - ○ A. water stress
   - ○ B. international trade
   - ○ C. transboundary pollution
   - ○ D. arithmetic population density

2. Which term describes a business that has operations all over the world?
   - ○ A. trade bloc
   - ○ B. common market
   - ○ C. micro-enterprise
   - ○ D. multinational corporation

3. Which country is a **major** center of sneaker design?
   - ○ A. Brazil
   - ○ B. Taiwan
   - ○ C. Saudi Arabia
   - ○ D. United States

4. Which country is a **major** producer of synthetic rubber?
   - ○ A. Brazil
   - ○ B. Taiwan
   - ○ C. Saudi Arabia
   - ○ D. United States

5. A company in Mexico ships fruit to the United States for sale without paying tariffs. This is an example of which of the following?
   - ○ A. free trade
   - ○ B. vertical trade
   - ○ C. subsistence agriculture
   - ○ D. comparative advantage

6. China looks to Japan for foreign investment and technology. Japanese consumers buy many goods made in China. The result is which of the following?
   - ○ A. ethnic diversity
   - ○ B. sustainable development
   - ○ C. supranational cooperation
   - ○ D. economic interdependence

7. The circle graphs below show where foreign investment went in two different years.

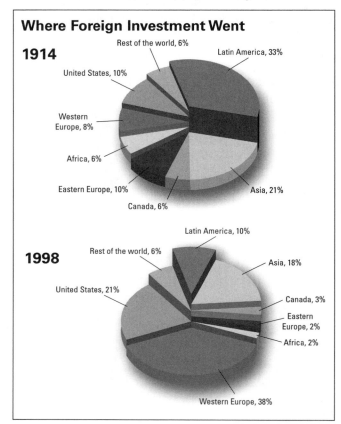

Where Foreign Investment Went

1914

Rest of the world, 6%
Latin America, 33%
United States, 10%
Western Europe, 8%
Africa, 6%
Eastern Europe, 10%
Canada, 6%
Asia, 21%

1998

Latin America, 10%
Rest of the world, 6%
Asia, 18%
United States, 21%
Canada, 3%
Eastern Europe, 2%
Africa, 2%
Western Europe, 38%

Which region of the world received the most foreign investment in 1914?
   - ○ A. Western Europe   ○ C. Africa
   - ○ B. Latin America   ○ D. Asia

8. According to the graphs above, which part of the world doubled its percentage of foreign investment between 1914 and 1998?
   - ○ A. the United States   ○ C. Eastern Europe
   - ○ B. Canada   ○ D. Africa

Applying Geography Skills: Analyzing Line Graphs

Use these graphs and your knowledge of geography to complete the tasks below.

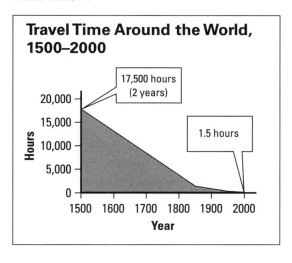

Travel Time Around the World, 1500–2000

17,500 hours (2 years)

1.5 hours

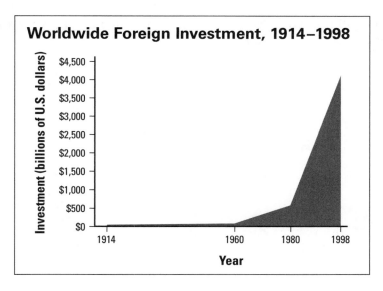

Worldwide Foreign Investment, 1914–1998

Both of these graphs show information that relates to globalization.

1. Examine the travel time graph. About how many hours did it take a sailing ship to travel around the world in 1500?

2. What form of transportation made it possible for people to circle the world in just 1.5 hours by 2000?

3. Examine the worldwide foreign investment graph. About how many billions of dollars were invested in foreign countries in 1914?

4. Between 1980 and 1998, many nations in Asia, Africa, and Latin American reduced their trade barriers. How did foreign investment change in this time period?

5. Examine the two line graphs to see what they have in common. Then describe what kind of information is best shown on this type of graph.

Test Terms Glossary
To **examine** means to study or analyze a subject in detail.

Exploring the Essential Question

What is globalization, and how does it affect people and places?

In Chapter 32, you explored the globalization of the sneaker industry. Now you will use what you learned. Use this diagram and your knowledge of geography to complete the task below.

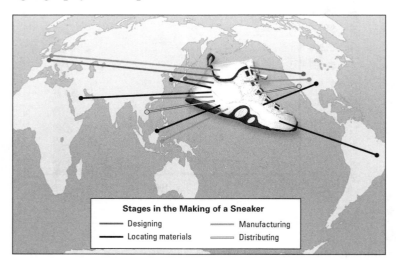

Stages in the Making of a Sneaker
——— Designing   ——— Manufacturing
——— Locating materials   ═══ Distributing

The Task: Creating a Political Cartoon on Globalization

Sneaker production is just one of many global industries. Your task is to create a political cartoon about either the positive or negative effects of globalization.

Step 1: On the table below, list two positive effects of globalization. Also list two negative effects. Circle the effect you will use for your cartoon.

Globalization

Positive effects	Negative effects

Step 2: On another sheet of paper, draw a political cartoon illustrating the effect you chose in Step 1. Your cartoon should include the following:
A. a drawing that shows how you think globalization either helps or hurts people or places
B. a caption, title, or speech balloon that summarizes your view

Applying Geography Skills: Sample Responses

1. 17,500 hours (2 years)
2. the space shuttle
3. Answers will vary. Students should note that relatively few U.S. dollars were invested in foreign countries in 1914.
4. Between 1980 and 1998, foreign investment rose rapidly, from about $500 billion to over $4 trillion.
5. Line graphs are best used to show change over time.

Exploring the Essential Question: Sample Response

Step 1: Responses will vary. At least two examples should be listed in each column.

Globalization

Positive effects	Negative effects
• New jobs and better standard of living	• Pollution in countries with less strict environmental laws
• Low prices for products people want or need to buy	• Unsafe or unhealthy working conditions in factories
• Fewer wars and a more peaceful world	• Loss of jobs when companies in developed countries move production offshore

Step 2: Responses will vary. The cartoon should show a point of view toward globalization. Details in the cartoon, caption, or title should tell how globalization creates positive or negative changes. It should have a caption or title expressing support for or against globalization.

Mastering the Content Answer Key

1. B	2. D	3. D	4. B
5. A	6. D	7. B	8. A

Applying Geography Skills Scoring Rubric

Score	General Description
2	Student responds to all parts of the task. Response is correct and clear.
1	Student responds to some parts of the task. Response is mostly correct.
0	Response does not match the task or is incorrect.

Exploring the Essential Question Scoring Rubric

Score	General Description
3	Student responds to all parts of the task. Response is correct, clear, and supported by details.
2	Student responds to most or all parts of the task. Response is generally correct but may lack details.
1	Student responds to at least one part of the task. Response may contain errors and lack details.
0	Response does not match the task or is incorrect.

Role Card 1

Your Name and Job
Huang Xu, supervisor of the fitting room (sewing room)

Job Responsibilities
- Make sure workers meet the production goal set by the managers: 2,400 pairs of shoes in 10 hours. If your workers can't meet their production target, you will be punished.
- Report any problems—such as workers arriving late, talking too much, or doing poor-quality work—to the factory manager.

Facts About Your Job
- Your factory follows workplace laws. It does not hire children under the age of 15, and it provides a safe and clean working environment.

- Your factory creates hundreds of jobs. It benefits the country's economy because people have more money to spend.
- Wages in this factory are much lower than in other parts of the world. However, workers here earn more than most other people in the country.

Be Prepared to Answer These Questions
- What is your name, and what is your job here at the factory?
- What can you tell us about conditions in your factory?
- Overall, do you think the effects of this factory are positive or negative? Why?

Role Card 2

Your Name and Job
Soo Lim, worker in the fitting room (sewing room)

Job Responsibilities
- You put together the upper part of the sneaker. You sew one piece of the upper onto another piece and pass it to the next worker.

Facts About Your Job
- You typically work 10 to 12 hours per day, 6 days a week. However, sometimes you must work up to 5 hours of overtime or work on your day off.
- Managers can deduct a day's pay if you are late four times. Some supervisors yell at you for laughing, talking, or breaking equipment.

- You are able to send money home to your family in the farming village where you grew up.

Be Prepared to Answer These Questions
- What is your name, and what is your job here at the factory?
- How would you describe the working conditions in this factory?
- How do you feel about working here? Why?

Role Card 3

Your Name and Job

Hong Lee, worker in the lasting room
(gluing room)

Job Responsibilities

- You work on one of the last phases of producing a sneaker. You glue the outer sole to the upper and put it into a machine that squeezes the two parts together.

Facts About Your Job

- You earn about 21¢ per hour. This is far more than what you could make working in the rice fields in your home village.

- You live with other female workers in a dormitory owned by the factory. You must pay rent at the dormitory, but it is located close to your job and also serves meals.

- In your factory, there is a suggestion box for written complaints.

Be Prepared to Answer These Questions

- What is your name, and what is your job here at the factory?

- How would you describe the working conditions in this factory?

- How do you feel about working here? Why?

Role Card 4

Your Name and Job

Chen Suo, worker in the lasting room
(gluing room)

Job Responsibilities

- You work on one of the last phases of producing a sneaker. You glue the outer sole to the upper and put it into a machine that squeezes the two parts together.

Facts About Your Job

- Once you worked overtime but were not paid the extra wages you were promised.

- You have been fined for taking a day off without prior notice. You have also been searched by a company security guard for stolen sneakers.

- A co-worker once tried to voice an opinion by dropping a note into the company complaint box. The manager punished the worker and fined her supervisor.

- You have heard from a relative in the United States that the company whose shoes you make pays a professional athlete $55,000 a day just to wear their products. You would have to work for almost 40 years to make that much money.

Be Prepared to Answer These Questions

- What is your name, and what is your job here at the factory?

- How would you describe the working conditions in this factory?

- How do you feel about working here? Why?

Read each section, and complete the corresponding notes.

32.3 Designing a Global Sneaker

1. On the map, draw a blue dot in each country involved in this step of producing a global sneaker.

2. List three ways the design of sneakers has changed since the 1950s.

   Today's sneakers are designed for many types of activities. New designs improve performance and comfort. Sneakers are also designed for fashion appeal.

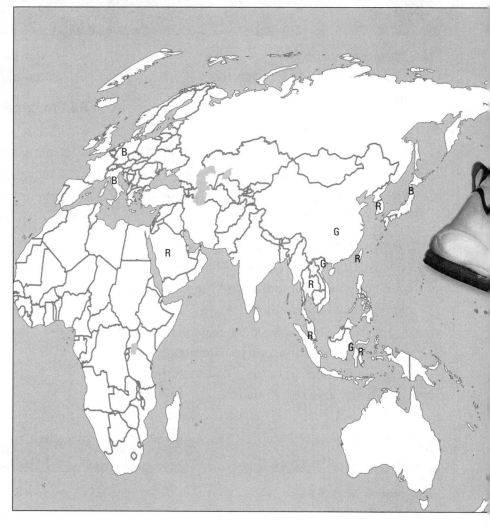

32.4 Locating Global Sneaker Materials

1. On the map, draw a red dot in each country involved in this step of producing a global sneaker.

2. What are the three parts of the sneaker? What materials is each part made of?

   The upper is made of natural materials (like cotton and leather) or synthetic materials (like nylon). The midsole is made of plastic and foam padding (both made from oil) and sometimes air bags of pressurized gas. The outer sole, or tread, is made of natural or synthetic (from coal or oil) rubber.

3. List a reason why each sneaker material might come from the locations listed.

   • leather from Texas and Venezuela: These are livestock centers.

   • foam padding from Saudi Arabia: This is an oil-rich country.

   • synthetic rubber from Taiwan: This country has factories to produce this material.

32.5 Manufacturing the Global Sneaker

1. On the map, draw a green dot in each country currently involved in this step of producing a global sneaker.

2. Where were sneakers manufactured until the 1960s? What changes occurred in the 1970s that caused sneaker companies to no longer make shoes at home?

   Until the 1960s, sneakers were made in the countries where they were sold: the United States, Britain, and Germany. In the 1970s, styles multiplied and designs became more complicated. More labor was needed to assemble the shoes, and costs began to rise.

3. List three reasons sneaker companies moved their production offshore to Asian countries.

   Asian countries offered large pools of low-wage workers, factories to make shoes, and ports for shipping.

32.6 Distributing the Global Sneaker

1. On the map, draw a typical sneaker distribution route from Asia to your state.
   Distribution route should go from Asia, to the U.S. west coast, to Memphis, to the student's state.

2. What three modes of transportation are used to move sneakers from Asia to stores in the United States? How is each mode used?

   Ships, trains, and trucks are used to transport sneakers from Asia to stores in the United States. Ships are used between Asia and the U.S. west coast, trains or trucks from the west coast to distribution centers like Memphis, and trucks from distribution centers to stores around the country.

3. What are three advantages of using freight containers to transport products?
   Freight containers are weatherproof and easy to stack, and big ships can carry many at once.

Oceania and Antarctica

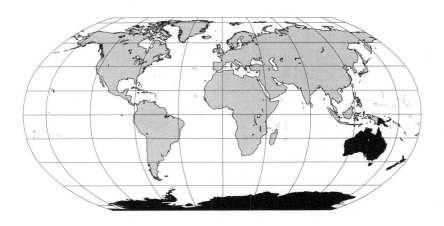

Relative and Absolute Location: What Makes Australia Unique?

Overview

In this lesson, students discover how Australia's absolute and relative location have helped to shape many aspects of life there. In a **Social Studies Skill Builder,** students will learn how six aspects of life in Australia have been affected by its absolute or relative location. They will then explore whether absolute location or relative location has had a greater impact on this island continent.

Objectives

Students will

- define and explain the importance of these key geographic terms: *continental drift theory, endangered species, exotic species, native species, threatened species.*
- examine how absolute location and relative location affect place.
- analyze how location has played a role in shaping aspects of life in Australia.
- investigate the impact of location and other factors on threatened species worldwide.

Materials

- *Geography Alive! Regions and People*
- Interactive Student Notebooks
- Transparencies 33A–33C
- Placards 33A–33E (3 sets)
- masking tape

Preview

1 **Project the top map on** *Transparency 33A: Preview 33.*
Help students analyze the map by asking,

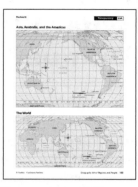

- What are some ways we could measure the distance between two places on this map?

- What are latitude and longitude lines? What purpose do they serve on a map or globe? (**Note:** You may wish to explain that latitude lines are approximately 69 miles apart. Longitude lines are farthest apart at the equator, where they too are 69 miles apart. However, these lines converge, or come together, at the poles, so they are not equidistant. Students can use these estimates to think about the next two questions.)

- How far do you think Australia is from the United States?

- How many hours might it take you to fly from New York City to Canberra, Australia?

2 **Explain the simulation.** Take the class outside, or clear a large area in the room. Explain that students will now simulate traveling from New York to three other cities, including Canberra, Australia. They will take side-to-side "slides" to represent moving across latitude lines and marching-like "steps" to represent moving down longitude lines. For every step or slide, they will have "traveled" 10 degrees latitude or 10 degrees longitude. (**Note:** If it is more feasible in your class, you could have students execute the "steps" and "slides" while standing in place beside their desks. If so, you may wish to choose a volunteer for each part of the simulation to actually complete the steps and slides so the class can compare the three distances traveled.)

3 **Have students simulate traveling from New York to Los Angeles, Honolulu, and Canberra.** Tell students they are starting in New York City. Have them simulate traveling each of the three distances as follows:

- *From New York to Los Angeles:* On the map, point out the two cities and their longitude and latitude coordinates. Explain that students should take $4\frac{1}{2}$ slides and a half step to represent traveling approximately 45 degrees of longitude and 5 degrees of latitude. (For half steps or slides, have students take a smaller step or slide than normal.) Ask, *About how far do you think you traveled?* Explain that the actual flying distance is about 2,500 miles.

- *From New York to Honolulu:* Students should take 8 slides and 2 steps to represent traveling approximately 80 degrees of longitude and 20 degrees of latitude. Ask, *About how far do you think you traveled?* Explain that the actual flying distance is about 5,000 miles.

- *From New York to Canberra:* Students should take $13\frac{1}{2}$ slides and $7\frac{1}{2}$ steps to represent traveling approximately 135 degrees of longitude and 75 degrees of latitude. (**Note:** Between the 10th and 11th slide, you may wish to point out that students have now crossed the International Dateline and have entered the Eastern Hemisphere. At the 4th step, you might mention that they have crossed the equator and entered the Southern Hemisphere.) Ask, *About how far do you think you traveled?* Explain that the actual flying distance is about 10,000 miles.

4 **Have students complete Preview 33 in their Interactive Student Notebooks.** Follow these steps:
- Project the second map on Transparency 33.
- Have students answer Questions 1–3 of Preview 33. For each question, have them share their ideas and add any new information to their answers. You might record the answers on a transparency of the page. Here are some possible answers:
Question 1: In the Southern Hemisphere, south of Asia, between the Pacific and Indian oceans, north of Antarctica, or using latitude/longitude coordinates: 20°S, 140°E.
Question 2, absolute location: The precise point where a place is located on Earth; students might have put an *A* next to "latitude and longitude coordinates," "20°S, 140°E."
Relative location: Where a place is located in relation to another place; students might have put an *R* next to "in the Southern Hemisphere," "south of Asia," "between the Pacific and Indian oceans," "north of Antarctica."
Question 3: climate, resources, animals, vegetation, land use, tourism, trade partners

Preview 33

5 **Explain the connection between the Preview and the upcoming activity.** Tell students that Australia's relative and absolute location has played a large role in shaping life there. In the upcoming activity, students will explore some specific aspects of life in Australia and examine how the country's location has influenced life there.

Graphic Organizer and Geoterms

1 **Introduce Chapter 33 in** *Geography Alive! Regions and People.* Explain that in this chapter, students will learn how Australia's unique location affects life there. Have them read Section 33.1. Then have them examine the photograph of the Australian outback, and ask,
- What kind of climate might you expect to find here?
- What kinds of animals might you expect to see?
- What else about this location might make living here unique?

2 Introduce the Graphic Organizer and the Essential Question. Have students examine the map and ask,

- What do you see?
- How is this map different from world maps you commonly see in textbooks or atlases?
- What can a map like this tell us about a place's location?

Have students read the accompanying text. Make sure they understand the Essential Question, *How does a country's location shape life within its borders?* You may want to post the Essential Question in the room or write it on the board for the duration of the activity.

3 Have students read Section 33.2. Then have them work individually or in pairs to complete Geoterms 33 in their Interactive Student Notebooks. Ask them to share their answers with another student, or have volunteers share their answers with the class.

Geoterms 33

Social Studies Skill Builder

1 Prepare the classroom. Create five stations around the room. At each station, post all three copies of *Placard 33A, 33B, 33C, 33D,* or *33E* on the walls. Space the three placards at each station about three feet apart to allow space for three pairs to work at a station at a time. If you have more than 30 students, consider making an additional copy of each placard.

2 Place students in mixed-ability pairs. You might prepare a transparency that shows them with whom they will work and where they will sit.

3 Explain the activity. Tell students that in this activity they will examine placards with visual information about Australia. Each placard represents a different aspect of life in Australia. Review these steps for the activity:

- Go to one of the stations and carefully analyze the visual information on a placard at that station.
- Discuss the questions at the bottom of the placard with your partner.
- Find and complete the matching section of Reading Notes 33.

Placards 33A–33E

4 Analyze one pair of images as a class.

- Project *Transparency 33B: British Influences in Australia.*
- In their pairs, have students analyze the two photographs. Point out the latitude and longitude coordinates given for each city, and ask students what they reveal about the difference in the locations of these two places. Then discuss the three questions at the bottom of the transparency.

Transparency 33B

- Have students turn to Section 33.3 in Reading Notes 33 and write their hypothesis in response to the first question: *Great Britain has had an influence on life in Australia. How do you think Australia's location may have played a role in this?*

- Have pairs read Section 33.3.

- Discuss possible answers to the question, and have students revise their hypotheses using what they've learned from the reading.

- Have students complete this statement in their Reading Notes: *Relative/absolute location (circle one) is more responsible for shaping British influences on Australia because....*

5 Conduct the Social Studies Skill Builder. Instruct pairs to go to one of the stations and begin the activity. After pairs have analyzed their first placard and read the corresponding section of the text (Placard 33A, Section 33.4; Placard 33B, Section 33.5; Placard 33C, Section 33.6; Placard 33D, Section 33.7; Placard 33E, Section 33.8), have them check with you to make sure they completed the Reading Notes correctly. (**Note:** Expect that most students will not have a correct or complete hypothesis to the first question after simply analyzing the placard. Reading the related section in the text will help them clarify their answers.) Continue the activity until all pairs have analyzed all five placards.

Reading Notes 33

6 Conduct a wrap-up activity.

- Create a spectrum by placing a 10- to 15-foot strip of masking tape along the floor at the front of the room. On the board above either end of the spectrum, write "Only Absolute Location Shapes Life" and "Only Relative Location Shapes Life." In the center, write "Both Shape Life Equally."

- Have pairs discuss this question: *Based on what you have learned, do you think absolute location or relative location has had a greater effect on shaping life in Australia?*

- Have one student from each pair come forward to stand on the spectrum in the place they think best answers the question.

- Facilitate a discussion by selecting students at various spots along the spectrum and having their seated partners justify their location.

- Finally, ask the class, *Which aspects of life are more affected by absolute location? Which aspects are more affected by relative location?*

(**Note:** You might also have students create a human spectrum based on this question: *Do you think absolute location or relative location has a greater effect on shaping your life?*)

Global Connections

1 Introduce the Global Connections. Have students read Section 33.9. Tell them that they will now explore one of the topics in the activity on a global scale.

2 Project *Transparency 33C: Global Connections.* Help students analyze the map by asking the following questions. Use the additional information given to enrich the discussion.

Transparency 33C

- **What does this map tell us?**
  It shows various places in the world where species are threatened and to what degree.

- **What do the colors on this map tell us?**
  The areas that are darker brown have the highest numbers of threatened species.

- **Which areas of the world seem to have the greatest number of threatened species? The least?**
  The United States, Latin America, Australia, and parts of Africa and Southeast Asia have high numbers of threatened species. Russia, Canada, and northern Africa have the least.

- **How do you think location and the endangerment of species are related?**

3 Have students compare the map of threatened species to a population density map. Have students examine the population density map of the world in the back of their books. Lead a discussion of these questions:

- **What do you notice about the population density of some of the locations where large numbers of species are threatened? What might this tell you?**
  In China and India, where human populations are very high, and in the United States, with a fairly high population density, threatened species' numbers are also high.

- **What do you notice about the population density of some of the locations where the fewest species are threatened? What might this tell you?**
  In Canada, Russia, and North Africa, where human populations are lower, threatened species' numbers are lower.

Explain that there are exceptions to this correlation. Europe, for example, has a high population density yet a low number of threatened species.

4 Have students read Section 33.10 and examine the rest of the information in the section. Then lead a discussion of these questions:

- **What do the areas with most of the threatened species have in common?**

- **Which factors pose the greatest dangers to threatened species?**

- **How does relative location affect a species' chances of survival?**

Processing

Have students turn to Processing 33 in their Interactive Student Notebooks. Read through the directions with them, and answer any questions they have. Students will need to consult the regional map of Canada and the United States in the Atlas at the back of their books. You may wish to brainstorm ideas for each of the five aspects of life before students do the assignment. (**Note:** Students may need additional resources to find information relating to local migration and trade partners as well as the wildlife, constellations, and environmental concerns near their community.)

Online Resources

For more information on Australia, refer students to Online Resources for *Geography Alive! Regions and People* at www.teachtci.com.

Assessment

Masters for assessment appear on the next three pages followed by answers and scoring rubrics.

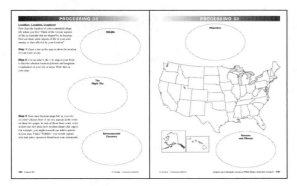

Processing 33

Mastering the Content

Shade in the oval by the letter of the best answer for each question.

1. According to this graph, which statement is an accurate description of Australia?

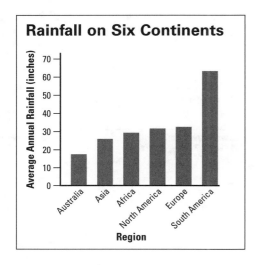

Rainfall on Six Continents

○ A. It is the flattest continent.
○ B. It is the smallest continent.
○ C. It is the most arid continent.
○ D. It is the most populous continent.

2. According to continental drift theory, which physical process brought Australia to its present position?
○ A. salinization
○ B. desertification
○ C. volcanic activity
○ D. tectonic movement

3. Which ethnic group first settled Australia?
○ A. Aborigine
○ B. Melanesian
○ C. Micronesian
○ D. Polynesian

4. Which of these first brought British settlers to Australia?
○ A. the discovery of gold
○ B. the unique flora and fauna
○ C. the founding of a prison colony
○ D. the "whites only" immigration policy

5. What is true of both kangaroos and koalas in Australia?
○ A. Both are exotic species.
○ B. Both are native species.
○ C. Both are extinct species.
○ D. Both are invasive species.

6. Which of these would be the **best** month to travel to Australia for a sun, sea, and sand vacation?
○ A. January
○ B. June
○ C. August
○ D. October

7. Rabbits in Australia are an example of which of the following?
○ A. a native species
○ B. an exotic species
○ C. a threatened species
○ D. an endangered species

8. Which of these has increased concern about skin cancer in Australia?
○ A. the ozone hole
○ B. continental drift
○ C. the reversed seasons
○ D. environmental degradation

Applying Geography Skills:
Describing Relative Locations

Use these maps and your knowledge of geography to complete the
tasks below.

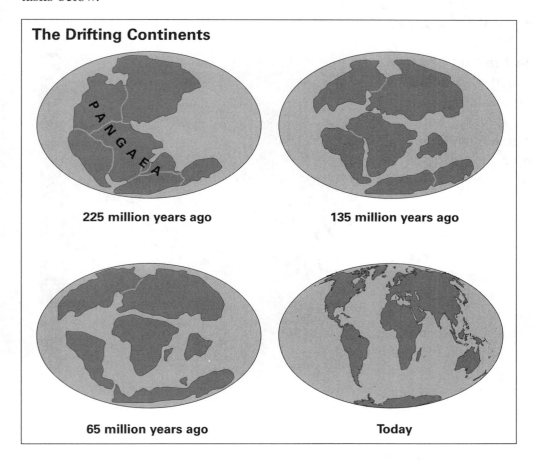

The Drifting Continents

225 million years ago   135 million years ago

65 million years ago   Today

1. On each map, write the letters *NA* on the land that became North
   America. (**Hint:** This will be easier if you start with today and work
   backward in time.)

2. On each map, write the letter *A* on the land that became Africa.

3. Describe the relative location of North America and Africa 225 million
   years ago.

4. Describe the relative location of North America and Africa today.

Exploring the Essential Question

How does a country's location shape life within its borders?

In Chapter 33, you explored how Australia's location has shaped life there. Now you will use what you learned. Use this poster and your knowledge of geography to complete the task below.

The Task: Creating a "Safe in the Sun" Poster

The Sid Seagull poster has been used in Australia for many years to fight skin cancer. It encourages people to "slip" on a shirt, "slop" on suntan lotion, and "slap" on a hat before going out in the sun. More recently, Australians have also been encouraged to "wrap" on a pair of sunglasses before going outside.

Australia is not the only country with a skin cancer problem. Experts estimate that one out of two Americans will develop some form of skin cancer in their lifetime. Yet most of those cancers could be prevented if Americans were better about protecting themselves from the sun. Your task is to persuade your friends to do just that by creating a "safe in the sun" poster.

Queensland Cancer Fund

Step 1: Choose a character to use for your poster. Your choice should appeal to your friends. Describe your character here.

Step 2: Think of a slogan for your poster. It should use words or phrases that will catch your friends' interest. It should also tell your friends how they can be safe in the sun. Write your slogan here.

Step 3: Sketch your poster on another sheet of paper.

Writing Tips: Creating a Catchy Slogan

A slogan is a catchy phrase that promotes an idea or a product. A good slogan is easy to understand. It is also easy to remember. Make your slogan short. But make sure it tells people what they can do to prevent skin cancer.

Applying Geography Skills: Sample Responses

1, 2.

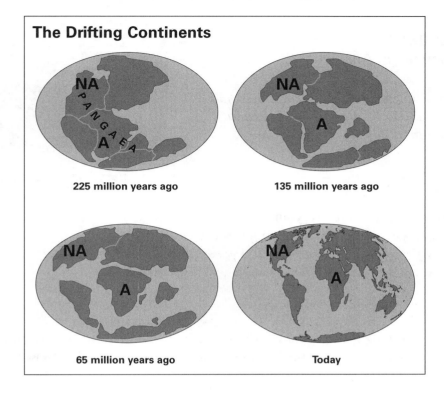

The Drifting Continents

225 million years ago

135 million years ago

65 million years ago

Today

Applying Geography Skills Scoring Rubric

Score	General Description
2	Student responds to all parts of the task. Response is correct and clear.
1	Student responds to some parts of the task. Response is mostly correct.
0	Response does not match the task or is incorrect.

3. North America was located to the northwest of Africa when both were part of Pangaea 225 millions of years ago.

4. Today, North America lies far to the west of Africa, with the Atlantic Ocean separating the two continents.

Exploring the Essential Question: Sample Response

Step 1: Students should describe a character for the poster.

Step 2: Students should state a slogan for the poster.

Step 3: Posters should include a catchy slogan and an indication of what people can do to prevent skin cancer.

Exploring the Essential Question Scoring Rubric

Score	General Description
3	Student responds to all parts of the task. Response is correct, clear, and supported by details.
2	Student responds to most or all parts of the task. Response is generally correct but may lack details.
1	Student responds to at least one part of the task. Response may contain errors and lack details.
0	Response does not match the task or is incorrect.

Complete the matching section of Reading Notes for each placard you analyze.

33.3 A Land Far from Great Britain
Transparency: British Influences in Australia

1. Write a possible answer to this question: *Great Britain has had an influence on life in Australia. How do you think Australia's location may have played a role in this?* Answers will vary.

2. Read Section 33.3. Use what you learn to revise your answer.
Australia was the farthest colony to which the British government could send prisoners. It was their colony for more than 200 years and has been greatly influenced by British culture, government, and language.

3. Finish this statement: (Relative) absolute location (circle one) *is more responsible for shaping British influences on Australia because* Australia was the farthest possible location relative to Britain to send prisoners.

33.4 New Relationships with Near Neighbors
Placard 33A: Immigrants to Australia

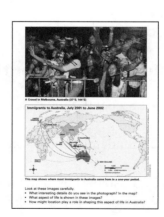

1. Write a possible answer to this question: *How do you think Australia's location plays a role in shaping who comes to live there?*
Answers will vary.

2. Read Section 33.4. Use what you learn to revise your answer.
Australia's close location to Asia and Africa helped to increase immigration from those continents. This, in turn, has created a plural society and sometimes tension between ethnic groups.

3. Finish this statement: (Relative) absolute location (circle one) *is more responsible for shaping who comes to live in Australia because* Australia's location has resulted in greater immigration from Asian nations.

33.5 Australia's Reversed Seasons
Placard 33B: Seasons in Australia

1. Write a possible answer to these questions: *How do you think Australia's location plays a role in shaping its seasons? How might Australia benefit from its seasons?* Answers will vary.

2. Read Section 33.5. Use what you learn to revise your answer.
Australia's location in the Southern Hemisphere means that its seasons are reversed from those in the Northern Hemisphere. This means that people from northern regions can vacation "Down Under" to escape winter where they live. And Australians can grow crops during their summer to ship to northern countries still experiencing winter.

3. Finish this statement: *Relative/absolute location (circle one) is more responsible for shaping seasons in Australia because* Australia's absolute location below the equator affects its seasons.

33.6 Australia's Amazing Wildlife
Placard 33C: Wildlife in Australia

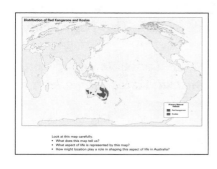

1. Write a possible answer to this question: *What role do you think Australia's location has played in shaping the kinds of wildlife found there?*
Answers will vary.

2. Read Section 33.6. Use what you learn to revise your answer.
Australia's isolated location has resulted in unique wildlife. Plants and animals found nowhere else in the world have adapted to Australia's sometimes harsh climate. However, many exotic species have been brought in that now endanger native species.

3. Finish this statement: *Relative/absolute location (circle one) is more responsible for shaping the kinds of wildlife found in Australia because* Australia's place on the globe has affected what types of native wildlife live there.

33.7 Living Under an Ozone Hole
Placard 33D: The Sun in Australia

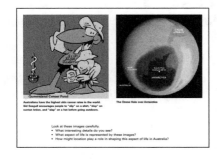

1. Write a possible answer to this question: *How do you think Australia's location impacts the effects of the sun on the people who live there?* Answers will vary.

2. Read Section 33.7. Use what you learn to revise your answer.
Australia's location near the equator as well as near the ozone hole over Antarctica has resulted in the highest rate of skin cancer in the world. Because Australians enjoy outdoor activities, Australia has used its "slip, slop, slap" campaign to educate people about the dangers of the sun.

3. Finish this statement: *Relative/absolute location (circle one) is more responsible for impacting the sun's effect on the people of Australia because* Australia's location below the equator and near the ozone hole has led to increased danger from the sun's rays.

33.8 Australia's Night Sky
Placard 33E: The Night Sky in Australia

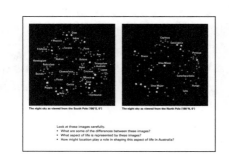

1. Write a possible answer to this question: *How do you think Australia's location affects its view of the night sky?* Answers will vary.

2. Read Section 33.8. Use what you learn to revise your answer.
Australia's location in the Southern Hemisphere means that people there see different constellations than people in Northern Hemisphere countries see.

3. Finish this statement: *Relative/absolute location (circle one) is more responsible for shaping Australia's view of the night sky because* Australia's position on the globe affects what is visible in its night sky.

The Pacific Islands: Adapting to Life Surrounded by Ocean

Overview

In this lesson, students learn how physical and human geography affect life on three types of islands in the Pacific Ocean. In a **Problem Solving Groupwork** activity, student groups create illustrated maps of one of three island types: continental islands, volcanic islands, and atolls. They then read and interpret the illustrated maps created by their classmates, comparing and contrasting them to learn what makes each type of island unique.

Objectives

Students will

- define and explain the importance of these key geographic terms: *atoll, continental island, lagoon, volcanic island.*

- explain how the ocean affects life on islands in the Pacific.

- create an illustrated map depicting how physical and human geography affect life on three types of islands: continental islands, volcanic islands, and atolls.

- evaluate the overutilization of ocean resources and explain what is being done to protect oceans today.

Materials

- *Geography Alive! Regions and People*
- Interactive Student Notebooks
- Transparencies 34A–34C
- Student Handout 34A (1 three-page set for every 4 students, plus 1 transparency of each map)
- Student Handout 34B (1 for every 4 students)
- butcher paper or white poster board (1 sheet for every 4 students)
- sheets of unlined white paper
- colored markers
- glue sticks
- scissors

Preview

1 Project *Transparency 34A: Preview 34* and have students complete Preview 34 in their Interactive Student Notebooks. Have students analyze the image and work with a partner to answer the questions in the Preview, which also appear below. Afterward, have pairs share their responses to each question.

- What is the large blue area? What do you think the green and brown dots in the blue area are?
- What islands, countries, or continents do you see?
- What are some ways these islands might be similar to one another?
- What are some ways these islands might be different from one another?
- How do you think your daily routine might be different if you lived on one of these islands?

2 Connect the Preview to the upcoming activity. Tell students that in this activity they will work in groups to create illustrated maps showing how physical and human geography affect life on three different types of islands.

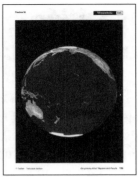

Transparency 34A   **Preview 34**

Essential Question and Geoterms

1 Introduce Chapter 34 in *Geography Alive! Regions and People*. Explain that in this chapter, students will learn how geography affects life on three types of islands. Have them read Section 34.1. Then ask them to identify details in the satellite image that represent ideas in the text they just read.

2 Introduce the Graphic Organizer and the Essential Question. Have students examine the illustration of the three types of islands. Ask,

- What are some ways these islands might be different from one another?
- What factors do you think might make life different on each type of island?

Have students read the accompanying text. Make sure they understand the Essential Question, *How do people adapt to life in an island region?* You may want to post the question in the classroom or write it on the board for the duration of this activity.

3 Have students read Section 34.2. Then have them work individually or in pairs to complete Geoterms 34 in their Interactive Student Notebooks. Ask them to share their answers with another student, or have volunteers share their answers with the class.

Geoterms 34

Problem Solving Groupwork

1 Introduce the activity. Tell students that they will now work in groups to become experts on one type of island and create an illustrated map that shows how physical and human geography affect life there.

2 Arrange students in mixed-ability groups of four. You may want to prepare a transparency that shows them whom to work with and where to sit. (**Note:** If your class cannot be evenly divided into groups of four, you might form one or two groups of three and assign them to Kwajalein Atoll, with one person covering the responsibilities of both the Physical Geographer and the Ocean Expert.)

3 Have students read Section 34.3 and complete the Reading Notes for that section. When they've finished, quickly discuss this question: *What are some ways that the ocean affects life on Pacific islands?*

Transparency 34B

4 Project *Transparency 34B: Illustrated Map of Michigan* **and review the elements of an illustrated map.** Ask, *What can you learn about the human and physical geography of Michigan by looking at this illustrated map?* Help students point out key words, phrases, and visual elements. Emphasize how the layout helps the viewer understand how the physical environment, including the water surrounding Michigan, affects how people live in that state. (**Note:** You may want to project this illustrated map as a model when students create their own.)

5 Assign island types and distribute materials. Assign each group one of the three island types by giving them each one of the three-page sets of *Student Handout 34A: Guidelines for Creating an Illustrated Map.* Depending on the class size, each island will be assigned to more than one group. Also give each group scissors, colored markers, glue sticks, unlined white paper, and butcher paper or white poster board.

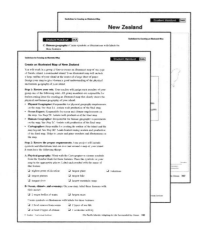

Student Handout 34A

6 Assign roles and review the steps for creating an illustrated map. Review the four roles with the class—Physical Geographer, Ocean Expert, Human Geographer, and Cartographer—and assign each student a role. Then review Steps 2 through 5 on Student Handout 34A. Point out that groups must get your initials for Steps 4 and 5 before moving on.

7 Monitor groups as they create their illustrated maps. Here are some tips for conducting the activity:

- *Student Handout 34A, Step 4:* Remind students that they are to make simple sketches of their symbols and illustrations. You might suggest an appropriate time limit for this step, such as 20 minutes, to help them work quickly.

- *Step 5:* Project the appropriate map from Student Handout 34A and have the group trace the island outline onto a large sheet of paper hung on the wall. Having more than one projector will move this process along more quickly. Since it will be difficult for all four students to work on the final copy at the same time, suggest that some create their illustrations on separate sheets of paper and glue them to the final map.

8 Have students post their completed maps. When all groups have finished their illustrated maps, have them post them in three areas, one for each island type.

9 Have students examine the maps, take notes, and then read Sections 34.4 to 34.6 to complete their Reading Notes.

- First ask students to go to the area that contains the maps of the island type on which they worked. Tell them to examine the other maps that were created for that type of island and to add any additional information they discover to that section of their Reading Notes.

- Second, have students rotate to the other collections of illustrated maps and take notes on the other two island types. Check that they complete the respective sections of the Reading Notes as thoroughly as possible.

- For the two island types they did not work on, have students read the corresponding sections to discover what they may have missed or misinterpreted by inspecting the maps and to correct their notes based on the reading.

10 Debrief the activity. Once students have completed their Reading Notes, have them return to their groups. Give each group a copy of *Student Handout 34B: Island Types* and have them cut it into three strips. Ask the questions below, allowing 30 seconds for groups to discuss a possible answer and justification for each. Then have groups hold up the strip with the island they think best answers the question. Ask a few volunteers to share their group's reasoning, and then reveal the correct answer. Consider giving extra points for correct answers.

- On this island, people can hike over glaciers or lie on the beach. *New Zealand*

- The landing strip at this airport takes up more than half the island. *Kwajalein*

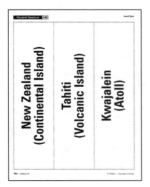

Student Handout 34B

- This island's capital is the southernmost in the world. *New Zealand*
- Volcanoes created the black sand beaches on this island. *Tahiti*
- This island is so low that no part of the land is taller than the palm trees found there. *Kwajalein*
- On this island, most of the land is too steep to grow food on. *Tahiti*
- This island chain surrounds the largest lagoon in the world. *Kwajalein Atoll*
- Long mountain ranges dominate the center of this island, which fans out to flat coastal plains used for farming and sheep grazing. *New Zealand*
- This island is made up of two inactive volcanoes connected by a narrow isthmus. *Tahiti*
- It rains nearly every day on this warm tropical island. The humidity rusts bikes very quickly, and the island even has its own "bicycle heaven." *Kwajalein*

Global Connections

1 Introduce the Global Connections. Have students read Section 34.7. Then explain that they will now learn about the causes and consequences of overfishing, one of the most pressing concerns regarding oceans today.

2 Project *Transparency 34C: Global Connections.* Have students analyze the map by discussing and sharing their answers to the questions below. Use the additional information given to enrich the discussion.

Transparency 34C

- **What do the dark blue areas on this map represent?** *The dark blue areas represent the parts of the ocean where commercial fishing can be regulated. All countries control the waters 200 nautical miles (230 miles) from their shorelines. Beyond these areas, commercial fishing is largely unregulated.*

- **What do the drawings in the ocean represent?** *They represent types of sea life that are overfished and are considered endangered in certain parts of the ocean.*

- **Why do you think overfishing occurs in some areas but not others?** *Only areas within 200 nautical miles from a country can be regulated by that county. That leaves a lot of unregulated areas. Ships from any country can fish in those waters, and there is no one there to enforce fishing regulations. These areas are often overfished.*

3 **Have students read Section 34.8 and examine the rest of the information in the section.** Then lead a discussion of these questions:

- **What is happening to the world's fish supply and why?**

- **What problems might overfishing cause?**

- **What can be done to prevent overfishing?**

Processing

Have students complete Processing 34 in their Interactive Student Notebooks.

Online Resources

For more information on the Pacific islands, refer students to Online Resources for *Geography Alive! Regions and People* at www.teachtci.com.

Assessment

Masters for assessment appear on the next three pages followed by answers and scoring rubrics.

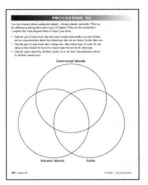

Processing 34

Mastering the Content

Shade in the oval by the letter of the best answer for each question.

1. How are continental islands different from other types of islands?

   ◯ A. They are mountainous.

   ◯ B. They are protected by coral reefs.

   ◯ C. They were once part of a larger landmass.

   ◯ D. They were formed by lava flowing on the seabed.

2. Which of these descriptions **best** fits a volcanic island?

   ◯ A. large and varied in landforms

   ◯ B. cone shaped with steep slopes

   ◯ C. ring shaped with a central lagoon

   ◯ D. low and sandy with little vegetation

3. A body of shallow water partly cut off from the ocean by coral reefs is called which of the following?

   ◯ A. a basin

   ◯ B. a bay

   ◯ C. a gulf

   ◯ D. a lagoon

4. Based on the climagraph below, which type of climate is found in Tahiti?

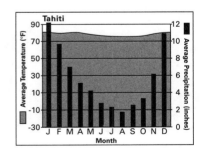

   ◯ A. tropical wet and dry

   ◯ B. marine west coast

   ◯ C. humid continental

   ◯ D. tropical wet

5. Oceans provide all of the following **except**

   ◯ A. food.

   ◯ B. medicines.

   ◯ C. fossil fuels.

   ◯ D. human habitat.

6. Which physical feature are you **least likely** to find on or near an atoll?

   ◯ A. reef

   ◯ B. river

   ◯ C. beach

   ◯ D. lagoon

7. Which of these conclusions is **best** supported by the map of Tahiti below?

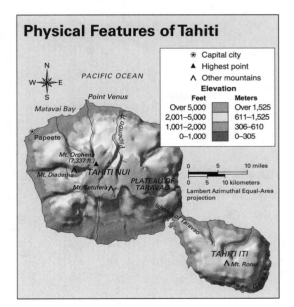

   ◯ A. It has few year-round rivers.

   ◯ B. It was formed by two volcanoes.

   ◯ C. It is often hit by tropical cyclones.

   ◯ D. It was once covered by grasslands.

8. Why are some species of ocean fish becoming endangered species?

   ◯ A. accidental pollution

   ◯ B. ozone depletion

   ◯ C. overfishing

   ◯ D. salinization

Applying Geography Skills:
Reading an Ocean Currents Map

Use this map and your knowledge of geography to complete the
tasks below.

Ocean Surface Currents

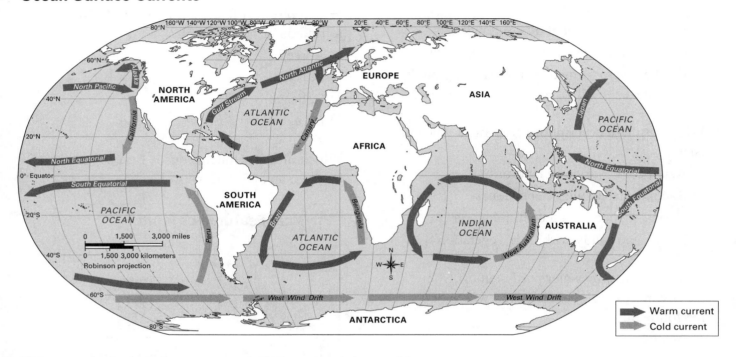

This map shows how ocean currents move around the world.

1. Examine the map carefully. Find and circle the names of three
   cold currents.

2. Examine the cold currents in the Northern Hemisphere. Describe
   the pattern of movement you see.

3. Examine the ocean currents in the Indian Ocean. Beginning at the
   equator, describe the pattern of movement you see. Tell what happens
   to the temperature of the current as it moves.

4. Explain how the ocean currents in the Indian Ocean affect climates
   in parts of Africa and Australia.

Exploring the Essential Question

How do people adapt to life in an island region?

In Chapter 34, you explored the physical geography of three types of Pacific islands. Now you will use what you learned. Use this illustration and your knowledge of geography to complete the task below.

The Task: Writing a Travel Article About a Pacific Island

This illustration shows the relative size and shape of three types of islands in the Pacific Ocean. Your task is to write a travel article about one of these types of islands. Travel articles appear in many newspapers and magazines. Their purpose is to interest readers in traveling to places they may know little about.

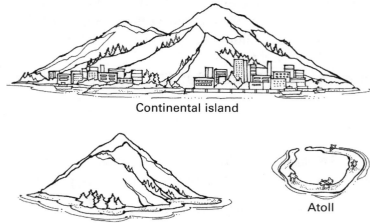

Continental island

Volcanic island

Atoll

Step 1: Circle the type of island you want to write about. Give your island a name. It can be a real island name or one that you make up for your article. Write its name here.

Step 2: List three physical features of your island. These should include landforms and bodies of water.

Step 3: List two facts about your island's climate. Base these facts on what you know about ocean currents and extreme weather in the Pacific.

Step 4: List three facts about life on your island. They might include facts about the economy, food, housing, recreation, or transportation.

Step 5: On another sheet of paper, write a short travel article about your island. Your article should include the following:
A. an opening paragraph that will excite readers to learn more about your island
B. a second paragraph about the physical features and climate of your island
C. a third paragraph about life on your island
D. a concluding paragraph that tells readers why they should visit your island

Writing Tips: Creating Word Pictures
Travel writers create word pictures of the places they write about. To do this, they use words that appeal to our five senses. Such words tell readers what things look like and how they sound, smell, taste, or feel.

Applying Geography Skills: Sample Responses

1. Students should have circled the names of three cold currents.
2. In the Northern Hemisphere, cold currents travel south toward the equator. They also curve toward the southwest.
3. Starting at the equator, the current flows counterclockwise, south along the east coast of Africa and then north again along the west coast of Australia. The current starts warm at the equator, loses heat as it moves east, and returns to the equator as a cool current.
4. The current warms the climate along the southeast coast of Africa and cools the climate along the west coast of Australia.

Exploring the Essential Question: Sample Response

Steps 1–4: Accept any reasonable answer based on the type of island identified.

Step 5: The article should include the elements listed in the prompt. These elements are identified by letter in the response below.

(A) I had heard good things about the island of Teal. But I was not prepared for my first sight of this island. As my plane approached the island, I saw crystal blue waters surrounding a majestic, black volcano. When the plane came in to land, I could see green fields edged by white sand beaches. Everything I had heard about Teal was coming true before my eyes.

(B) A thin band of sparkling white sand surrounds the island like a bracelet. Inside that band, a deep, green forest marches up the steep mountain slopes. The lush forest is home to brightly colored birds and sweet-smelling flowers. Small trails lead to waterfalls that cascade down cliffs to deep blue pools. The warm sunny days often end with a short downpour. At times, the rain sounds like a drum beating on rooftops. Then the skies clear again.

(C) Near the beach is a quiet village. Its friendly people still fish in traditional ways. They also plant crops on any flat land they can find. Teal's people are very welcoming to the few tourists who come here. Visitors are honored guests at local celebrations. On those occasions, the smell of roasting fish and vegetables fills the air. Everyone dances to island music.

(D) My few days on Teal were unforgettable. Yours will be too. For a step back in time, Teal is a perfect vacation destination.

Mastering the Content Answer Key

1. C	2. B	3. D	4. A
5. D	6. B	7. B	8. C

Applying Geography Skills Scoring Rubric

Score	General Description
2	Student responds to all parts of the task. Response is correct and clear.
1	Student responds to some parts of the task. Response is mostly correct.
0	Response does not match the task or is incorrect.

Exploring the Essential Question Scoring Rubric

Score	General Description
3	Student responds to all parts of the task. Response is correct, clear, and supported by details.
2	Student responds to most or all parts of the task. Response is generally correct but may lack details.
1	Student responds to at least one part of the task. Response may contain errors and lack details.
0	Response does not match the task or is incorrect.

Create an Illustrated Map of New Zealand

You will work in a group of four to create an illustrated map of one type of Pacific island: a continental island. Your illustrated map will include a large outline of your island in the center of a large sheet of paper. Design your map to give viewers a good understanding of the physical and human geography of your island.

Step 1: Review your role. Your teacher will assign each member of your group one of the following roles. All group members are responsible for brainstorming ideas for creating an illustrated map that clearly shows the physical and human geography of your island.

- **Physical Geographer:** Responsible for physical geography requirements on the map. See Step 2A. Assists with production of the final map.

- **Ocean Expert:** Responsible for ocean and climate requirements on the map. See Step 2B. Assists with production of the final map.

- **Human Geographer:** Responsible for human geography requirements on the map. See Step 2C. Assists with production of the final map.

- **Cartographer:** Responsible for creating the outline of the island and the map legend. See Step 2D. Leads brainstorming session and production of the final map. Helps to create and place symbols and illustrations on the map.

Step 2: Review the project requirements. Your project will include symbols and illustrations laid out over and around a map of your island. It must have the following things:

A. Physical geography: Work with the Cartographer to choose symbols from the Symbol Bank for these features. Place the symbols on your map in the appropriate places. Label each symbol with the name of that feature.

❏ highest point of elevation ❏ largest plain ❏ volcanoes

❏ largest plateau ❏ largest lake

❏ longest river ❏ largest mountain range

B. Ocean, climate, and economy: On your map, label these features with their names:

❏ 2 major bodies of water ❏ largest strait

Create symbols or illustrations with labels for these features:

❏ 2 food sources from ocean ❏ 2 types of sea life

❏ at least 2 types of climate ❏ 1 economic activity

C. Human geography: Create symbols or illustrations with labels for these features:

❏ 3 forms of recreation   ❏ capital city

❏ largest city on each island   ❏ 2 forms of transportation

❏ 1 type of housing   ❏ 2 sources of food from land

D. Cartography: Create the following map features. Select the appropriate symbols for your map from the Symbol Bank.

❏ a compass rose

❏ a map scale

❏ a map title

❏ a map legend with symbols for
- land physical features
- ocean physical features
- major cities

Symbol Bank

Symbol	Feature	Symbol	Feature
◸	Mountain	◹	Plain
▲	Highest point	◌	Lagoon
⬕	Volcano	⊓	Plateau
⬗	Lake	⊙	City (100,000–499,999)
∫	River	◉	City (500,000–1,000,000)
◿	Strait	☆	Capital city

Step 3: Complete the Reading Notes for Section 34.4. Read Section 34.4 on New Zealand. Use this section to gather background information on the physical and human geography affecting life on your island type. As you read, complete Reading Notes 34.4.

_____ **Step 4: Brainstorm ideas and create a rough draft of your map.** Make sure to include all items on the checklists in Step 2. Quickly brainstorm appropriate symbols and illustrations. Sketch them on the outline of your island on the third page of this handout. Get your teacher's initials for this step before moving on.

_____ **Step 5: Create your final map.** The Cartographer will create the outline of your island and the map legend. Each expert will create the symbols and illustrations and the labels for his or her area of expertise (physical geography, human geography, or ocean). All group members will work with the Cartographer to lay out the final map. Use color and creative touches to make it visually appealing. When you are done, have your teacher review your work and initial this step.

New Zealand

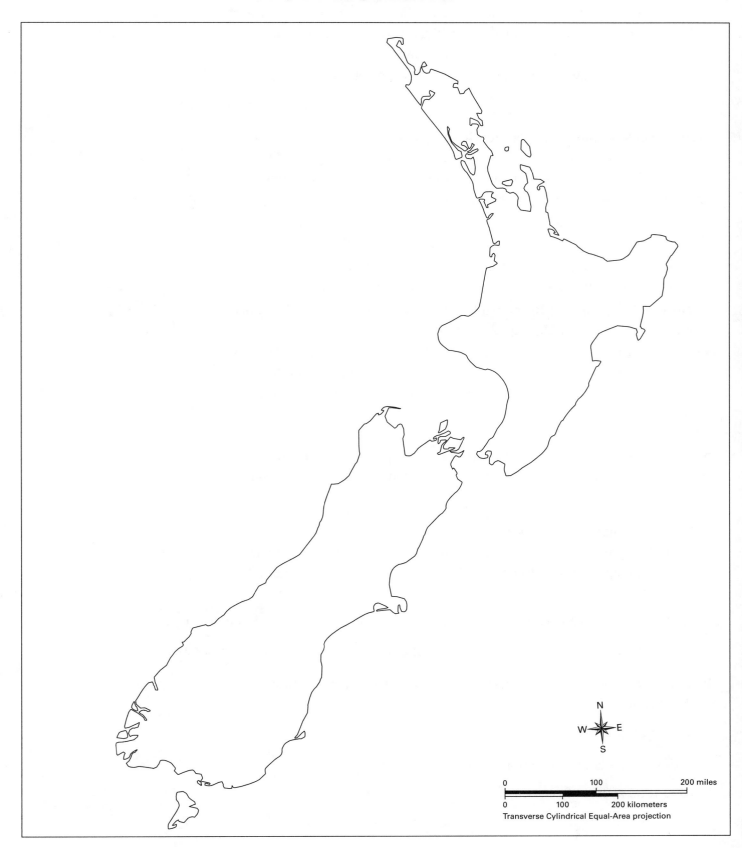

0   100   200 miles

0   100   200 kilometers

Transverse Cylindrical Equal-Area projection

Create an Illustrated Map of Tahiti

You will work in a group of four to create an illustrated map of one type of Pacific island: a volcanic island. Your illustrated map will include a large outline of your island in the center of a large sheet of paper. Design your map to give viewers a good understanding of the physical and human geography of your island.

Step 1: Review your role. Your teacher will assign each member of your group one of the following roles. All group members are responsible for brainstorming ideas for creating an illustrated map that clearly shows the physical and human geography of your island.

- **Physical Geographer:** Responsible for physical geography requirements on the map. See Step 2A. Assists with production of the final map.
- **Ocean Expert:** Responsible for ocean and climate requirements on the map. See Step 2B. Assists with production of the final map.
- **Human Geographer:** Responsible for human geography requirements on the map. See Step 2C. Assists with production of the final map.
- **Cartographer:** Responsible for creating the outline of the island and the map legend. See Step 2D. Leads brainstorming session and production of the final map. Helps to create and place symbols and illustrations on the map.

Step 2: Review the project requirements. Your project will include symbols and illustrations laid out over and around a map of your island. It must have the following things:

A. Physical geography: Work with the Cartographer to choose symbols from the Symbol Bank for these features. Place the symbols on your map in the appropriate places. Label each symbol with the name of that feature.

❏ highest point of elevation   ❏ major isthmus   ❏ longest river

❏ coastal cliffs   ❏ 4 mountains   ❏ largest bay

B. Ocean, climate, and economy: On your map, label these features with their names:

❏ major bodies of water

Create symbols or illustrations with labels for these features:

❏ 2 food sources from ocean   ❏ 2 economic activities

❏ 2 types of sea life   ❏ 2 types of climate

C. Human geography: Create symbols or illustrations with labels for these features:

❏ 3 forms of recreation ❏ 1 form of transportation

❏ 1 type of traditional clothing ❏ capital city

❏ 2 types of housing ❏ 2 sources of food from land

D. Cartography: Create the following map features. Select the appropriate symbols for your map from the Symbol Bank.

❏ a compass rose

❏ a map scale

❏ a map title

❏ a map legend with symbols for
  • land physical features
  • ocean physical features
  • major cities

Symbol Bank

Symbol		Symbol	
△	Mountain	▨	Plain
▲	Highest point	◌	Lagoon
🌋	Volcano	⊓	Plateau
🗺	Lake	☉	City (100,000–499,999)
〰	River	◉	City (500,000–1,000,000)
▨	Strait	☆	Capital city

Step 3: Complete the Reading Notes for Section 34.5. Read Section 34.5 on Tahiti. Use this section to gather background information on the physical and human geography affecting life on your island type. As you read, complete Reading Notes 34.5.

_____ **Step 4: Brainstorm ideas and create a rough draft of your map.** Make sure to include all items on the checklists in Step 2. Quickly brainstorm appropriate symbols and illustrations. Sketch them on the outline of your island on the third page of this handout. Get your teacher's initials for this step before moving on.

_____ **Step 5: Create your final map.** The Cartographer will create the outline of your island and the map legend. Each expert will create the symbols and illustrations and the labels for his or her area of expertise (physical geography, human geography, or ocean). All group members will work with the Cartographer to lay out the final map. Use color and creative touches to make it visually appealing. When you are done, have your teacher review your work and initial this step.

Tahiti

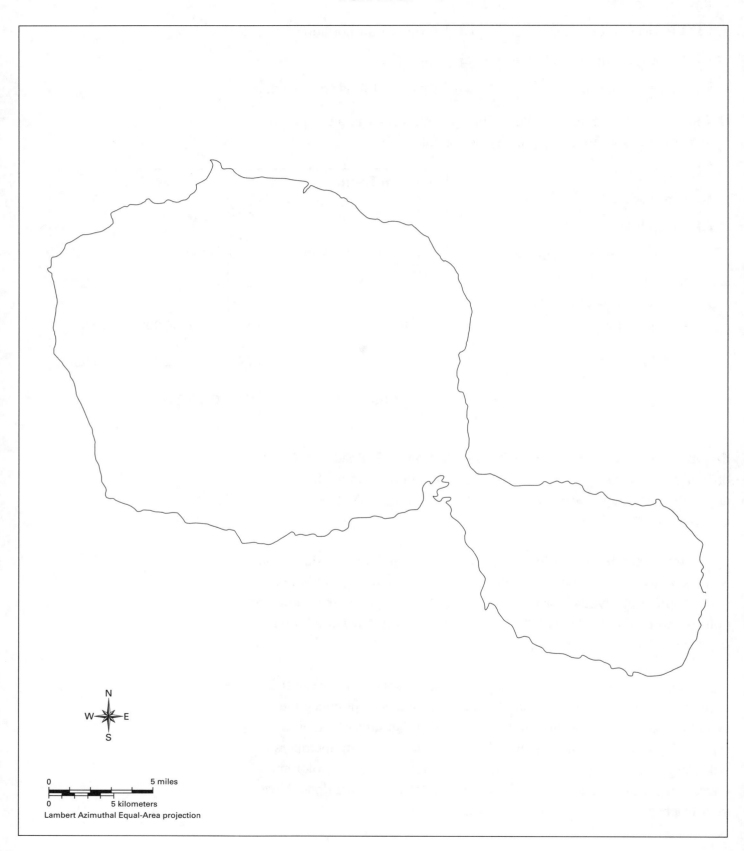

Create an Illustrated Map of Kwajalein Atoll

You will work in a group of four to create an illustrated map of one type of Pacific island: an atoll. Your illustrated map will include a large outline of your island in the center of a large sheet of paper. Design your map to give viewers a good understanding of the physical and human geography of your island.

Step 1: Review your role. Your teacher will assign each member of your group one of the following roles. All group members are responsible for brainstorming ideas for creating an illustrated map that clearly shows the physical and human geography of your island.

- **Physical Geographer:** Responsible for physical geography requirements on the map. See Step 2A. Assists with production of the final map.

- **Ocean Expert:** Responsible for ocean and climate requirements on the map. See Step 2B. Assists with production of the final map.

- **Human Geographer:** Responsible for human geography requirements on the map. See Step 2C. Assists with production of the final map.

- **Cartographer:** Responsible for creating the outline of the island and the map legend. See Step 2D. Leads brainstorming session and production of the final map. Helps to create and place symbols and illustrations on the map.

Step 2: Review the project requirements. Your project will include symbols and illustrations laid out over and around a map of your island. It must have the following things:

A. Physical geography: Work with the Cartographer to choose symbols from the Symbol Bank for these features. Place the symbols on your map in the appropriate places. Label each symbol with the name of that feature.

- ❏ major bodies of water   ❏ 19 islands

B. Ocean, climate, and economy: Create symbols and illustrations with labels for these features:

- ❏ 2 food sources from the ocean   ❏ at least 2 types of climate

- ❏ 2 types of sea life   ❏ 1 economic activity

C. Human geography: Create symbols or illustrations with labels for these features:

- ❏ 3 forms of recreation
- ❏ 2 types of seasonal clothing
- ❏ 2 types of housing
- ❏ 1 form of transportation
- ❏ 2 sources of food from land

D. Cartography: Create the following map features. Select the appropriate symbols for your map from the Symbol Bank.

- ❏ a compass rose
- ❏ a map scale
- ❏ a map title
- ❏ a map legend with symbols for
  - land physical features
  - ocean physical features
  - major cities

Symbol Bank

⟨△⟩	Mountain	⟨▨⟩	Plain
⟨▲⟩	Highest point	⟨◌⟩	Lagoon
⟨🌋⟩	Volcano	⟨⎍⟩	Plateau
⟨◠⟩	Lake	⊙	City (100,000–499,999)
⟨∿⟩	River	◉	City (500,000–1,000,000)
⟨≋⟩	Strait	☆	Capital city

Step 3: Complete the Reading Notes for Section 34.6. Read Section 34.6 on Kwajalein Island. Use this section to gather background information on the physical and human geography affecting life on your island type. As you read, complete Reading Notes 34.6.

_____ **Step 4: Brainstorm ideas and create a rough draft of your map.** Make sure to include all items on the checklists in Step 2. Quickly brainstorm appropriate symbols and illustrations. Sketch them on the outline of your island on the third page of this handout. Get your teacher's initials for this step before moving on.

_____ **Step 5: Create your final map.** The Cartographer will create the outline of your island and the map legend. Each expert will create the symbols and illustrations and the labels for his or her area of expertise (physical geography, human geography, or ocean). All group members will work with the Cartographer to lay out the final map. Use color and creative touches to make it visually appealing. When you are done, have your teacher review your work and initial this step.

Kwajalein Atoll

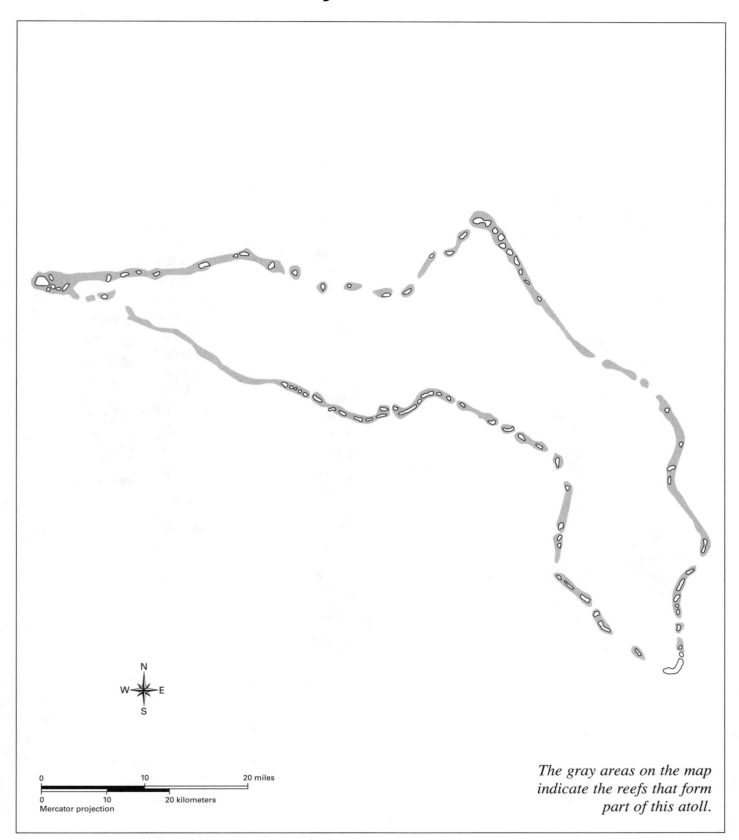

N
W E
S

0   10   20 miles
0   10   20 kilometers
Mercator projection

*The gray areas on the map
indicate the reefs that form
part of this atoll.*

New Zealand (Continental Island)

Tahiti (Volcanic Island)

Kwajalein (Atoll)

34.3 The Ocean Shapes Life in the Pacific

Read Section 34.3, and complete the notes below.

- Around the map, write two facts to explain how ocean surface currents work. Use a line to connect each fact to the appropriate part of the map. An example is done for you.

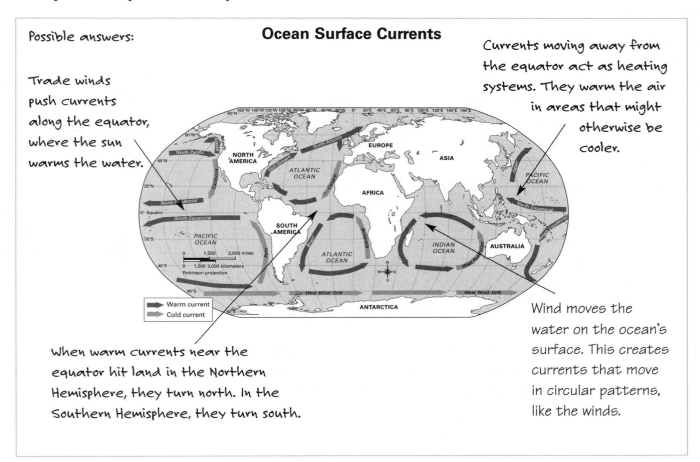

Possible answers:

Ocean Surface Currents

Currents moving away from the equator act as heating systems. They warm the air in areas that might otherwise be cooler.

Trade winds push currents along the equator, where the sun warms the water.

When warm currents near the equator hit land in the Northern Hemisphere, they turn north. In the Southern Hemisphere, they turn south.

Wind moves the water on the ocean's surface. This creates currents that move in circular patterns, like the winds.

- Explain why islands in the Pacific have warm temperatures and lots of rain. Pacific islands are mostly in warm equatorial waters. Warm air can hold a lot of moisture. Warm ocean water evaporates easily to provide that moisture. As the wet, warm air rises, it forms rain clouds. This means the islands in the area have tropical wet climates where it rains a lot. Islands farther from the equator are cooler and drier.

- In the space below, quickly sketch and label four resources found in the Pacific.
  Sketches might include fish (food), sea sponges or marine snails (medicine), oysters (pearls), metal ores, oil, or natural gas.

34.4 Life on a Continental Island: New Zealand

Step 1: Examine the continental island maps your class created.
Take notes below based on what you learn from the maps.

Step 2: Read Section 34.4. Use what you learned in both
Sections 34.2 and 34.4 to correct and add to your notes below.

- Around the drawing of a continental
  island, write two facts about this type
  of island. Draw a line from each fact to
  an appropriate part of the island. Add
  to the drawing if it helps illustrate your
  facts. An example is done for you.

Answers will vary.

*Large cities can usually
be found on continental
islands.*

- Listed below are four features of New Zealand. Describe each feature.
  Include at least two facts in each of your descriptions.

physical features: *Mountains dominate New Zealand's two large islands.
The North Island has rivers, lakes, hot springs, and geysers. On the South
Island, the Southern Alps are covered by snow all year and the west coast
has fjords. New Zealand also has lots of fertile land.*

climate: *Temperatures are moderate all year. Most days are sunny, but the islands
receive regular rain. The warm, moist winds blow from west to east. The western
slopes of the mountains can get more than an inch of rain daily. The eastern side
gets only 25 inches a year.*

economy: *Sheep are a major industry. Fishing is another important part of New Zealand's
economy. The islands also attract many tourists.*

human adaptations: *Most New Zealanders live on the North Island and in cities. People wear
cooler clothes in the summer and warmer clothes in the winter. There is outdoor recreation like
skiing, hiking, surfing, sailing, swimming, fishing, kayaking, and white-water rafting. People travel
by car, train, bus, and airplane.*

- Which features make New Zealand a classic continental island? *New Zealand was once part
  of a larger landmass. The movement of tectonic plates broke the landmass apart to form
  Antarctica, Australia, and several continental islands. Like most continental islands, New
  Zealand is relatively large.*

34.5 Life on a Volcanic Island: Tahiti

Step 1: Examine the volcanic island maps your class created.
Take notes below based on what you learn from the maps.

Step 2: Read Section 34.5. Use what you learned in both
Sections 34.2 and 34.5 to correct and add to your notes below.

- Around the drawing of a volcanic island,   *Answers will vary.*
  write two facts about this type of island.
  Draw a line from each fact to an appropriate
  part of the island. Add to the drawing if
  it helps illustrate your facts. An example
  is done for you.

Volcanic islands are created
when volcanoes break through
the ocean floor. Lava and ash
build up on the ocean floor,
rising to above sea level.

- Include at least two facts in each of your descriptions.

  physical features: Tahiti is made up of two inactive volcanoes, Tahiti
  Nui (Big Tahiti) and Tahiti Iti (Small Tahiti). An isthmus connects them.
  The land on both parts rises steeply from the coast to the volcano
  craters. There are waterfalls and cliffs on the steep land.

  climate: Tahiti has two seasons. The wet season, from November to April,
  brings most of the annual rain, and temperatures are in the 80s. During
  the dry season, from May to October, temperatures are slightly lower.

  economy: Only Tahiti's coastal plain is flat enough to grow crops, like breadfruit, coconut palms,
  citrus fruits, and orchids. Because of its growing population, Tahitians import most of what they
  eat. The economy depends on the ocean, which attracts tourism, produces black pearls, and
  supports commercial fishing.

  human adaptations: Most Tahitians live on Tahiti Nui, where the crowded city of Papeete is.
  Other parts are less built up, and some people still live in traditional villages. Houses are larger
  and sturdier than in the past. Casual, modern clothes have replaced the traditional pareu. For
  recreation, people scuba dive, snorkel, surf, hike, ride horses, and hang glide. They travel to and
  from Tahiti on planes and use cars and buses on the island.

- What features make Tahiti a classic volcanic island? Tahiti is made up of two inactive volcanoes.
  The volcanoes are cone shaped, with steep slopes rising to high peaks.

34.6 Life on an Atoll: Kwajalein Island

Step 1: Examine the atoll maps your class created. Take notes below based on what you learn from the maps.

Step 2: Read Section 34.6. Use what you learned in both Sections 34.2 and 34.6 to correct and add to your notes below.

- Around the drawing of an atoll, write two facts about this type of island. Draw a line from each fact to an appropriate part of the island. Add to the drawing if it helps illustrate your facts. An example is done for you.

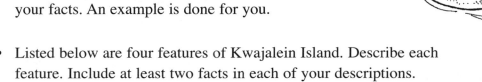

Answers will vary.

Atolls have very low elevations.

- Listed below are four features of Kwajalein Island. Describe each feature. Include at least two facts in each of your descriptions.

physical features: Kwajalein is the largest coral atoll in the world. Its 97 islands cover only 6.5 square miles. The atoll surrounds a large lagoon. It has a very low elevation. Because the island is so small and low, there are no rivers or springs.

climate: Kwajalein has a tropical wet climate. Temperatures are almost always in the 80s, and rain falls daily during both the wet and "dry" seasons. Showers don't last as long during the drier months. Tropical storms can cause storm surges, but coral reefs protect the islands from flooding.

economy: There is little agriculture, but coconut palms, breadfruit, and arrowroot are grown. Copra, or dried coconut meat, is the main product, and fish is an important food. The economy is based on the U.S. military base located on the island. Tourism is also important.

human adaptations: Fourteen of the atoll's islands are inhabited. Most travel on Kwajalein Island is on bicycles, which rust quickly in the wet weather. Ferries and planes link people to the other islands and the outside world. Residents live in trailers, concrete and wooden houses, and dome houses, all of which are owned by the U.S. military. They wear casual, modern clothes and enjoy scuba diving, sailing, windsurfing, sport fishing, and common American activities like volleyball, softball, and bowling.

- What features makes Kwajalein Atoll a classic atoll?
  Kwajalein Atoll is a low-lying ring of coral islands and reefs surrounding a shallow lagoon.

Antarctica: Researching Global Warming at the Coldest Place on Earth

Overview

In this lesson, students explore how Antarctica is affected by world climate changes. In a **Writing for Understanding** activity, they "visit" Antarctica to discover why this unique and barren land is so ideal for the study of global warming. After collecting evidence at three research stations, they write a dialogue debating the theory of global warming.

Objectives

Students will

- define and explain the importance of these key geographic terms: *biome, global warming, greenhouse effect, ice shelf.*
- discover why Antarctica is an ideal place for a wide variety of research, especially that concerning global warming.
- examine how global warming may be affecting Antarctica's temperature, ice shelves, and penguin populations.
- investigate how global climate change could affect the rest of the world.

Materials

- *Geography Alive! Regions and People*
- Interactive Student Notebooks
- Transparencies 35A–35D
- Information Master 35 (1 transparency)
- Station Labels 35A–35C (1 of each)
- Station Directions 35A–35C (3 of each)
- Station Materials 35A (3 copies of the thermometer readings and 3 of the dialogue)
- Station Materials 35B (6 transparencies of the grid, 3 copies of each satellite image, and 3 copies of the dialogue)
- Station Materials 35C (10 copies of each nest photograph and 3 of the dialogue)
- CD Tracks 23–28
- paper towels or cloths
- 6 transparency markers in at least 2 colors
- 3 or more calculators

Preview

1 Have students complete Preview 35 in their Interactive Student Notebooks. When they've finished, ask them to nominate one item from the list that they think is most clearly an exaggeration. Dramatically reveal the correct answers, one at a time. In reality, every item on the list is a fact about Antarctica.

Preview 35

2 Explain the connection between the Preview and the upcoming activity. Tell students that in the upcoming activity they will learn more about Antarctica's unique environment, how researchers study that environment, and how it may be affected by changes in the global climate. In the activity, students will "visit" three research stations in Antarctica, collect data, and analyze whether the data support or throw doubt on the theory of global warming.

Essential Question and Geoterms

1 Project the top half of *Transparency 35A: Flight to Antarctica* **and play CD Track 23, "Preparing to Leave Christchurch, New Zealand."** This track introduces students to the classroom activity—a research trip to Antarctica—and directs them to do some background reading while they wait to board the plane.

Transparency 35A

2 Have students read Section 35.1 in *Geography Alive! Regions and People.* Then ask them to identify sentences or phrases in the text that reflect aspects of the photograph of a researcher in Antarctica.

3 Introduce the Graphic Organizer and the Essential Question. Have students examine the illustration of the two researchers. Ask,

- Who are these two figures?
- What issue are they debating?
- What information might geographers look for to try to determine whether global warming is occurring?

Have students read the accompanying text. Make sure they understand the Essential Question, *How might global warming affect the environment in the world's coldest places?* You may want to post the Essential Question in the room or write it on the board for the duration of the activity.

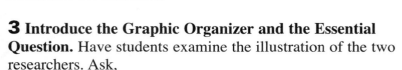

4 Have students read Section 35.2. Then have them complete Geoterms 35 in their Interactive Student Notebooks, individually or in pairs. Have them share their answers with another student, or have volunteers share their answers with the class.

Geoterms 35

Writing for Understanding

Phase 1: Traveling to Antarctica

1 Set up the classroom. Clear an open space in the center of the room for students to sit on the floor during their "flight" to Antarctica. (**Note:** Consider making the flight more realistic by making the classroom colder. Lower the thermostat, open doors or windows, or turn on a fan or an air conditioner. You might also have students bring in ECW—extreme cold weather—gear, such as heavy jackets and gloves.)

2 Place students in mixed-ability pairs. You might prepare a transparency showing them who their research partners are. Have partners sit together on the floor. Make sure they pack a copy of *Geography Alive! Regions and People,* their Interactive Student Notebooks, and a pencil.

3 Project the bottom half of Transparency 35A and play CD Track 24, "Boarding Flight 1136 to McMurdo Base in Antarctica." When the geographer from Argentina begins to read his "speech," direct students to follow along by reading Section 35.3. Afterward, have partners work together to complete this section of Reading Notes 35.

4 Repeat Step 3, projecting the top half of *Transparency 35B: Arriving in Antarctica* **and playing CD Tracks 25 and 26, "Supporters and Doubters of the Global Warming Theory."** When the geographers from New Zealand and Russia are introduced on the track, have students follow along by reading Sections 35.4 and 35.5, respectively. After each track, have partners complete the corresponding Reading Notes.

5 Project the bottom half of Transparency 35B and play CD Track 27, "Welcome to McMurdo Base." Then wrap up Phase 1 of the activity by asking students,

- What interesting things have you learned so far about Antarctica?
- What have you learned about the geographers who conduct research in Antarctica?
- Why is Antarctica a good place to study global warming?
- Do all geographers agree that global warming is occurring? Why or why not?

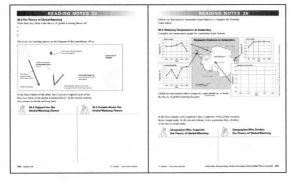

Reading Notes 35

Transparency 35B

Phase 2: Gathering Research on Global Warming in Antarctica

1 Set up the classroom. Create three Antarctica research stations —Amundsen-Scott, Rothera, and Palmer—along three walls of the classroom. For each research station, create three work areas for students by placing two desks together and pushing them up against the wall. Use these checklists to set up each station:

Amundsen-Scott Station

- Place *Station Label 35A: Amundsen-Scott Station* high on the wall.
- At each of the three work areas, tape a copy of *Station Directions 35A: Research at Amundsen-Scott Station* to the wall.
- At each work area, place one copy of *Station Materials 35A: Temperature Readings at Amundsen-Scott Station* and one of *Station Materials 35A: Amundsen-Scott Dialogue* on the desks.

Rothera Station

- Place *Station Label 35B: Rothera Station* high on the wall.
- At each of the three work areas, tape a copy of *Station Directions 35B: Research at Rothera Station* to the wall.
- At each work area, place two transparencies of *Station Materials 35B: Grid for Analyzing Satellite Images,* one copy of *Station Materials 35B: Satellite Image 1,* one copy of *Station Materials 35B: Satellite Image 2,* and one copy of *Station Materials 35B: Rothera Dialogue* on the desks.
- At each work area, place a damp cloth (for wiping the transparencies clean) and two transparency markers in different colors. Place at least one calculator at the station. (**Note:** Optionally, ask each pair of students to bring a calculator with them.)

Palmer Station

- Place *Station Label 35C: Palmer Station* high on the wall.
- At each of the three work areas, tape a copy of *Station Directions 35C: Research at Palmer Station* to the wall.
- At each work area, place one copy of *Station Materials 35C: Palmer Dialogue* on the desks.
- Place at least one calculator at the station.
- On the floor next to the station or in a hallway or area right outside the classroom, create an Adelie penguin colony by randomly placing 10 copies each of *Station Materials 35C: Adelie Penguin Nests 1–5* on the floor.
- Set up a CD player near the Adelie penguin colony. Cue it to CD Track 28, "Adelie Penguin Sounds."

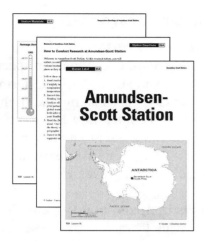

Station Label 35A
Station Directions 35A
Station Materials 35A

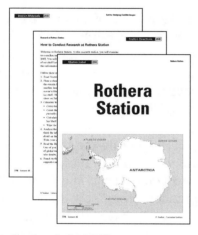

Station Label 35B
Station Directions 35B
Station Materials 35B

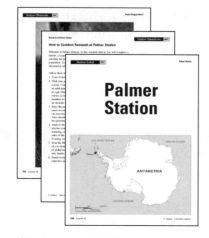

Station Label 35C
Station Directions 35C
Station Materials 35C

2 Introduce Phase 2 of the activity. Have students sit with their partners. Explain that they will now visit three research stations in Antarctica and complete important fieldwork at each. To do this fieldwork, they will need their textbooks and Interactive Student Notebooks. Explain that each research station has three "work areas," with space and materials for two pairs at each work area; each station can thus accommodate 12 students in all. Tell students to follow these steps:

• Go to a research station, and find space at one of the work areas.

• Carefully read and complete each task on the Station Directions posted there.

• Once you have completed *all* the tasks on the Station Directions, have the teacher check your work. If complete, go to a new station.

3 Have students complete their Antarctic fieldwork. While students are visiting the three stations, keep the activity running smoothly by doing the following:

• Make sure no more than two pairs are at any one work area.

• If students are waiting, direct them to an open work area at that station or to another station.

• When students bring their completed work to you, use Guide to Reading Notes 35 to quickly check their graphs (Amundsen-Scott Station) or math calculations (Rothera and Palmer stations). If correct, just make sure they have completed the remainder of the notes, and send them to the next station. If their graph or math calculations are incorrect, or if they have not completed the remainder of the notes, have them return to the station to redo or complete their work.

4 Review the Reading Notes. Once most or all students have visited all three research stations, use the Guide to Reading Notes to review their Reading Notes as a class. You may want to make transparencies of the blank Reading Notes pages and have students share their answers out loud as you record them. Alternatively, have volunteers come up and write their answers on the transparencies. Have students make necessary corrections or additions to their notes as you review them.

5 Project *Information Master 35: Writing a Dialogue* and review the directions for the writing assignment. Answer any questions students have. (**Note:** Consider giving students a copy of Information Master 35 to use as a checklist of what must be included in their writing assignments. After they have written their first drafts, they should have another person—parent, guardian, older sibling, or friend—use the checklist to make sure they have included all the required elements.)

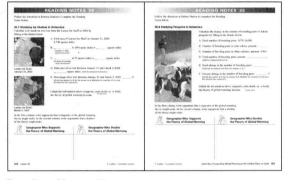

Reading Notes 35

Information Master 35

Global Connections

1 Introduce the Global Connections. Have students read Section 35.9. Then explain that they will now analyze possible consequences of global warming.

2 Project *Transparency 35C: Global Connections.* Have students analyze the three maps by discussing and sharing their answers to the questions below. Use the additional information given to enrich the discussion.

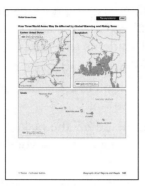

Transparency 35C

- **What do the various colors on these maps represent?**

- **Based on these maps, what parts of the world do you think would be most affected by a 20-foot rise in sea level?**

- **How might such a rise in sea level affect how people live? How you live?**

  If seas rose only 3 feet, the world's coastal cities, which have more than half of the world's population, would be flooded. Low-lying countries like Bangladesh could be wiped out. Cities near river deltas, such as Cairo, Egypt, and New Orleans, United States, may be hit hard, too. Flooding could destroy crops, homes, and highways. Salt water would push upstream, possibly contaminating drinking water.

- **What might cause sea levels to rise so dramatically?**

  If Earth's air temperature rises by only 1.5°F, experts believe that the ice covering parts of the Earth, like Greenland, could begin to melt. The sea level might rise as much as 3 feet. If the Greenland Ice Sheet were to melt completely, the sea level could rise 20 feet or more.

3 Project *Transparency 35D: Global Connections.* Have students analyze the cartogram by discussing and sharing their answers to these questions:

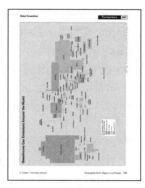

Transparency 35D

- **What interesting details do you see in this cartogram?**

- **Which countries are adding the most greenhouse gases to the environment, in total? How can you tell?**

- **Which countries are adding the most greenhouse gases to the environment, per person? How can you tell?**

- **What might the countries that add the most greenhouse gases to the environment have in common?**

4 Have students read Section 35.10. Then lead a discussion of the questions below. Encourage students to use information from the maps and cartogram to support their answers.

- **How might rising sea levels be connected to greenhouse gases?**

- **Are the countries that produce the most greenhouse gases the ones that will be most affected by rising sea levels?**

- **What can people do to reduce the greenhouse gases they add to the environment?**

Processing

There is no Processing assignment for this activity. The dialogue that students write functions as a Processing assignment.

Online Resources

For more information on Antarctica and global warming, refer students to Online Resources for *Geography Alive! Regions and People* at www.teachtci.com.

Assessment

Masters for assessment appear on the next three pages followed by answers and scoring rubrics.

Mastering the Content

Shade in the oval by the letter of the best answer for each question.

1. What is a biome?
   ○ A. an arid continent
   ○ B. a large watershed
   ○ C. an ice cap habitat
   ○ D. a large ecosystem

2. Which of the following is the **best** definition of an ice shelf?
   ○ A. a huge iceberg that floats free in the ocean
   ○ B. a floating sheet of ice that is attached to a coast
   ○ C. a vast glacier that is up to a mile and a half thick
   ○ D. a moving ice stream that flows across an ice cap

3. According to the theory of global warming, which part of Earth is growing warmer over time?
   ○ A the core
   ○ B. the ocean floor
   ○ C. the surface
   ○ D. the upper mantle

4. Which of the following **best** describes what the greenhouse effect does?
   ○ A. traps energy from the sun in the atmosphere
   ○ B. traps smoke from factories in the atmosphere
   ○ C. traps moisture from clouds in the atmosphere
   ○ D. traps dust from windstorms in the atmosphere

5. Global warming is predicted to lead to all of the following **except**
   ○ A. rising sea levels.
   ○ B. expanding ice caps.
   ○ C. widespread crop failures.
   ○ D. newly endangered species.

6. Scientists who doubt the global warming theory support their view by pointing out that some
   ○ A. penguin populations are shrinking.
   ○ B. greenhouse gases are increasing.
   ○ C. ice cap glaciers are growing.
   ○ D. floating ice shelves are breaking up.

7. One way that scientists learn about the climate of Antarctica thousands of years ago is by studying
   ○ A. ice cores from glaciers.
   ○ B. the growth of ice shelves.
   ○ C. the shrinking of the ozone hole.
   ○ D. changes in penguin populations.

8. Which of these conclusions is **best** supported by the information on the map below?

Bangladesh

Mymensingh

Dhaka

Chittagong

▪ Areas submerged by a 20-foot rise in sea level

   ○ A. Much of Bangladesh is densely populated.
   ○ B. Much of Bangladesh is in a rain shadow.
   ○ C. Much of Bangladesh is dotted by oases.
   ○ D. Much of Bangladesh is low-lying land.

Applying Geography Skills:
Analyzing a Political Cartoon

Use this political cartoon and your knowledge of geography to complete the tasks below.

This political cartoon was created in 2002.

1. Examine the first panel of the cartoon. Identify who the people on the stage and in the audience are. What props has the cartoonist used to help the reader identify each group of people?

2. Read the first two panels. What are the speakers talking about?

3. Look at all four panels together. Describe the action that takes place on stage and in the audience.

4. Summarize the point that the cartoonist is making.

Test Terms Glossary

To **describe** means to provide details about something, such as what happened.

To **summarize** means to briefly present the main points of a subject.

Exploring the Essential Question

How might global warming affect the environment in the world's coldest places?

In Chapter 35, you explored global warming and how it might affect Antarctica. Now you will use what you learned. Use this map and your knowledge of geography to complete the task below.

The Task: Writing an Essay About the Impact of Rising Sea Levels on the United States

Global warming could have a major impact on life in the United States. This map shows some areas in the eastern U.S. that might be affected by global warming. The dark areas would be under water if the ocean were to rise 20 feet. Your task is to write an essay on the problems the country would face if this happened.

Step 1: List two problems that the country might face if sea levels were to rise 20 feet.

Eastern United States

Areas submerged by a 20-foot rise in sea level

Boston
New York City
Washington, D.C.
Charleston
Savannah
St. Augustine
Mobile
Houston
New Orleans
Miami
Corpus Christi

Step 2: List at least one possible way of dealing with each problem you identified above.

Step 3: On another sheet of paper, write a four-paragraph essay on the problems that rising sea levels could cause in the United States. Your essay should include the following:

- an introductory paragraph with a thesis statement that tells the reader what you plan to prove or explain.
- two body paragraphs. Each paragraph should discuss a different problem that the country might face if there were a 20-foot rise in sea level. Describe each challenge, and discuss the country's response to that challenge.
- a concluding paragraph that restates your thesis.

Writing Tips: Restating Your Thesis
A good essay begins with a thesis statement. The thesis statement lays out the position that the writer plans to prove or explain. At the end of the essay, the writer restates the thesis statement. This means repeating it using different words.

Applying Geography Skills: Sample Responses

1. The people on the stage are scientists; the people in the audience are representatives of the media, such as newspaper and television reporters. The lab coats and graphs help to identify the scientists; the cameras and notebooks help to identify the reporters.
2. The speakers are talking about both sides of the global warming debate.
3. The two scientists begin to debate, but as the one who doubts the theory of global warming begins to speak, the reporters begin to walk out until there is only one left.
4. The cartoonist is making the point that media representatives are not always interested in reporting both sides of the global warming debate. Instead, some reporters focus on scary news, not on helping people hear both sides of an issue.

Exploring the Essential Question: Sample Response

Step 1: Problems might include flooded cities, loss of homes, damage to ports, loss of farmland, displaced people, disappearing beaches, and damaged transportation systems.

Step 2: Answers should relate to the challenges listed in Step 1. Examples include moving cities to higher ground, building levees around low-lying cities, creating emergency housing for displaced people, and building bridges or causeways for roads in flooded zones.

Step 3: The essay should include all the elements listed in the prompt.

Mastering the Content Answer Key

1. D	2. B	3. C	4. A
5. B	6. C	7. A	8. D

Applying Geography Skills Scoring Rubric

Score	General Description
2	Student responds to all parts of the task. Response is correct and clear.
1	Student responds to some parts of the task. Response is mostly correct.
0	Response does not match the task or is incorrect.

Exploring the Essential Question Scoring Rubric

Score	General Description
3	Student responds to all parts of the task. Response is correct, clear, and supported by details.
2	Student responds to most or all parts of the task. Response is generally correct but may lack details.
1	Student responds to at least one part of the task. Response may contain errors and lack details.
0	Response does not match the task or is incorrect.

Amundsen-Scott Station

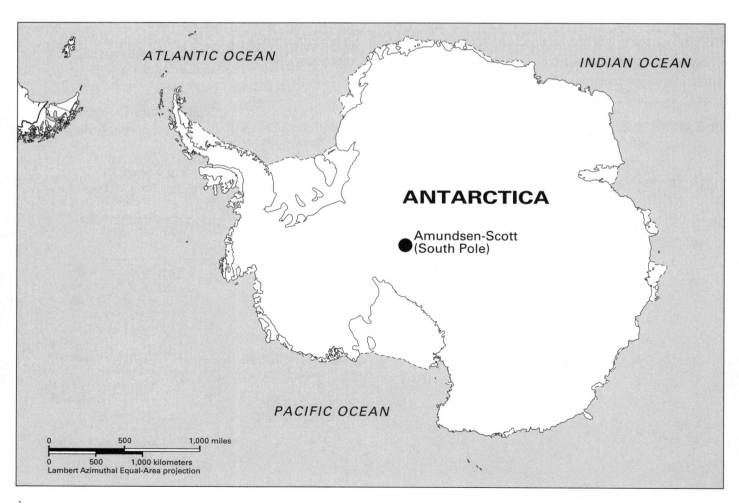

How to Conduct Research at Amundsen-Scott Station

Welcome to Amundsen-Scott Station. At this research station, you will collect, record, and analyze data on the average annual temperature at various locations in Antarctica since 1960. You will also listen to geographers as they debate what this information tells us about global warming.

Follow these steps:

1. Read Section 35.6 in your book.

2. *Carefully* inspect the five thermometers. They show the average annual temperature at this research station from 1960 to 2000. Note that these temperatures are in *negative* degrees.

3. Record this temperature information in the blank graph in your Reading Notes.

4. Analyze all four temperature graphs in your Reading Notes. With your partner, discuss whether you think they *support* the theory of global warming, cast *doubt* on the theory, or could be evidence for both sides of the debate. Record your conclusion and explanation in your Reading Notes.

5. Read the *Dialogue Between Geographers at Amundsen-Scott Station* aloud. One of you should read the part of the geographer who supports the theory of global warming. The other should read the part of the geographer who doubts it.

6. Based on the dialogue, write arguments in your Reading Notes that a supporter and a doubter of the theory might make.

Average Annual Temperature at Amundsen-Scott Station

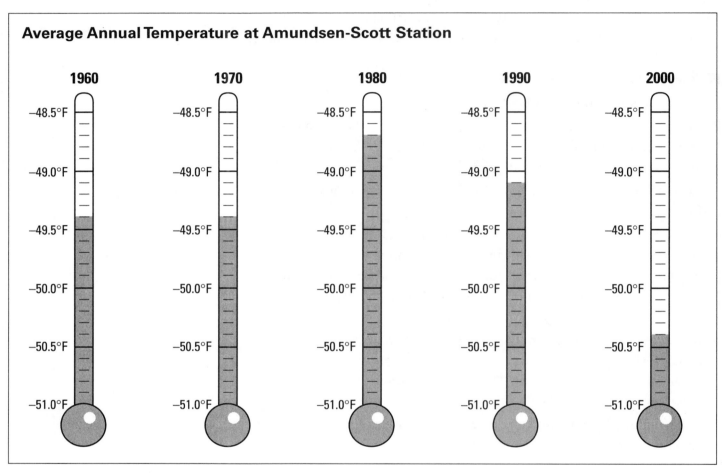

Source: *British Antarctica Survey: National Environmental Resource Council,* www.antarctica.ac.uk/.

Dialogue Between Geographers at Amundsen-Scott Station

Geographer Who Supports the Theory of Global Warming: Just look at these data. It's clear we are seeing warming in Antarctica. The average temperature at two of the stations has risen by 2 or 3 degrees in the last 40 years. And I read a study recently about the Antarctic Peninsula. Temperatures there have risen about 4.5°F in the last 60 years. It was predicted this would happen—and indeed it *is* happening.

Geographer Who Doubts the Theory of Global Warming: Now wait a minute. Imagine laying a grid over all of Antarctica. You would find that less than 40 percent of the grid squares show signs of warming. The rest would actually show cooling. You mention that temperatures have risen on the Antarctic Peninsula. True, but further inland, they have actually fallen 1.2°F in the past 20 years.

Geographer Who Supports the Theory of Global Warming: Let me remind you that Antarctica is a very large landmass. It is hard to generalize from one part of it to another. However, I don't think you can deny the findings that several lakes there are not as frozen as they used to be. Many of these lakes are experiencing thawing for longer periods each summer—sometimes by as much as 30 days longer.

Geographer Who Doubts the Theory of Global Warming: Those temperatures are by no means a "trend." In fact, just last week I read about the West Antarctic Ice Sheet. For years we've been told that the huge sheets of ice that cover Antarctica are melting. But the thickness of this ice sheet was measured recently. And it doesn't appear to be melting at all—in fact, it's getting thicker.

Rothera Station

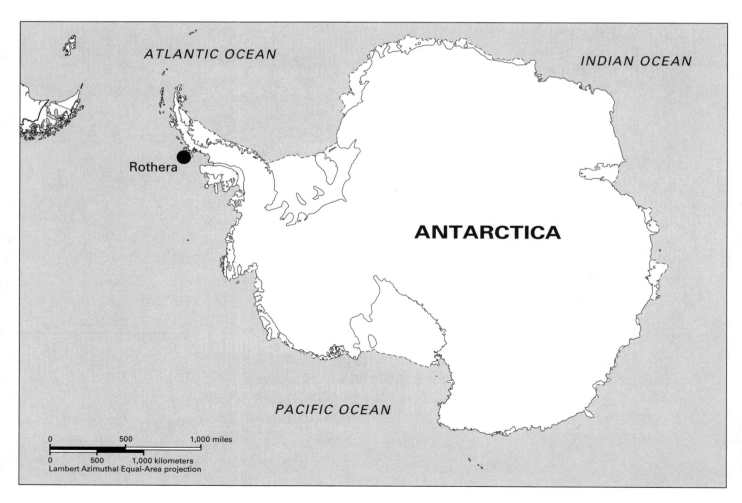

ATLANTIC OCEAN

INDIAN OCEAN

Rothera

ANTARCTICA

PACIFIC OCEAN

0   500   1,000 miles

0   500   1,000 kilometers
Lambert Azimuthal Equal-Area projection

How to Conduct Research at Rothera Station

Welcome to Rothera Station. At this research station, you will examine two satellite images taken during the breakup of the Larsen Ice Shelf in 2002. You will use this information to calculate the area and percentage of ice shelf lost. You will also listen to geographers as they debate what this information tells us about global warming.

Follow these steps:

1. Read Section 35.7 in your book.

2. Place a clean transparency grid on top of *Satellite Image 1*. Make sure the outside borders of the grid line up precisely with the edges of the satellite image. On the image, the Larsen Ice Shelf is white and the ocean is black. Use a transparency marker to outline the edges of the ice shelf. Then, on the same grid, use a different color to outline the ice sheet on *Satellite Image 2*.

3. Calculate how much ice was lost from the Larsen Ice Shelf.

   • Color the area between the two lines you traced.

   • Count the number of *fully* colored squares. Then count the number of *partially* colored squares. Enter these numbers in your Reading Notes.

   • Calculate the total area of ice lost from the Larsen Ice Shelf during this time period. Then calculate the percentage of ice lost.

   • Wipe the transparency clean.

4. Analyze the ice shelf data. With your partner, discuss whether you think the information *supports* the theory of global warming, casts *doubt* on the theory, or could be evidence for both sides of the debate. Write your conclusion and explanation in your Reading Notes.

5. Read the *Dialogue Between Geographers at Rothera Station* aloud. One of you should read the part of geographer who supports the theory of global warming. The other should read the part of the geographer who doubts it.

6. Based on the dialogue, write arguments in your Reading Notes that a supporter and a doubter of the theory might make.

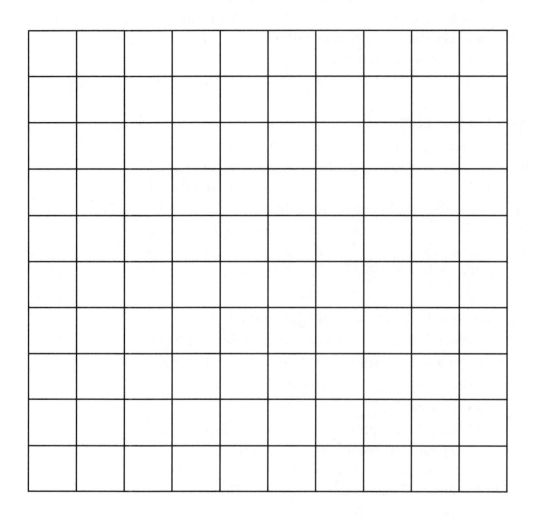

Satellite Image of Larsen Ice Shelf
January 31, 2002

Satellite Image of Larsen Ice Shelf
March 5, 2002

Dialogue Between Geographers at Rothera Station

Geographer Who Supports the Theory of Global Warming: These data clearly show that ice shelves are breaking apart at an alarming rate. In the last 30 years, almost 7,000 square miles of ice from Antarctic shelves has been lost. We know that global warming has caused warmer summer temperatures. These warmer temperatures have lengthened the "melt season" of ice shelves. So, we've seen more ice shelves break apart.

Geographer Who Doubts the Theory of Global Warming: Yes, but this is nothing new. Ice shelves break apart all the time. Icebergs break off, or calve, quite often in the summer months. But it's too soon to blame global warming for the collapse of these ice shelves. All we've learned really is that a warmer summer will probably lead to the breakup of more ice shelves.

Geographer Who Supports the Theory of Global Warming: I completely disagree. With global warming, more melting is occurring than ever before. For example, one ice shelf on the Antarctic Peninsula has shrunk from about 6,000 square miles in 1986 to its current 1,700 square miles.

Geographer Who Doubts the Theory of Global Warming: Wait just a minute. We *know* there is warming on the Antarctic Peninsula. But this is only a small area of Antarctica. And our temperature records for other parts of Antarctica don't go back very far. We really don't know if the breakup of ice shelves on other parts of the continent is related to warming trends. In fact, we don't even know if warming trends are occurring in these other places at all.

Palmer Station

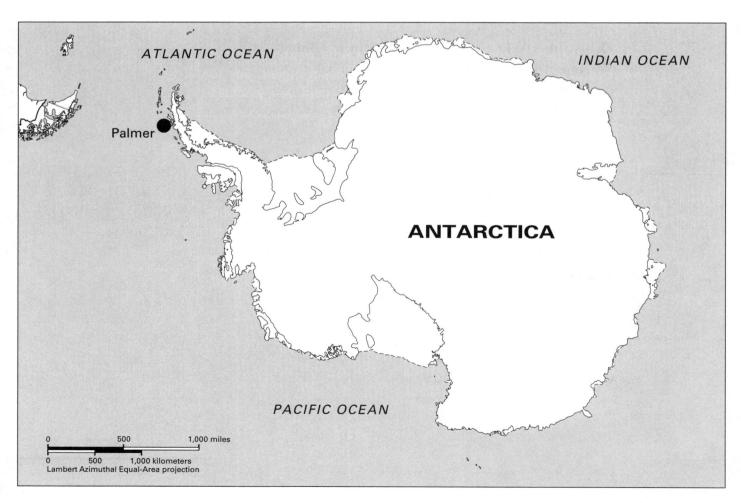

ATLANTIC OCEAN

INDIAN OCEAN

Palmer ●

ANTARCTICA

PACIFIC OCEAN

0   500   1,000 miles

0   500   1,000 kilometers
Lambert Azimuthal Equal-Area projection

How to Conduct Research at Palmer Station

Welcome to Palmer Station. At this research station, you will complete a census, or population count, of Adelie penguins in the area. You will then calculate the percentage increase or decrease in the local Adelie penguin population. You will also listen to geographers as they debate what this information tells us about global warming.

Follow these steps:

1. Read Section 35.8 in your book.

2. With your partner, find and examine the nests in the Adelie penguin colony. Count the number of *active* penguin nests. An active nest has an adult penguin in it. (If you're lucky, you might also be able to see an egg.) Each active nest is equal to one breeding pair of penguins. To ensure accuracy, each of you should do your own count. Compare your numbers to see if they are within 2 of each other. If they are, you have an accurate count. If not, count again more carefully.

3. Enter the number of breeding pairs you counted in the appropriate space in your Reading Notes. (Remember, each active nest equals one breeding pair.) Then calculate the total number of breeding pairs. Also calculate the total increase or decrease in pairs since 1975 and the percentage increase or decrease in pairs since 1975.

4. Analyze the Adelie penguin census data. With your partner, discuss whether you think the information *supports* the theory of global warming, casts *doubt* on the theory, or could be evidence for both sides of the debate. Record your conclusion and explanation in your Reading Notes.

5. Read the *Dialogue Between Geographers at Palmer Station* aloud. One of you should read the part of the geographer who supports the theory of global warming. The other should read the part of the geographer who doubts it.

6. Based on the dialogue, write arguments in your Reading Notes that a supporter and a doubter of the theory might make.

© Teachers' Curriculum Institute

Dialogue Between Geographers at Palmer Station

Geographer Who Supports the Theory of Global Warming: As you can see, the Adelie penguin population is decreasing. This is strong evidence of global warming. A warmer climate leads to less sea ice. Sea ice acts like a lid over the ocean and reduces evaporation. So, less ice means more evaporation. More evaporation and warmer air lead to more snow. This extra snow blankets the penguins' breeding grounds. It doesn't melt in time for the penguins to raise healthy chicks. So, without bare ground to nest on, the penguin population suffers.

Geographer Who Doubts the Theory of Global Warming: That's not what's happening. Adelie numbers are falling, I agree. But it's because we humans continue to interfere with their habitats. We've built research stations near their colonies. Our trash and pollution disrupt their habitats. We've let tourists wander through their breeding grounds, as well. We are slowly crowding the penguins out of their homes. Global warming has nothing to do with this.

Geographer Who Supports the Theory of Global Warming: On the contrary, it's *all* about global warming. Look, Adelies feed on krill, a small sea animal. Krill feed on plankton, which grow on the bottom of sea ice. As the climate in Antarctica warms and the ice melts, there is less plankton. This results in less krill for the Adelies to eat. Global warming is throwing this delicate ecosystem out of balance.

Geographer Who Doubts the Theory of Global Warming: I'll agree that fewer krill could hurt the Adelie population. But krill numbers are dwindling for other reasons. Since the early 1980s, some countries are catching and harvesting large amounts of krill near Antarctica. Over 130,000 tons of krill are being caught by humans every year. There is good reason to believe that overfishing of krill by humans, not global warming, is hurting these penguins.

Write a Dialogue Between Two Geographers

Write a dialogue between two Antarctic geographers. One of them supports the theory of global warming. The other doubts it. Follow these steps:

1. Begin your dialogue with these lines:

   Supporter: *The evidence from Antarctica I've seen clearly shows that global warming is occurring. How can you continue to doubt that it is happening?*

   Doubter: *I've looked at some of the same evidence. My conclusions are different.*

   Supporter:

2. Have each geographer speak at least five more times in the dialogue. Each time, they should present a specific argument and at least one concrete piece of evidence to support it. Use your Reading Notes to help you.

3. Be sure to include

   • information on each of the three research topics: temperatures, ice shelves, and penguins.

   • at least three of the Geoterms from the chapter: *biome, global warming, greenhouse effect,* and *ice shelf.*

   • any of the *optional* Antarctica slang terms that are appropriate (see the glossary below).

Glossary of Antarctica Slang

A-factor: The Antarctic factor; the extra difficulties presented by life in Antarctica

Big Eye: Difficulty sleeping due to the amount of daylight each day

dingle: Good weather, relatively high temperatures (above freezing), and low winds

ECW: Extreme cold weather; used to describe the protective clothing worn by researchers, including parkas, boots, and thick mittens

fidlet: Someone spending his or her first summer in Antarctica

the field: Anywhere in Antarctica that isn't a research station. (*"I'm going out in the field to gather some data."*)

freshies: Fresh fruit and vegetables brought in by air or ship

the ice: A common nickname for Antarctica. Being in Antarctica is referred to as being "on the ice."

scradge: Food

35.3 The Theory of Global Warming

What three key ideas is the theory of global warming based on?

1. Earth's climate is getting warmer.
2. This warming trend is mainly the result of human activity, not natural causes.
3. Global warming is harmful to people and biomes.

Fill in the five missing pieces on the diagram of the greenhouse effect.

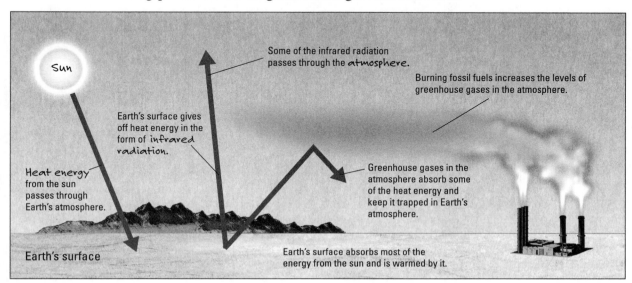

Some of the infrared radiation passes through the atmosphere.

Burning fossil fuels increases the levels of greenhouse gases in the atmosphere.

Earth's surface gives off heat energy in the form of infrared radiation.

Heat energy from the sun passes through Earth's atmosphere.

Greenhouse gases in the atmosphere absorb some of the heat energy and keep it trapped in Earth's atmosphere.

Earth's surface

Earth's surface absorbs most of the energy from the sun and is warmed by it.

In the first column of the table, list a reason to support each of the three key ideas of the global warming theory. In the second column, list a reason to doubt each key idea.

35.4 Support for the Global Warming Theory	35.5 Doubts About the Global Warming Theory
Possible answers: • Climate and glacier records show rising surface temperatures and melting glaciers. Polar ice studies show rising greenhouse gas levels. • Scientists trace these changes back to the Industrial Revolution. Today, use of coal, oil, and natural gas adds more than 4 billion tons of carbon dioxide to the air every year. • Some experts warn that plants and animals may be unable to adapt to warmer conditions. Crop failures may lead to hunger. Higher seas may flood islands and coastal cities.	Possible answers: • Some experts doubt that surface temperatures are rising. Buildings and pavement absorb more heat, so what looks like global warming could be just city warming. • Changes in the sun's energy or ocean currents could be the cause of Earth's warming, rather than human activity. • Global warming might be beneficial, producing warmer winters in cold areas. Areas that are too cold for crops could become farmland. More carbon dioxide in the air may increase plant growth.

Follow the directions at Amundsen-Scott Station to complete the Reading Notes below.

35.6 Studying Temperatures in Antarctica

Complete the temperature graph for Amundsen-Scott Station.

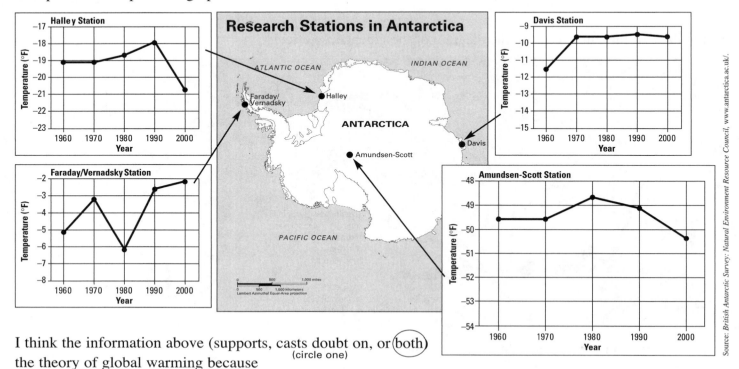

I think the information above (supports, casts doubt on, or (both)) the theory of global warming because (circle one)

Possible answer: Temperature readings at two stations, Amundsen-Scott and Halley, do not show a clear warming trend, while readings at Davis and Faraday/Vernadsky do.

In the first column, write arguments that a supporter of the global warming theory might make. In the second column, write arguments that a doubter of the theory might make.

Geographer Who Supports the Theory of Global Warming	Geographer Who Doubts the Theory of Global Warming
• Temperatures on the Antarctic Peninsula have risen about 4.5°F in the last 60 years. • Many Antarctic lakes are thawing for longer periods each summer, up to 60 days longer.	• Less than 40 percent of Antarctica shows signs of warming. The rest shows that temperatures are falling. • The West Antarctic Ice Sheet was recently measured and in fact is getting thicker.

Follow the directions at Rothera Station to complete the Reading
Notes below.

35.7 Studying Ice Shelves in Antarctica

Calculate how much ice was lost from the Larsen Ice Shelf in 2002 by
filling in the blanks below.

Larsen Ice Shelf,
January 31, 2002

Larsen Ice Shelf,
March 5, 2002

A. Total area of Larsen Ice Shelf on January 31, 2002:
   2,749 square miles

B. ___4 squares___ x 100 square miles = ___400___ square miles
   (number of *fully*
   colored squares)   +

C. ___12 squares___ x 50 square miles = ___600___ square miles
   (number of *partially*
   colored squares)

D. Total area of ice lost between January 31 and March 5, 2002:
   ___1,000___ square miles (Add the answers to B and C.)

E. Percentage of ice lost between January 31 and March 5, 2002: _about 36_ %
   (Divide the answer to D by the answer to A. Multiply the result by 100 to turn
   the decimal into a percent.)

I think the information above (supports, casts doubt on, or both)
                                              (circle one)
the theory of global warming because
Possible answer: According to the data, 36% of the Larsen Ice Shelf was
lost in 2002. Warmer temperatures seems a likely reason why an ice shelf
would break up as this one did.

In the first column, write arguments that a supporter of the global warming
theory might make. In the second column, write arguments that a doubter
of the theory might make.

Geographer Who Supports the Theory of Global Warming	**Geographer Who Doubts the Theory of Global Warming**
• In the last 30 years, almost 7,000 square miles of ice from Antarctic shelves has been lost.	• Ice shelves break apart all the time. Icebergs break off quite often in the summer.
• One ice shelf shrank from about 6,000 square miles in 1986 to just 1,700 square miles.	• We know there is warming on the Antarctic Peninsula. But this is only a small area of Antarctica. And temperature records for other parts of Antarctica don't go back very far.

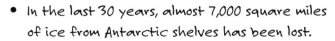
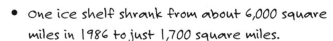

Follow the directions at Palmer Station to complete the Reading
Notes below.

35.8 Studying Penguins in Antarctica

Calculate the change in the number of breeding pairs of Adelie
penguins by filling in the blanks below.

A. Total number of breeding pairs, 1975: 16,000

B. Number of breeding pairs in *your* colony, present: ___40___

C. Number of breeding pairs in other colonies, present: 4,960

D. Total number of breeding pairs, present: _____5,000_____
(Add the answers to B and C.)

E. Total change in the number of breeding pairs: ___11,000___
(Subtract the answer to A from the answer to D.)

F. Percent change in the number of breeding pairs: ___-69___ %
(Divide the answer to E by the answer to A. Multiply the result by 100 to turn
the decimal into a percent.)

I think the information above (⟨supports⟩, casts doubt on, or both)
the theory of global warming because   (circle one)
Possible answer: The number of Adelie penguins is falling so rapidly
because their habitat is growing too warm and causing snow to fall
on their breeding areas.

In the first column, write arguments that a supporter of the global warming
theory might make. In the second column, write arguments that a doubter
of the theory might make.

Geographer Who Supports the Theory of Global Warming	**Geographer Who Doubts the Theory of Global Warming**
• Sea ice reduces evaporation. Less ice means more evaporation. More evaporation and warmer air lead to more snow, which covers the penguins' breeding grounds and harms the population. • Adelies feed on krill, and krill feed on plankton, which grow on sea ice. As the climate in Antarctica warms and the sea ice melts, there is less plankton, and so less krill for the Adelies.	• Adelie numbers are falling because of human interference. Research stations, trash, pollution, and tourists disrupt their habitats. • Krill are dwindling because some countries are harvesting over 130,000 tons every year near Antarctica.

Options for Students with Special Needs

The diverse needs of students are inherently addressed in the pedagogy of the TCI Approach, which taps multiple intelligences, creates cooperative interaction, and spirals learning from basic knowledge to higher-order thinking. Still, there may be times when an individual or a group of students would benefit from differentiated instruction during portions of the lessons in this program. Read through the following tips for ways to adapt the lesson activities in *Geography Alive! Regions and People* to suit the particular special needs of your students.

The Nile River: A Journey from Source to Mouth

English Language Learners

Provide additional support for the Social Studies Skill Builder by reading aloud the directions on Information Master 19 as students follow along. Model the steps as needed to ensure that all students understand what to do.

Learners Reading and Writing Below Grade Level

Reduce the amount of writing in the Processing assignment. Students might answer only two or three of their four questions. They might create a bulleted list of details to support their answers.

Learners with Special Education Needs

In Step 3 of the Social Studies Skill Builder, as students are introduced to the activity, make and project a transparency of page 1 of the Reading Notes. Use the coordinates of Lake Albert (2°N, 31°E) to model how to use latitude and longitude to determine absolute location. Then have students practice the skill by using the coordinates on Placard 19I to locate Lake Victoria on the map in their Reading Notes.

In the Social Studies Skill Builder, reduce the number of stations each pair visits from ten to only six or seven. Use Guide to Reading Notes 19 to share information with them about the stations they did not visit.

Advanced Learners

As an alternative to the Processing activity, have students create an annotated map about a river system other than the Nile. Use the world map of river systems in Section 19.8 of the textbook, and have students follow these guidelines:

- Draw a physical map of the river system. Include a title, compass rose, scale, and latitude and longitude lines.
- Identify five to eight key physical or human changes experienced by the river system as it flows across Earth's surface. Mark and label each feature, include a visual, and write a caption that describes what the feature is and how the river system changes at that location.

Students may use the annotated map of the Nile River from their Reading Notes as a model.

Life in the Sahara and the Sahel: Adapting to a Desert Region

English Language Learners

After students have speculated how the physical geography of the Sahara influences people's daily activities, review the concept of *adaptation* by discussing students' own environment. Have students provide examples of how physical geography has influenced their own daily routines and activities. For example, they might share how their clothing choices are an adaptation to their climate. This discussion serves to foreshadow the tasks required in the Processing.

Learners Reading and Writing Below Grade Level

Provide additional support to help students complete the Reading Notes. Give students photocopies of Sections 20.3 to 20.5 to highlight as they read, using one color for details that show physical characteristics and another color for adaptations made by people. Point out that this will help them complete the Reading Notes, in which they must identify the physical characteristics of and the adaptations people have made to each environment.

Learners with Special Education Needs

For the act-it-outs in the Response Group activity, consider encouraging some groups to choose a Host to introduce the physical environment and to identify what each student's role is during the act-it-out. The Host could prepare a cue card to read before the group presents their act-it-out; for example:

My group is going to act out an adaptation to the [desert/oases/Sahel]. Playing the part of [description of part] is [student]. Playing the role of [description of part] is [student]. And finally, playing the role of [description of part] is [student]. Watch to guess what adaptation we are acting out.

Give students a choice of drawing, writing, or speaking to complete the Processing. Students might prepare a bulleted list of adaptations. Each bullet could include an explanation of why people make that adaptation; for example, *wearing sunglasses: to protect against the constant sun.*

Advanced Learners

As an extension of the Global Connections, have students use the world map in the textbook to select another desert region and then research how desertification has affected it. Then have students create a pamphlet, with these elements:

- a title
- a map of the region
- a section with a written description of the physical characteristics of the region, an illustration, and a caption
- a section with a written description of the adaptations people have made to living in the region, an illustration, and a caption
- a section with a written description of current threats to the region (such as desertification), an illustration, and a caption
- creative touches to make the pamphlet appealing

Micro-entrepreneurs: Women's Role in the Development of Africa

English Language Learners

Support students as they prepare their writing assignment by modeling the directions on Student Handout 21. After distributing the handout to students, have them follow along as you demonstrate each step of the directions.

Have students peer-check each other's first drafts. After students complete a first draft of the text and images for their pamphlets, have them exchange these drafts and their copies of Student Handout 21 with another student. Each peer-checker should read the draft and use the writer's handout to *check off* each of the required elements they find. Afterward, have peer-checkers explain to writers what required elements they did and did not find in the rough draft. Have writers use this information to include any missing elements in their final drafts.

Learners Reading and Writing Below Grade Level

Have students preread their assigned section of the chapter by reading the section head and subheads, analyzing the images, and reading the captions. Afterward, have them discuss or write their responses to these prereading questions:

- What micro-enterprise do you think the women in this section have created?

- How do you think their micro-enterprise works?

- How do you think their micro-enterprise has helped improve their lives and the lives of others?

Learners with Special Education Needs

The night before the class discussion, give students the four discussion questions found in Step 6 of the Writing for Understanding activity. Encourage students to think about and prepare (written) responses beforehand. They can either read their responses during the class discussion or have another group member read the responses for them. Depending on the student, these written responses could be used as an alternative writing assignment.

Advanced Learners

Have students read all three micro-entrepreneur case studies (Sections 21.3, 21.4, and 21.5). For their promotional pamphlets, have students include information from all three sections. Suggest they use two standard-size sheets of paper (or one 11-by-17-inch sheet) for their pamphlets.

Students might include a section in their pamphlets on micro-credit organizations. This section could include information on the following questions:

- Who created the first micro-credit organizations?

- When and where were they created?

- How do micro-credit organizations work?

- Whom do micro-credit organizations tend to work with and why?

Nigeria: A Country of Many Cultures

English Language Learners

For the Preview, discuss as a class some of the ways that students might choose to divide Nigeria into three regions. Once various methods have been discussed, have student pairs talk about and choose one of the options.

Provide students with a copy of Guide to Reading Notes 22. Omit key words and phrases for them to fill in as they read. For the physical environment in the northern region, the notes might read as follows:

> *There is a _____-month dry season. From October to March, little _____ falls and lakes and _____ dry up.*

Learners Reading and Writing Below Grade Level

Provide students with a partially completed Guide to Reading Notes, omitting some of the photograph letters and some of the notes. For example, you might provide students with the notes for "Physical Environment" in the north region, but delete the photograph letter. For "Ethnic Groups" in the north, you might provide the photograph letter, but only partially completed notes with key words omitted.

Learners with Special Education Needs

For the Social Studies Skill Builder, assist pairs in which one of the students may be physically unable to visit the graphics walls. Provide color photocopies of the placards, and have those pairs use these copies to participate in the activity.

Give students a partially completed Web page template for the Processing assignment. Set up the template by creating a line for a title, placing the three photographs on the page with captions, and allowing room for students to write a paragraph about each region next to the photo. Remind students that they still need to create links for each region as well.

Advanced Learners

Extend the Global Connections section by having students further investigate one of the armed ethnic conflicts in Africa. Have students choose one of the conflicts shown on the Global Connections map. Encourage them to conduct research to determine (a) what caused the conflict, (b) what happened during the conflict, and (c) the result of the conflict. Have them provide a written summary or an oral presentation to the class about the conflict.

Resources and Power in Post-apartheid South Africa

English Language Learners

For the Preview, distribute incomplete cue cards that students can use to help them participate in the analysis of the photograph. Prepare several identical cue cards for each spiral question. Here are some examples of prompts that could become cue cards for the image:

- *I think the purpose of this sign is _____ because...*
- *I think whites feel _____ because...*
- *I think blacks feel _____ because...*
- *This picture might have been taken in _____ because....*

Give students photocopies of Sections 23.4 to 23.7. Encourage them to highlight all the ways life has improved in South Africa since the end of apartheid in yellow and all the ways life has not improved in green. As they complete the Reading Notes for these sections, remind them that the things they highlighted in yellow can be used as evidence for Step 2 of the Reading Notes, while what they highlighted in green can be used for Step 3.

Learners Reading and Writing Below Grade Level

Provide students with additional support as they complete their Reading Notes. Photocopy the Guide to Reading Notes pages with some key words and phrases omitted. Have students fill in the missing words or phrases after they read each section. A few examples are provided below.

- Section 23.4: *Blacks like Nelson Mandela were jailed for _____, but they helped end this policy.*
- Section 23.5: *In 1998, the government passed the _____, opening job opportunities to _____ South Africans. It required businesses to hire blacks, coloreds, Asians, women, and the disabled.*
- Section 23.6: *Because of apartheid, over _____ nonwhites never went to high school, and over _____ had no schooling at all. This has led to high levels of _____ among nonwhites.*
- Section 23.7: *Many more nonwhites now have access to _____ .*

Learners with Special Education Needs

Give students the spiral questions for each image in the Visual Discovery activity ahead of time. As the class analyzes each transparency, students can record the responses to those questions. Have students use this to help them as they complete their Reading Notes.

Consider completing the Reading Notes as a class. Make a transparency of each page of the Reading Notes. Have pairs work together on Step 2 of the Reading Notes. Then, as a class, record their answers on the transparency. Allow students to add to their notes as the class discusses. Then have pairs work on Step 3 before discussing it as a class.

Advanced Learners

During the act-it-outs in the Visual Discovery activity, challenge students by asking additional questions. Tell students ahead of time that you will ask them additional questions that are not on the handout. Remind them that they should answer these questions from their character's point of view. Here are some examples:

- How has your life changed since the end of apartheid?
- Do you consider yourself better or worse off than during the apartheid era?
- Is South Africa as a whole better off since the end of apartheid? Why or why not?
- What additional changes or improvements do you think need to happen in the post-apartheid era?

Oil in Southwest Asia:
How "Black Gold" Has Shaped a Region

English Language Learners

Make transparencies of Student Handouts 24A–24C. During Step 3 of the Response Group activity, use the transparency of Student Handout 24A to answer the questions as a class rather than in small groups. Take time to define vocabulary that students may struggle with and to answer any questions. Then explain Critical Thinking Question A and let groups prepare for the class discussion. Encourage groups to write down at least two justifications for their choice. Allow Presenters to refer to these notes during the class discussion. Repeat this process for Student Handouts 24B and 24C.

Learners Reading and Writing Below Grade Level

Assign students a peer tutor when placing students in groups for the Response Group activity. Consider creating some groups of four. Peer tutors can help with the following aspects of this activity:

- working through the questions on Student Handouts 24A–24C
- reading Sections 24.3 to 24.5
- completing Reading Notes 24
- completing Processing 24

Learners with Special Education Needs

Simplify Reading Notes 24 using the Guide to Reading Notes. Consider these options:

- Have students complete only the map portion of the Reading Notes. Then provide them with a copy of the Guide to Reading Notes and let them read the answers provided.
- Provide students with a copy of the Guide to Reading Notes with the map portion completed. Provide partial answers to the questions by omitting key words or by creating partial sentences to complete.

Adjust the requirements of the Processing assignment to read as follows:

- Around the map, write at least one example of how oil has affected Southwest Asia.
- Your sentences should mention at least one country in Southwest Asia.

Encourage students to refer to Geoterms 24 while they complete this assignment.

Advanced Learners

Enrich the Processing assignment. After students have read the directions to Processing 24, encourage them to use specific data from the Global Data Bank as they annotate the map.

Extend the Global Connections by having students research other sources of renewable energy. Working individually or in groups of two or three, have students research and create a poster explaining the viability of various renewable resources in their state (such as solar, wind, hydroelectric, and geothermal). Posters should include

- the name of the renewable resource.
- a diagram of how the resource produces energy.
- a U.S. map showing what areas of the country have this valuable resource.
- a paragraph explaining why this resource is or is not a good source of renewable energy for the state.

Istanbul: A Primate City Throughout History

English Language Learners

Preview any difficult vocabulary in this chapter with students. Create visual cue cards and cloze sentences using the vocabulary to help students become more familiar with it.

Ask students if they know another meaning for the word *primate*. Check that all students are clear about which meaning the word has in the context of this lesson.

Learners Reading and Writing Below Grade Level

For the Reading for Understanding portion of the lesson, copy Sections 25.3 to 25.5 of the text. Highlight phrases in each section that point out the key features of primate cities. Distribute a copy to mixed-ability pairs of students at their desks. For example, in Section 25.3, you might highlight the following:

• *A primate city... has at least twice as many people as the next largest city in the country.*

• *Primate cities act like magnets. They attract people from surrounding towns and villages.*

Learners with Special Education Needs

Pair students during and after the Experiential Exercise, with one student acting as a peer tutor as appropriate.

Advanced Learners

Have students research and write a response to this question: *Which is the most powerful and important primate city in the world?* After students have completed the Global Connections section, list three great primate cities—Mexico City, Paris, and Tokyo, for example. Assign each student one of these cities and ask them to gather evidence to prove that their assigned city is the most powerful and important primate city in the world. After students complete their work, hold a class debate on the question.

The Aral Sea: Central Asia's Shrinking Water Source

English Language Learners

Assign students a peer tutor. Peer tutors can help with the following aspects of this lesson:

- working through the questions in Preview 26
- reading the student handout that provides background information on their topic
- completing Reading Notes 26
- completing Processing 26

Encourage students to make a cue card for use during their presentations. On the card, students should write any lines they are assigned to speak during their group's presentation.

Learners Reading and Writing Below Grade Level

Use Guide to Reading Notes 26 to offer additional structure for students as they complete Reading Notes 26. Provide partial answers for the questions in Sections 26.3 to 26.5. Omit key words or provide partial sentences that give students some additional clues as they read these sections and watch the corresponding presentations.

Give students individual copies of the student handout that provides background information for the topic they have been assigned, and encourage them to highlight details in four or five colors. The colors should correspond to the four or five questions under "Segment 1" on the handout For example, for the question *Who will you be interviewing?*, students highlight in a particular color that question and anything in the "Background Information" portion that provides information about their interviewee.

Learners with Special Education Needs

Before the Problem Solving Groupwork activity, examine Student Handout 26 with students and encourage them to choose a role they feel comfortable with. Help them choose roles that match their unique learning styles and individual strengths. In some situations, you might set up a group of five and allow two students to share a role, or make one student an assistant for one of the roles. Also, make sure students understand all of the steps involved in preparing their documentaries.

Provide additional structure for Processing 26. Consider predrawing a basic, unlabeled map of water sources for your area. Have students create a key for this map, using colors that can add additional meaning to it. Also have them label any water sources that you have drawn in.

Advanced Learners

Extend the Global Connections by having students research another region of the world experiencing water stress. Working individually or in groups of two or three, have students create a public awareness advertisement for another region in the world that, like the Aral Sea region, is battling a shortage of fresh water. Advertisements should include

- the name of the region being affected.
- a brief explanation of why this region is experiencing a water shortage.
- a few examples of how the people in this region are being affected.
- an illustration or a map that provides additional details about this location.
- one suggestion for what could be done in this region to alleviate some of the water stress (*optional*).

Waiting for the Rains:
The Effects of Monsoons in South Asia

English Language Learners

Assign a peer to help students work through Preview 27. Ask the peer tutor to help point out some of the important elements of the climagraph. Pairs might also discuss some of the answers to the questions.

Learners Reading and Writing Below Grade Level

Provide individual copies of Information Master 27. Highlight important direction words—such as *cut, assemble,* and *find*—so that students are better able to follow along during the activity.

Photocopy Sections 27.3 to 27.6 for students. As students read, encourage them to highlight in one color anything they believe is an effect of that particular climate on the people who live there. In a second color, have students highlight anything they believe is an example of how people have adapted to that climate. Make sure they understand the distinction between *effect* and *adaptation* before they begin. This will help them as they complete the "Effects and Adaptations" pieces of their puzzles.

Learners with Special Education Needs

Provide additional structure for students as they complete the puzzles. Give students a copy of Guide to Reading Notes 27 with two pieces of each puzzle showing, and have them complete the remainder of the puzzles.

Consider providing a partially completed climagraph for students to use as they complete Processing 27. The climagraph could have all of the precipitation bars filled in, or the temperature line graph completed, or a few months completed for students to use as a model.

Advanced Learners

Extend Processing 27 by having students locate another U.S. city whose climate is influenced by one of the topics discussed in this lesson. Working individually or in groups of two or three, have students use the Internet and a U.S. physical features map to locate a city whose climate might be influenced by one of the following:

• the orographic effect
• a rain shadow
• monsoon winds

Then have students go to www.worldclimate.com to find out temperature and precipitation information for that city. Ask them to create a climagraph for their chosen city and to write a short paragraph describing the climate and explaining what affects the climate in this region.

Tech Workers and Time Zones: India's Comparative Advantage

English Language Learners

Assist students with writing the feature article by providing them with sentence starters. Here are examples of sentence starters for each paragraph of the article:

- Introduction: *India has recently become a leader in the world by….*
- Paragraph 1: *Two factors that have allowed India to become a leader in the global IT revolution are….*
- Paragraph 2: *The IT revolution has affected people from Bangalore in the following ways….*

Learners Reading and Writing Below Grade Level

Provide students with a copy of Guide to Reading Notes 28 with occasional words in each section omitted. Students can fill in the blanks as they read the text and listen to the online meetings.

Simplify the Writing for Understanding feature article on Information Master 28 by reducing the details and illustrations students need to include. Revised directions might read as follows:

- A paragraph that explains one factor that has allowed India to become a leader in the IT revolution.
- A paragraph that explains how the IT revolution has affected a person from Bangalore.
- One image (photograph, map, or graph) that shows something you wrote about. Give the image a short caption.

Learners with Special Education Needs

To help students with the feature article assignment, consider providing intermediate due dates. For example, have a separate due date for each of these parts:

- first draft of the introduction paragraph
- first draft of the second and third paragraphs
- images

You might also give students a copy of Information Master 28, with key directions highlighted. Also consider giving students a copy to share with parents or aides that may assist them with this assignment outside of class.

Advanced Learners

Have students expand the feature article by researching two positive effects and two negative effects that the outsourcing of IT jobs to India has had on the United States. Invite students to add an additional paragraph to their feature article describing these effects.

Mount Everest: Climbing the World's Tallest Physical Feature

English Language Learners

Have the class create and display a poster-size, illustrated dictionary for difficult or new terms. Before beginning Phase 1 of the Experiential Exercise, post a sheet of butcher paper on the wall. Divide the paper into four sections, one for each phase of the activity. In each section, list any of the challenging vocabulary and unfamiliar physical features for that phase. Assign one term to each group of students. Ask them to find the term in the chapter, define it in their own words, and draw a simple illustration to represent the term. Some suggested terms:

- Phase 1: *Acute Mountain Sickness, porter*
- Phase 2: *serac, crevasse, avalanche, sirdar*
- Phase 3: *crampon, Death Zone*
- Phase 4: *summit, Hillary Step*

Learners Reading and Writing Below Grade Level

Use Guide to Reading Notes 29 to offer additional structure for students as they complete the Reading Notes. Provide partial answers for the second and third questions in each section by omitting key words or providing sentence prompts that give students clues about what to look for as they read these sections.

In the Processing, students complete four journal entries describing the experience of climbing Mount Everest. Provide additional structure by having students first answer the following questions for each entry:

- At what elevation did you begin? End?
- What are two interesting details about the geography of this section of the climb?
- What is one challenge that climbers face during this section of the climb?
- What are three adjectives that describe how climbers must feel during or after completing this section of the climb?

Learners with Special Education Needs

Create the role of sirdar (head Sherpa) for the Experiential Exercise. Have one or two students sit outside of the climbing area, as if they are the sirdar remaining in Base Camp. For each phase of the Experiential Exercise, ask the sirdar to closely observe the "climbing" in Step 3, as if he or she were receiving detailed radio dispatches about the climb. Have the sirdar record the ways teams did or did not work well together, the number of climbers lost to injury, and any other interesting details. Before you debrief the activity in Step 4, have the sirdar report highlights of the climb to the class, delivering the report as if sending a radio dispatch from Base Camp to climbers in camps at higher elevations.

Advanced Learners

Extend the Global Connections by having students, individually or in pairs, select a World Heritage site that is of interest to them and design a sample Web page for the site. The Web page should have these elements:

- a web address and page title
- a description of the World Heritage site
- an explanation of why this site was placed on the World Heritage list and what type of site it is—cultural, natural, or mixed
- a visual of the site with a caption
- a locator map

Students might begin at the World Heritage Committee site, whc.unesco.org/.

China: The World's Most Populous Country

English Language Learners

In Step 4 of Reading Notes 30 for each section, groups discuss to what extent they would recommend the plan highlighted in that section. After reviewing the task with the class, give students time to complete Step 4 individually so they can then participate in their group discussions with a prepared response. Have students mark the spectrum in pencil and write down ideas for support on scrap paper.

Learners Reading and Writing Below Grade Level

Photocopy Sections 30.3 to 30.5 for students, and have students use color to identify details that will help them complete their Reading Notes. They could use one color to highlight the title "The Challenge" and important details describing the challenge, a second color for "The Proposed Solution" and important details describing the solution, a third color to highlight "The Benefits" and examples of benefits, and a fourth color for "The Costs" and examples of costs.

Have students complete an outline of their main ideas for Step 3 of the Processing instead of writing complete sentences. For example, an outline response for Question 1 might be as follows:

Challenges:
- need for more economic development
- lower standard of living
- not enough doctors or teachers

Learners with Special Education Needs

Provide students with data from the Global Data Bank for Steps 1 and 2 of the Processing. For Step 1, create a list from the Global Data Bank of the countries with large and rapidly growing populations. Have students use this list to pick the five countries to label on their world maps. For Step 2, make a transparency of the Processing ahead of time with the data for China filled in. Project the transparency and allow students to copy the information into their own tables.

Advanced Learners

As an extension to the Processing, have students write a letter for Step 3 instead of answering the three questions. Ask them to write a five-paragraph letter addressed to the United Nations Population Division, including a proper salutation and closing, as well as the following:

- an introduction in which they identify and describe their country
- a first paragraph in which they address Question 1
- a second paragraph in which they address Question 2
- a third paragraph in which they address Question 3
- a conclusion in which they summarize their main points

Population Density in Japan: Life in a Crowded Country

English Language Learners

Simplify Preview 31. For Question 1, consider providing a list of six statements, three correct and three incorrect. Instead of having students create five facts, have them decide which three statements are correct and write them in their Interactive Student Notebooks. Three sample facts are given Step 2 of the Preview instructions in the Lesson Guide. The three incorrect statements could include the following:

- Japan is a relatively large country.
- Japan borders the Asian nations of Russia and South Korea.
- Japan has many flat, wide-open spaces.

Learners Reading and Writing Below Grade Level

Provide added support for students as they complete Reading Notes 31. Photocopy Guide to Reading Notes 31, omitting the check marks next to each of the bulleted statements for students to complete after they read each section. For Step 3 of each section of Reading Notes, omit key words for students to fill in after they have read the section. For example, a summary for Section 31.3 might read as follows:

> *Crowded rush hours led to the creation of an efficient _____ system with some of the fastest _____ in the world. Parking garages stack _____ on top of one another to use less _____.*

Learners with Special Education Needs

Give students additional support as they complete Processing 31 by completing Steps 1 to 3 for them. Provide students with an outline map of their state, with the most densely populated areas shaded in and the five largest cities labeled. Have students complete Steps 4 and 5 on their own.

Advanced Learners

Extend the Processing assignment. In addition to having students examine population density in their own state, have them choose a nearby state that they believe has a different population density. Have them complete Steps 1, 2, and 3 of the Processing for this additional state. Then have them write a paragraph about how population density might affect these states.

The Global Sneaker: From Asia to Everywhere

English Language Learners

Create simple cue cards for the spiral questions in the Visual Discovery activity. For each spiral question you plan to ask, write an incomplete answer on a cue card. Create several identical cards for each spiral question. During the lesson, distribute these to students, instructing them to analyze an image and complete the statements on their cards. Students can read from these cards in response to the questions you ask. Cue cards for Transparency 32A, for example, might read as follows:

- *An interesting detail I see in this image is _____.*
- *I think the time period of this image is _____.*
- *Basketball games and shoes today look different in the following ways: _____.*
- *I think 1950s sneakers were designed in _____.*
- *I think today's sneakers are designed in _____.*

Consider adding nonspeaking roles to the act-it-out for Transparency 32C. Have students play the roles of additional sneaker factory workers. You can ask simple yes-or-no questions that they can respond to by simply nodding or shaking their heads. Some questions to ask these workers might be these:

- *Do you enjoy working in this factory?*
- *Do you think the working conditions in this factory are satisfactory?*
- *Do you think factories like this are good for your country?*

Learners Reading and Writing Below Grade Level

Provide additional support for students as they complete Reading Notes 32. Reduce the number of questions that students must complete for each section from three to two. Give students a copy of Guide to Reading Notes 32 at the completion of the lesson and allow them to use it to complete the third question. Also consider providing some students with partial answers for the questions you assign them, omitting key words that they can fill in once they have read the appropriate section.

Simplify Step 3 of the Processing assignment by asking students to complete sentence starters about the choropleth map they created. Sentence starters could include the following:

- *Most of the products I found in my home come from…*
- *I think this is true because…*
- *Few of the products I found in my home come from…*
- *I think this is true because…*

Learners with Special Education Needs

Assign a "student pointer" during the analysis of each image in the Visual Discovery activity. These students can come to the front of the room and point to details that other students identify as important or interesting. Give each student pointer a sheet of paper to place over each detail on the screen. Then have them take three steps away from the screen, keeping the detail centered on the paper. This will magnify the detail for the rest of the class.

Prepare a hint sheet to help students complete Reading Notes 32. On it, list in random order all the possible answers provided in Guide to Reading Notes 32. Students can refer to the hint sheet as they complete the questions.

Advanced Learners

Invite students to take the Processing assignment one step further in one of these ways:

- Find out where 40 items at home were produced, and record the name of each item and the country where it was made.
- Find out where 20 items from the grocery store were produced, and record the name of each item and the country where it was made. Create a separate choropleth map and set of "Why?" or "Where?" questions for these items.

Relative and Absolute Location: What Makes Australia Unique?

English Language Learners

Provide additional structure for Processing 33 by giving students a hint sheet with key words or phrases to help them complete their three examples. For example, if a native species in your area is a certain kind of snake, write *snake* on the hint sheet to prompt them to look for snake species native to your area. Give similar hints for environmental concerns, stars you might see in your night sky, locations that people in your area migrate from, nearby locations that serve as trading partners, and climate patterns.

Learners Reading and Writing Below Grade Level

For the Social Studies Skill Builder, provide a photocopy of Section 33.1 for students. Highlight the definitions of *absolute location* and *relative location*. Also consider having students create simple illustrations of the terms to use as cues as they complete the activity.

Learners with Special Education Needs

For the Social Studies Skill Builder, consider asking students to visit just three of the five placards. For the stations they don't visit, provide students with Guide to Reading Notes 33 to use to fill in any information they need to complete their Reading Notes.

Provide additional structure for Reading Notes 33 by photocopying Guide to Reading Notes 33 with key words omitted that students can fill in as they read each section.

Advanced Learners

Extend Processing 33 by having students find examples for all five aspects on the spoke diagram. As an additional assignment, have students choose at least two other aspects of their society that are affected by location; for example:

- types of food grown and prepared
- types of jobs available
- types of housing or construction
- common vacation locations or recreation activities

In addition, have students identify whether absolute or relative location is more influential for each example they give.

The Pacific Islands: Adapting to Life Surrounded by Ocean

English Language Learners

Before the Problem Solving Groupwork activity, examine Student Handout 34A with students. Consider assigning English language learners the roles of Physical Geographer or Cartographer, which are more visual and rely less on written information.

Learners Reading and Writing Below Grade Level

Provide additional support for students as they create their illustrated maps in Step 7 of the Problem Solving Groupwork activity. Give these students a copy of the reading section pertaining to their island, highlighting information that they can use to help create their maps.

Learners with Special Education Needs

Form some groups of five for the Problem Solving Groupwork activity. Allow two students to share the duties of one of the four roles.

Provide students with additional support as they complete their Reading Notes. Photocopy the Guide to Reading Notes for Sections 34.4 to 34.6. As students view other illustrated maps for their assigned island type, as well as the maps groups created for the other island types, they can highlight or circle details in the Reading Notes that they notice portrayed on the maps.

Advanced Learners

Extend the Processing assignment by having students complete the Venn diagram and then write two paragraphs in which they compare and contrast the three island types. The first paragraph should focus on how the island types are similar, while the second paragraph should focus on how the island types are different.

Antarctica: Researching Global Warming at the Coldest Place on Earth

English Language Learners

To support students in reading Station Directions 35A–35C independently, highlight the most important words or phrases for each step. Encourage students to focus on reading the highlighted words and phrases.

Learners Reading and Writing Below Grade Level

Scaffold the writing assignment by giving students a partially completed dialogue containing five responses for one of the two geographers (either the doubter or the supporter). Have students complete the dialogue by writing the responses for the other geographer. Use or adapt statements from Station Materials 35A–35C to create the five completed statements you provide.

Learners with Special Education Needs

Set up station materials at desks or on the walls at a level that all students can read and access them. Alternatively, if you have students who have difficulty moving freely around the room, make an extra set of materials for each station and bring them to the student and his or her partner to use at their desks. For Palmer Station, students will still have to visit the "penguin colony" to complete their penguin census. Be sure to make the penguin colony as accessible as possible.

Advanced Learners

Have students find their own temperature information for Amundsen-Scott Station. Instead of providing them with the temperature information and completed graphs in the Reading Notes, have them research temperature data from various locations in Antarctica and graph it themselves. This Web site lists temperature data for several stations in Antarctica: www.antarctica.ac.uk/met/gjma/. Temperature data at this site is given for each year, so students can create more accurate graphs by graphing the average annual temperature at each station in five-, two-, or even one-year increments. This work can be done at computer stations in the classroom or for homework.

Credits

Lesson Guide

Cover
background: Yann Arthus-Bertrand/Corbis. **insets, left:** Frank Krahmer/Corbis. **center left:** Ludovic Maisant/Corbis. **center:** Olivier Coret/Corbis. **center right:** Carl Purcell/Corbis. **right:** ©Joseph Sohm-Visions of America/Corbis.

Lesson 19
p. 470: Qin Zhong Yu. **p. 471:** Len Ebert.

Lesson 20
p. 487: Qin Zhong Yu. **p. 489:** Len Ebert.

Lesson 21
p. 504: United Nations. **p. 507, top:** Robert Harding. **p. 507, bottom:** United Nations. **p. 508, top:** Fountain Publishers Ltd., Uganda. **p. 508, bottom:** Dr. Earl Scott.

Lesson 22
p. 520, left: Eye Ubiquitous-Hutchison. **p. 521, center:** Victor Englebert. **p. 521, right:** Victor Englebert.

Lesson 23
p. 533, top: Qin Zhong Yu. **p. 535:** Qin Zhong Yu. **p. 539, left:** Peter Turnley/Corbis. **p. 539, right:** Qin Zhong Yu. **p. 540, left:** Louise Gubb/Corbis SABA. **p. 540, right:** Qin Zhong Yu. **p. 541, left:** Gideon Mendel/Corbis. **p. 541, right:** Qin Zhong Yu. **p. 542, left:** Per-Anders Pettersson/Getty Images. **p. 542, right:** Qin Zhong Yu.

Lesson 24
p. 555: Qin Zhong Yu. **p. 557, center:** Qin Zhong Yu. **p. 560:** Qin Zhong Yu. **p. 561:** Qin Zhong Yu.

Lesson 25
p. 575: Len Ebert.

Lesson 26
p. 588: Qin Zhong Yu. **p. 589:** Qin Zhong Yu. **p. 606, top:** Len Ebert. **p. 607:** Len Ebert.

Lesson 27
p. 617: Qin Zhong Yu. **p. 618:** Qin Zhong Yu. **p. 619:** Qin Zhong Yu. **p. 622, top left:** Reuters/Corbis. **p. 622, top right:** Jayanta Shaw/Reuters Pictures Archive. **p. 623, top left:** Wally McNamee/Corbis. **p. 623, top right:** Farjana K. Godhuly-AFP/Getty Images. **p. 623, graphs:** Qin Zhong Yu. **p. 625, top right:** Qin Zhong Yu. **p. 625, bottom:** Farjana K. Godhuly-AFP/Getty Images. **p. 626, top right:** Qin Zhong Yu. **p. 626, bottom:** Reuters/Corbis. **p. 627, top right:** Qin Zhong Yu. **p. 627, bottom:** Jayanta Shaw/Reuters Pictures Archive. **p. 628, top right:** Qin Zhong Yu. **p. 628, bottom:** Wally McNamee/Corbis.

Lesson 28
p. 636, right: Qin Zhong Yu. **p. 638, left:** Qin Zhong Yu. **p. 638, right:** Len Ebert. **p. 640, top:** Jagadeesh-Reuters/Corbis. **p. 640, bottom:** Jagadeesh Nv-Reuters/Corbis. **p. 640, frame:** Qin Zhong Yu. **p. 641, top:** Clay McLachian/IPN. **p. 641, bottom:** Network Photographers/Alamy. **p. 641, frame:** Qin Zhong Yu. **p. 642, top:** AFP/Getty Images. **p. 642, bottom:** Reuters/Corbis. **p. 642, frame:** Qin Zhong Yu.

Lesson 29
p. 653: Doug Roy. **p. 657:** Qin Zhong Yu. **p. 659:** Qin Zhong Yu. **p. 663:** Doug Roy. **pp. 664–667:** Qin Zhong Yu.

Lesson 30
p. 676, left: Qin Zhong Yu. **pp. 681–683:** Qin Zhong Yu.

Lesson 31
p. 694, left: Roger Ressmeyer/Corbis. **p. 694, right:** Robert Essel NYC/Corbis. **p. 700:** Qin Zhong Yu. **p. 701:** Qin Zhong Yu.

Lesson 32
p. 710: Qin Zhong Yu. **p. 711:** Qin Zhong Yu. **p. 712, inset:** Qin Zhong Yu. **p. 717, inset:** Qin Zhong Yu.

Lesson 33
p. 728: Qin Zhong Yu. **p. 730:** Queensland Cancer Fund.

Lesson 34
p. 743: Len Ebert. **pp. 746, 749, 752:** Len Ebert. **pp. 756–758:** Len Ebert.

Lesson 35
p. 767: ASAY. Reprinted by permission of the Gazette in Colorado Springs. **p. 772:** Qin Zhong Yu. **p. 773:** Len Ebert. **p. 777:** USIDC. **p. 778:** USIDC. **p. 779:** Len Ebert. **p. 782:** Skip Jeffery/Bruce Coleman Inc. **p. 783:** Wolfgang Kaehler/Corbis. **p. 784:** Skip Jeffery/Bruce Coleman Inc. **p. 785:** Skip Jeffery/Bruce Coleman Inc. **p. 786:** Peter Essick/Aurora. **p. 787:** Len Ebert. **p. 789, top:** Qin Zhong Yu. **p. 789, bottom:** Len Ebert. **p. 790, graphs:** Qin Zhong Yu. **p. 790, bottom:** Len Ebert. **p. 791, top:** USIDC. **p. 791, center:** USIDC. **p. 791, bottom:** Len Ebert. **p. 792, top:** Peter Essick/Aurora. **p. 792, bottom:** Len Ebert.

Placards

Lesson 19
19A: Erich Lessing/Art Resource, NY. **19B:** Lloyd Cluff/Corbis. **19C:** Corbis. **19D:** NASA. **19E:** Robert Caputo/Aurora. **19F:** Paul Almasy/Corbis. **9G:** Michael Nicholson/Corbis. **19H:** NASA. **19I:** Chinch Gryniewicz-Ecoscene/Corbis. **19J:** NASA.

Lesson 22
22A, top: Eye Ubiquitous-Hutchison. **22A, bottom left and right:** Victor Englebert. **22B, top:** Bruce Paton/Panos Pictures. **22, bottom left:** Jacob Silverberg/Panos Pictures. **22B, bottom right:** Gilbert Liz/Corbis. **22C, top left:** Reunion des Musees Nationaux/Art Resource, NY. **22C, top right:** Bob Burch/Bruce Coleman Inc. **22C, bottom:** Getty Images. **22D, top:** Marc & Evelyn Bernheim/Woodfin Camp & Assoc. **22D, bottom left:** Paul Almasy/Corbis. **22D, bottom right:** Ed Kashi/Corbis.

Lesson 33
33A, top: Andrew Stephenson/Wildlight. **33B, top:** Getty Images. **33B, bottom:** Paul A. Souders/Corbis. **33D, left:** Queensland Cancer Fund. **33D, right:** NASA. **33E:** Qin Zhong Yu.

DATE DUE